Landscapes
and
Language

English for American
Academic Discourse

Landscapes and Language

English for American Academic Discourse

KAY LYNCH CUTCHIN

GAIL PRICE ROTTWEILER

AJANTA DUTT
all of
Rutgers University

ST. MARTIN'S PRESS
New York

Editorial director, ESL-ELT: Tina Carver
Assistant editor: Kimberly Wurtzel
Managing editor: Erica T. Appel
Project editor: Deirdre Hare
Production supervisor: Joe Ford
Art direction and cover design: Lucy Krikorian
Text design: Dorothy Bungert
Cover art: Linda Montgomery

Library of Congress Catalog Card Number: 97-65185

Manufactured in the United States of America.

3 2 1 0 9 8
f e d c b a

For information, write:
St. Martin's Press, Inc.
175 Fifth Avenue
New York, NY 10010

ISBN: 0-312-13724-9

Acknowledgments
Acknowledgments and copyrights appear at the back of the book on page 231, which constitutes an extension of the copyright page.

Contents

· ·

· ·

. . . .

Chapter Five *Bias and Discovery 190*

Preface

Landscapes and Language is an anthology for students whose native language is not English. It is also beneficial for all students developing skills in academic English. It introduces critical and analytical work appropriate for college writing classes, helping students make connections in academic discourse both conceptually and linguistically. The readings are grouped around specific issues that concern all people—identity, dignity, environment, power. They address related ideas in different situational contexts, enabling students to use the concepts, rhetorical and grammatical structures, and words necessary to get across their points, and thereby broaden their linguistic frame of reference.

Three readings are grouped together within each chapter—works of fiction or autobiographical experience, followed by a discursive or academic essay. Each chapter is organized around a topic heading that characterizes the readings. Students' perspectives on the topic will be revised as each reading introduces another idea or another perspective on a previous idea. For example, the sequence in Chapter 1, entitled "Context and Identity," draws students' attention to the different attachments people have to family, language, and environment and to how these feelings can be experienced personally and written about academically. The readings provide models of the different ways by which English speakers and writers explore topics of universal interest.

Each reading has a *Preview* in the form of a question or activity that requires students to think about a particular issue before reading about it from another's point of view. This is accompanied by a *Word Preview,* which directs students to focus on relevant vocabulary and become familiar with much of it before beginning the readings. Each reading is followed by three sets of guided questions—*Word Focus, English Craft,* and *Interpretive Journal. Word Focus* highlights vocabulary items in its *Vocabulary Gloss* of text-specific words and phrases, idiomatic expressions, and key vocabulary; it is followed by *Vocabulary Questions* that ask students to think about word meanings, structure, and usage. *English Craft* questions call attention to the various ways in which English lexical, grammatical, and discourse conventions create meaning. *Interpretive Journal* questions address ideas or associations stimulated by the content of the text. In combination, the readings and guided questions engage students with a range of ideas and language issues.

EXPERIENCE, AUTHOR POSITION, AND TEXT

It requires a cognitive and linguistic effort to move from experiencing something directly, to reporting that experience, and then to analyzing that experience. Both the selection and arrangement of readings in *Landscapes and Language* model a change from the storytelling or narrative mode to one of personal interpretation and then to academic discussion. Although individual chapters vary slightly in composition, the fifteen readings in this anthology reflect three types of writing: fiction, personal narratives, and academic essays.

Fiction places the writer in the role of storyteller. The storyteller does not always reveal why particular interactions have taken place, because the purpose of the story is to give the listener (or reader) an experience as either an observer or a participant.

Personal narratives slightly shift the role of the author. The text does not recount in third person but draws the reader into the experience as interpreted by the author. The personal narrative establishes an individual's relationship to an event or condition and makes both the teller of the story and the reader thoughtful participants in the experience.

Academic essays involve a more objective distance on the part of both author and reader. Authors frame the core issue, their thesis claim, from their point of view in terms of the way they interpret ideas and conflicts. The thesis claim is then developed through appropriate supporting evidence and interpretation. Readers are expected to perceive the events, attitudes, and ideas as relevant and connected not only to themselves or one group of people, but also to entire sets of people and various concepts.

Landscapes and Language demonstrates recursiveness in many forms and at many levels. The reader is asked to adopt different positions with respect to an event or situation, and then to revisit those experiences according to those articulated in a reading. By progressing through each chapter's readings and sequence of essay assignments, the reader perceives the problems and conflicts in the texts as concentric circles that are continually widening and deepening the central issue.

Landscapes and Language offers students a vehicle whereby experimentation with English enables them to address complex ideas. When students read a story or a narrative, they may empathize with it and perhaps tell their own story in response. When they read a more formal essay, however, they experience a kind of modeling essential to academic writing. Like the span of a bridge, the language that the students use to respond to these different texts helps them get from one place to another and to return to places left behind.

LANGUAGE AND EMPOWERMENT

Encounters with vocabulary and content that begin as a barrier (because of their unfamiliarity) can become a means by which students connect with the texts they are reading. *Landscapes and Language* demonstrates respect for readers and their experiences, perspectives, and even, perhaps, their mis-conceptions. The reading selections represent different styles of written English that are accessible to students; they also represent forms of lan-guage by which students can express their own ideas and concerns. In ad-dition, the readings demonstrate significant connections between language and the social conditions and cultural sentiments that shape language. This variety not only puts the students in touch with a cross-section of human experience on many continents, but it also discloses a vital landscape that often transcends ethnic and cultural particularism. As students respond to the experiences of the different writers through an assortment of perceptual filters or verbal lenses (i.e., their own perspectives as well as those gained through the guided questions), they begin to reinterpret their own experi-ences as part of a larger conceptual and linguistic framework. *Landscapes and Language* allows students to take part in the readings, giving every student from every culture a distinct voice.

HOW CAN INSTRUCTORS USE *LANDSCAPES AND LANGUAGE*?

Instructors can present the material in *Landscapes and Language* within the framework of individual readings, individual chapters, or combinations of readings from various chapters, depending on the needs of an individual class or group of students. Because every text is followed by its own sets of guided questions, instructors can be flexible in the way they assign the read-ings. Moreover, the readings put students in touch with issues of universal concern: the relationships between people and the physical and cultural worlds they inhabit, and the resourcefulness of humankind in finding iden-tity, value, and dignity within challenging environments.

We believe that *Landscapes and Language* can engage students in the self-reflective activities that characterize reading and writing for general academic purposes. We also hope that as students develop and refine their writing skills, they will discover new and different ways of seeing the world.

ACKNOWLEDGMENTS

This book is the result of the combined efforts of many people, including colleagues and students. To each one of these individuals, we want to offer our respect and gratitude. We also want to thank our respective families and friends who supported us throughout this project.

The faculty and staff of Rutgers University's English as a Second Language/Program in American Language Studies (ESL/PALS) have been invaluable. We are indebted to Eva-Maria Morin, who has been involved in this project from the beginning and has offered her expertise at all levels. Along with encouraging us, she has contributed to the book by suggesting readings and by carefully editing the text. We would like to thank Marian Eberly, whose experienced insights and thoughtful reactions helped us resolve problems. Our thanks also to Anca Rosu for her suggestions and questions in editing various drafts of this book. We would like to thank Alma Doran for photocopying, seeking permissions, and providing ongoing support of the project.

It was a pleasure to work with St. Martin's Press. The following reviewers offered valued suggestions: Steven Brown, Youngstown State University; Sally Gearhart, Santa Rosa Junior College; Adele G. Hansen, University of Minnesota; Jan Peterson, Edmonds Community College; Mark D. Rentz, Arizona State University; Howard Sage, New York University; Catherine Sajna, Hawaii Pacific University; and Margaret E. Sokolik, U.C. Berkeley.

Kay Lynch Cutchin
Gail Price Rottweiler
Ajanta Dutt

Conversation with Students

Reading a book is an adventure. Like a white-water rafting trip or back-country camping expedition, the adventure offered by *Landscapes and Language* challenges your ideas and skills and gives you the opportunity to broaden and improve them.

Landscapes and Language calls on you to look at reading, writing, and thinking as an opportunity to engage in this challenge. It asks you to risk creating a new mental landscape against which you register experiences—your own and those of others. For example, you may read about someone else's experiences or ideas, perhaps in a style of English that is different from what you are used to and, therefore, difficult to understand at first. However, the guided questions will help you overcome these difficulties and give you a better understanding of each reading. You may then make connections between the texts you read and your own knowledge of similar experiences. You will have the opportunity to share your opinions, interpretations, and written work with your peers and, in turn, to offer your own reflections in response to theirs. You will also have the opportunity to take risks in and with the English language; while doing so, you will confront temporary misunderstandings and errors. However, you will discover that these barriers are opportunities that help you reach new meanings and interpretations.

As you take these risks, you may sometimes find yourself in situations that seem strange. You might find yourself rejecting your initial reaction to certain issues. You may need to shift your focus by moving in and out of one area of language to another—from a word, to an idea, to a sentence, to a language convention such as punctuation, to the organization of content, and perhaps back again to a particular word. These challenges, though frustrating at times, will bring opportunities for discovery.

How can you make discoveries through writing? You do so by focusing on ideas and by experimenting with how words, phrases, sentence structure, and textual organization create different meanings and messages about those ideas. For example, you begin by constructing a sentence that expresses an opinion or observation. You then examine what happens to the meaning of that sentence when you change words, the arrangement of words, or the basic structure of the sentence. As you continue to experiment with language and meaning, you will find that you have started a conversation with a text.

OVERVIEW OF THE BOOK

Landscapes and Language contains fifteen readings in different forms and styles of English. Many of these texts contain words from different dialects of English or foreign languages. Some, the texts by Menchú and O'Flaherty, for example, follow British conventions in spelling and punctuation. The subject matter of the readings links different parts of the world, and the genres represent three major types of writing: fiction, personal narratives, and academic essays. The fiction selections—short stories or excerpts from novels—each tell a story; the personal narratives reveal the author's interpretation of events; and the academic essays represent an author's critical study of an issue.

Each reading is introduced by a *Preview* question or activity and a *Word Preview* in the form of a list of words that are used in the text. Each reading is followed by guided questions: *Word Focus, English Craft,* and *Interpretive Journal.* These guides will encourage you to think and write about ideas prompted by the text you have just read. They will focus your attention on some of the ways that English works, and they will help you understand and use unfamiliar words. Each guided question gives you a different point of entry into the text in order to help you begin your discussion. Collectively, these guides provide many opportunities to express ideas and experiences in writing.

Each reading is also part of a chapter of three texts that involve a common topic. The last reading in each chapter is intended to lead you directly into a discussion that brings together ideas related to the first two readings. The *Sequence of Essay Assignments* at the end of each chapter draws your attention to some aspect of the ideas expressed in the chapter title. These assignments will require you to relate those ideas to one or more of the texts that you have read. As you make these connections, you will take an important step toward academic discourse.

Getting Started

EXPECTATIONS

Landscapes and Language invites you to *interact with texts, make claims, frame discussions,* and *write essays.*

What is a text, and what does it mean to interact with a text? Think of a meaning of *text* that you are probably most familiar with—the textbook for a course. In such a case, the text is both the book itself and the content of the book—what is written in it. You interact with this book when you open it, read some part of it, and then close it again. However, a text is also any act of thought, speech, or writing that is the focus of your attention or discussion. In this sense, a text could be the language you use in telling a friend about a surprise you had last week, or it could be your journal entry about a particular incident. The text can also be the short story you just read or the paragraph that you are writing in response to it. By moving your attention from one text to the other, or from individual words to an entire paragraph or section, you are also moving in and out of the acts of speech and writing.

What is a *claim?* A claim is a statement you make that expresses an opinion or interpretation based on information, facts, or experiences. In *Landscapes and Language* we will be referring to three specific uses of claims. A *thesis claim* acts as the focus of an essay. It is a statement involving a belief that you can explore by integrating different kinds of supporting information. The scope of the thesis claim is the entire essay. In other words, the thesis claim is like a large umbrella that covers your entire essay and to which you keep connecting in different ways. For instance, the sentence "Learning to communicate in a new language takes courage" is a thesis claim *you* can make as a writer. A *topic sentence claim* organizes the content of a paragraph; in an essay, it connects to the thesis claim. *Supporting claims* provide evidence: for example, the names and ideas of other people who also think the issue is important, what they say about it, and what implications that claim might have in their lives and in yours. Like a picture frame, your claims focus and connect ideas to build your discussion.

Landscapes and Language, then, involves moving in and out of different parts of a text in a thoughtful way. It involves interpreting experiences you may have had and read about in a story or personal narrative, categorizing these interpretations, and evaluating how they connect to related ideas. This process of making, connecting, and supporting claims in writing is called *a conversation with a text.* By engaging in such a conversation, you create a new text—your own text—which you expand by thinking and writing about the ideas and experiences that are present in other texts.

HOW TO APPROACH THE READINGS

You may find some of these readings easy to approach because the words, situations, and topics will be familiar. You may find others difficult. Remember, there is something unfamiliar about new readings for everyone. However, successful readers build on their initial understanding through rereading, discussing, and writing. They try to connect their own knowledge of an event, idea, or experience to a point that an author has made. Although their initial connection may have little to do with the major focus of a story or an essay, nonetheless it is an entry into the text. It is the beginning of a conversation between the reader's ideas and those of the author of the text. Ultimately, this conversation can lead the reader into further discovery about the text, other people's ideas, and the reader's own perspectives about the world.

You do not have to understand every word or look up every word in order to have a conversation with a text. Just as it is possible to converse with people you have met for the first time, it is also possible to have a conversation with the readings in this book without understanding every word and idea. Keep in mind that you need to talk to people many times before you know them well; likewise, you will also need to read these texts many times. Much of your understanding of these readings will depend on your patience as a reader, your willingness to explore ideas, and your desire to work with language that can express those ideas.

HOW TO APPROACH THE SEQUENCE OF ESSAY ASSIGNMENTS

Part of the adventure of finding yourself in a new place or experiencing a familiar place in a new way is that it makes you question your relationship to that place. Taking a trip across a country or a continent from east to west, for example, brings you through many startlingly different landscapes. You might travel from mountains to deserts to cities to the sea. You might keep a diary to record your impressions and reactions, or you might talk about your experience to a friend, a relative, or a classmate. You might think about two or three distant landscapes at the same time and compare your impressions and reactions. In many ways, imagining such a trip represents what you do mentally when you use *Landscapes and Language.* As your textual landscapes change, so does the language.

As you work through the sequence of essay assignments, your reaction to them will change because each reading adds a new dimension to the ideas you are thinking and writing about. Such a process is recursive; that is, it turns back on itself. You revisit places in the readings and you revise your ideas, statements, or claims. As you revise, you come across a slightly different problem, new evidence, and perhaps a fresh perspective. Each time you revisit a text, you create a different text of your own.

HOW TO APPROACH ESSAY WRITING

Just as the readings create different landscapes by bringing together different writing styles and perspectives, so do the academic essays you write. The essays you write in connection with this book may result from an *English Craft* or *Interpretive Journal* question, the essay question at the end of each reading, an assignment from the *Sequence of Essay Assignments* at the end of each chapter, or an assignment given by your instructor. These essays will share one important characteristic: they will be interpretive essays, focusing on the discussion of ideas.

Reading and writing are adventures that can combine knowledge with pleasure. We encourage you, then, to read for knowledge and also for pleasure. Reading helps you discover the writer in yourself. That discovery carries with it the surprise of adventure and the reward of experience.

Chapter 1

Context and Identity

We identify ourselves through the people we know, the objects we own and use, and the places where we live. All these factors— people, objects, and places—give us a sense of who we are and where we belong. They provide a context of meaning within which we grow, develop, and interact.

ABOUT THE AUTHORS

Sandra Cisneros (b. 1954)

Mexican American author Sandra Cisneros's short story "No Speak English" is from her collection of vignettes entitled *The House on Mango Street* (1983). In it, the narrator, Esperanza Cordero, depicts the isolation, fear, and sense of entrapment that many immigrants feel when they begin a new life in a new environment.

Liam O'Flaherty (1896–1984)

Irish author Liam O'Flaherty's short story "Going into Exile" is about two young adults leaving their homeland, Ireland, to live and work in the United States. Although their emigration holds out a better economic promise for their mother and father and all the children, this promise comes at a substantial cost to the family.

Eva Hoffman (b. 1945)

When she was a child, Eva Hoffman emigrated from Poland to Canada with her family. The excerpt "Paradise" is a childhood memoir from her autobiography *Lost in Translation: A Life in a New Language* (1989). In seeking refuge from the strangeness she feels in Canada, Hoffman thinks back to her life in Poland.

Sandra Cisneros

No Speak English

Preview

The word *transition* means change, a movement from one situation to another. Describe a transition that you have experienced—such as moving from one school to another, or even from adolescence to adulthood—and discuss how this change has affected you.

Word Preview

You can familiarize yourself with the following words by looking them up in the dictionary. You can broaden your knowledge of these words by pronouncing them and understanding how they are used in context.

fuchsia (3)	startled (9)	tin (17)
hollyhocks (9)	hysterical (15)	

1   Mamacita is the big mama of the man across the street, third-floor front. Rachel says her name ought to be *Mamasota,* but I think that's mean.

2   The man saved his money to bring her here. He saved and saved because she was alone with the baby boy in that country. He worked two jobs. He came home late and he left early. Every day.

3   Then one day Mamacita and the baby boy arrived in a yellow taxi. The taxi door opened like a waiter's arm. Out stepped a tiny pink shoe, a foot soft as a rabbit's ear, then the thick ankle, a flutter of hips, fuchsia roses and green perfume. The man had to pull her, the taxicab driver had to push. Push, pull. Push, pull. Poof!

4   All at once she bloomed. Huge, enormous, beautiful to look at, from the salmon-pink feather on the tip of her hat down to the little rosebuds of her toes. I couldn't take my eyes off her tiny shoes.

5   Up, up, up the stairs she went with the baby boy in a blue blanket,

the man carrying her suitcases, her lavender hatboxes, a dozen boxes of satin high heels. Then we didn't see her.

6   Somebody said because she's too fat, somebody because of the three flights of stairs, but I believe she doesn't come out because she is afraid to speak English, and maybe this is so since she only knows eight words. She knows to say: *He not here* for when the landlord comes, *No speak English* if anybody else comes, and *Holy smokes*. I don't know where she learned this, but I heard her say it one time and it surprised me.

7   My father says when he came to this country he ate hamandeggs for three months. Breakfast, lunch and dinner. Hamandeggs. That was the only word he knew. He doesn't eat hamandeggs anymore.

8   Whatever her reasons, whether she is fat, or can't climb the stairs, or is afraid of English, she won't come down. She sits all day by the window and plays the Spanish radio show and sings all the homesick songs about her country in a voice that sounds like a seagull.

9   Home. Home. Home is a house in a photograph, a pink house, pink as hollyhocks with lots of startled light. The man paints the walls of the apartment pink, but it's not the same you know. She still sighs for her pink house, and then I think she cries. I would.

10   Sometimes the man gets disgusted. He starts screaming and you can hear it all the way down the street.

11   Ay, she says, she is sad.

12   Oh, he says, not again.

13   ¿Cuándo, cuándo, cuándo? she asks.

14   ¡Ay, Caray! We *are* home. This *is* home. Here I am and here I stay. Speak English. Speak English. Christ!

15   ¡Ay! Mamacita, who does not belong, every once in a while lets out a cry, hysterical, high, as if he had torn the only skinny thread that kept her alive, the only road out to that country.

16   And then to break her heart forever, the baby boy who has begun to talk, starts to sing the Pepsi commercial he heard on T.V.

17   No speak English, she says to the child who is singing in the language that sounds like tin. No speak English, no speak English, and bubbles into tears. No, no, no as if she can't believe her ears.

WORD FOCUS

VOCABULARY GLOSS

¡Ay, Caray!: *(Spanish) an exclamation of exasperation (14)*
¿Cuándo?: *(Spanish) "When?" (13)*
hamandeggs: *three words—ham and eggs (7)*
Holy smokes: *an expression of surprise (6)*

VOCABULARY QUESTIONS

1. This story begins by using three terms to describe the woman and her relationship to the man—"Mamacita," "big mama," and "Mamasota" (1). What other words and phrases in the story help you understand these terms and provide a picture of the woman and her relationship to the man? Look at the entire story in order to get to the meaning of these terms.

2. The woman in this story seems unhappy. What words in the story describe how the woman feels about living in the United States? Make a list of these words, and use them to write a few sentences describing the characters in the text.

ENGLISH CRAFT

1. In academic English, the most basic sentence is an independent clause: it is made up of a subject and verb, or a subject and verb with either a direct object or subject complement. Knowing basic sentence patterns helps you evaluate and revise your own sentences. Here are six basic English sentence patterns:

1.	**Subject**	**Verb**	
	Mamacita	cries.	
2.	**Subject**	**Verb**	**Direct Object**
	The boy	sings	Pepsi commercials.
3.	**Subject**	**Verb**	**Subject Complement**
	a. Mamacita	is	a lonely *woman.*
	b. Mamacita	is	lonely.

	Subject	**Verb**	**Indirect Object**	**Direct Object**
4.	The man	gave	Mamacita	a new home.

5.	*Subject*	*Verb*	*Direct Object*	*Object Complement*
	Rachel	called	Mamacita	Mamasota.

6.	*Subject*		*Verb*	*(Direct Object)*
	a.	*	Speak!	—
	b.	*	Speak	English!

a. Study the six basic sentence patterns outlined above. Then identify the patterns in the sentences that follow. Keep in mind that some patterns outlined above are not represented and that one sentence may contain two different patterns.

- The man saved his money to bring her here (2).
- He saved and saved because she was alone with the baby boy in that country (2).
- Home is a house in a photograph . . . (9).
- The man paints the walls of the apartment pink . . . (9).

b. Use several of these different sentence patterns to write a paragraph commenting on Cisneros's text.

c. If a sentence is missing either the subject or verb, it is incomplete and considered a *fragment* even though it may begin with a capital letter and end with a period. A fragment, therefore, may look like a sentence but does not contain an independent clause. According to this definition, the following example from Cisneros is a fragment: "Huge, enormous, beautiful to look at, from the salmon-pink feather on the tip of her hat down to the little rosebuds of her toes" (4). Rewrite this fragment as a complete sentence.

2. Making nouns from adjectives and verbs is a valuable way of talking about difficult or complex topics. For example, the adjective *unhappy* can take the noun form *unhappiness*.

Adjective	*Noun*
unhappy	unhappiness
Sample Sentence:	Mamacita was <u>unhappy</u> about living in the United States.
	Mamacita's <u>unhappiness</u> can be seen in her actions.

---

* The subject *you* in commands is usually understood rather than stated.

Look at the following adjectives. (1) Write a sentence using them as adjectives. (2) Now change the words *homesick* and *hysterical* into nouns, and write another sentence using them as nouns. (3) Choose your own adjective-noun pair, and then write sentences using them.

Adjective	*Noun*
homesick	_____
hysterical	_____

Sentence 1 (adjective form): _____

Sentence 2 (noun form): _____

Sentence 3 (adjective form, your choice): _____

Sentence 4 (noun form, your choice): _____

INTERPRETIVE JOURNAL

1. The narrator says that Mamacita does not come out of her apartment because she is afraid to speak English. Discuss the fears that Mamacita may have about speaking English. If English is your second language or if you have tried to learn another language, write about your own fears of speaking to others in a new language.

2. Describe the different ways Mamacita and her husband see the place where they are living now and the place they left behind. What does Mamacita do in order to feel at home in her new place?

3. Discuss why Mamacita's heart breaks when she hears her son sing a Pepsi commercial.

ESSAY QUESTION

People identify strongly with the persons, places, and objects in their environment. That is, the place where people grow up becomes a part of them, and peoples' identities, in turn, are shaped by this interaction. Look closely at the text "No Speak English," and discuss how a shift in environment—moving from one place to another—affects Mamacita and her family.

Liam O'Flaherty
Going into Exile

Preview

Write about a choice you made in the past that your parents either objected to or supported. Describe the feelings and reasons you and your parents had regarding this choice.

Word Preview

You can familiarize yourself with the following words by looking them up in the dictionary. You can broaden your knowledge of these words by pronouncing them and understanding how they are used in context.

turf (1)	ruminative (15)	creels (32)
frieze (3)	flayed (18)	whitewash (38)
pretence (3)		

1   Patrick Feeney's cabin was crowded with people. In the large kitchen men, women, and children lined the walls, three deep in places, sitting on forms, chairs, stools, and on one another's knees. On the cement floor three couples were dancing a jig and raising a quantity of dust, which was, however, soon sucked up the chimney by the huge turf fire that blazed on the hearth. The only clear space in the kitchen was the corner to the left of the fireplace, where Pat Mullaney sat on a yellow chair, with his right ankle resting on his left knee, a spotted red handkerchief on his head that reeked with perspiration, and his red face contorting as he played a tattered old accordion. One door was shut and the tins hanging on it gleamed in the firelight. The opposite door was open and over the heads of the small boys that crowded in it and outside it, peering in at the dancing couples in the kitchen, a starry June sky was visible and, beneath the sky, shadowy

Editor's note: Liam O'Flaherty uses British conventions in spelling and punctuation.

grey crags and misty, whitish fields lay motionless, still and sombre. There was a deep, calm silence outside the cabin and within the cabin, in spite of the music and dancing in the kitchen and the singing in the little room to the left, where Patrick Feeney's eldest son Michael sat on the bed with three other young men, there was a haunting melancholy in the air.

2   The people were dancing, laughing and singing with a certain forced and boisterous gaiety that failed to hide from them the real cause of their being there, dancing, singing and laughing. For the dance was on account of Patrick Feeney's two children, Mary and Michael, who were going to the United States on the following morning.

3   Feeney himself, a black-bearded, red-faced, middle-aged peasant, with white ivory buttons on his blue frieze shirt and his hands stuck in his leather waist belt, wandered restlessly about the kitchen, urging the people to sing and dance, while his mind was in agony all the time, thinking that on the following day he would lose his two eldest children, never to see them again perhaps. He kept talking to everybody about amusing things, shouted at the dancers and behaved in a boisterous and abandoned manner. But every now and then he had to leave the kitchen, under the pretence of going to the pigsty to look at a young pig that was supposed to be ill. He would stand, however, upright against his gable and look gloomily at some star or other, while his mind struggled with vague and peculiar ideas that wandered about in it. He could make nothing at all of his thoughts, but a lump always came up his throat, and he shivered, although the night was warm.

4   Then he would sigh and say with a contraction of his neck: "Oh, it's a queer world this and no doubt about it. So it is." Then he would go back to the cabin again and begin to urge on the dance, laughing, shouting and stamping on the floor.

5   Towards dawn, when the floor was crowded with couples, arranged in fours, stamping on the floor and going to and fro, dancing the "Walls of Limerick," Feeney was going out to the gable when his son Michael followed him out. The two of them walked side by side about the yard over the grey sea pebbles that had been strewn there the previous day. They walked in silence and yawned without need, pretending to be taking the air. But each of them was very excited. Michael was taller than his father and not so thickly built, but the shabby blue serge suit that he had bought for going to America was too narrow for his broad shoulders and the coat was too wide around the waist. He moved clumsily in it and his hands appeared altogether too bony and big and red, and he didn't know what to do with them. During his twenty-one years of life he had never worn anything other than the homespun clothes of Inverara, and the shop-made clothes appeared as strange to him and as

uncomfortable as a dress suit worn by a man working in a sewer. His face was flushed a bright red and his blue eyes shone with excitement. Now and again he wiped the perspiration from his forehead with the lining of his grey tweed cap.

6   At last Patrick Feeney reached his usual position at the gable end. He halted, balanced himself on his heels with his hands in his waist belt, coughed and said, "It's going to be a warm day." The son came up beside him, folded his arms and leaned his right shoulder against the gable.

7   "It was kind of Uncle Ned to lend the money for the dance, father," he said. "I'd hate to think that we'd have to go without something or other, just the same as everybody else has. I'll send you that money the very first money I earn, father . . . even before I pay Aunt Mary for my passage money. I should have all that money paid off in four months, and then I'll have some more money to send you by Christmas."

8   And Michael felt very strong and manly recounting what he was going to do when he got to Boston, Massachusetts. He told himself that with his great strength he would earn a great deal of money. Conscious of his youth and his strength and lusting for adventurous life, for the moment he forgot the ache in his heart that the thought of leaving his father inspired in him.

9   The father was silent for some time. He was looking at the sky with his lower lip hanging, thinking of nothing. At last he sighed as a memory struck him. "What is it?" said the son. "Don't weaken, for God's sake. You will only make it hard for me." "Fooh!" said the father suddenly with pretended gruffness. "Who is weakening? I'm afraid that your new clothes make you impudent." Then he was silent for a moment and continued in a low voice: "I was thinking of that potato field you sowed alone last spring the time I had the influenza. I never set eyes on that man that could do it better. It's a cruel world that takes you away from the land that God made you for."

10   "Oh, what are you talking about, father?" said Michael irritably. "Sure what did anybody ever get out of the land but poverty and hard work and potatoes and salt?"

11   "Ah, yes," said the father with a sigh, "but it's your own, the land, and over there"—he waved his hand at the western sky—"you'll be giving your sweat to some other man's land, or what's equal to it."

12   "Indeed," muttered Michael, looking at the ground with a melancholy expression in his eyes, "it's poor encouragement you are giving me."

13   They stood in silence fully five minutes. Each hungered to embrace the other, to cry, to beat the air, to scream with excess of sorrow. But they stood silent and sombre, like nature about them, hugging their

woe. Then they went back to the cabin. Michael went into the little room to the left of the kitchen, to the three young men who fished in the same curragh with him and were his bosom friends. The father walked into the large bedroom to the right of the kitchen.

14   The large bedroom was also crowded with people. A large table was laid for tea in the centre of the room and about a dozen young men were sitting at it, drinking tea and eating buttered raisin cake. Mrs. Feeney was bustling about the table, serving the food and urging them to eat. She was assisted by her two younger daughters and by another woman, a relative of her own. Her eldest daughter Mary, who was going to the United States that day, was sitting on the edge of the bed with several other young women. The bed was a large four poster bed with a deal canopy over it, painted red, and the young women were huddled together on it. So that there must have been about a dozen of them there. They were Mary Feeney's particular friends, and they stayed with her in that uncomfortable position just to show how much they liked her. It was a custom.

15   Mary herself sat on the edge of the bed with her legs dangling. She was a pretty, dark-haired girl of nineteen, with dimpled, plump, red cheeks and ruminative brown eyes that seemed to cause little wrinkles to come and go in her little low forehead. Her nose was soft and small and rounded. Her mouth was small and the lips were red and open. Beneath her white blouse that was frilled at the neck and her navy blue skirt that outlined her limbs as she sat on the edge of the bed, her body was plump, soft, well-moulded and in some manner exuded a feeling of freshness and innocence. So that she seemed to have been born to be fondled and admired in luxurious surroundings instead of having been born a peasant's daughter, who had to go to the United States that day to work as a servant or maybe in a factory.

16   And as she sat on the edge of the bed crushing her little handkerchief between her palms, she kept thinking feverishly of the United States, at one moment with fear and loathing, at the next with desire and longing. Unlike her brother she did not think of the work she was going to do or the money that she was going to earn. Other things troubled her, things of which she was half ashamed, half afraid, thoughts of love and of foreign men and of clothes and of houses where there were more than three rooms and where people ate meat every day. She was fond of life, and several young men among the local gentry had admired her in Inverara. But . . .

17   She happened to look up and she caught her father's eyes as he stood silently by the window with his hands stuck in his waist belt. His eyes rested on hers for a moment and then he dropped them without smiling, and with his lips compressed he walked down into the kitchen.

She shuddered slightly. She was a little afraid of her father, although she knew that he loved her very much and he was very kind to her. But the winter before he had whipped her with a dried willow rod, when he caught her one evening behind Tim Hernon's cabin after nightfall, with Tim Hernon's son Bartly's arms around her waist and he kissing her. Ever since, she always shivered slightly when her father touched her or spoke to her.

18   "Oho!" said an old peasant who sat at the table with a saucer full of tea in his hand and his grey flannel shirt open at his thin, hairy, wrinkled neck. "Oho! indeed, but it's a disgrace to the island of Inverara to let such a beautiful woman as your daughter go away, Mrs. Feeney. If I were a young man, I'll be flayed alive if I'd let her go."

19   There was a laugh and some of the women on the bed said: "Bad cess to you, Patsy Coyne, if you haven't too much impudence, it's a caution." But the laugh soon died. The young men sitting at the table felt embarrassed and kept looking at one another sheepishly, as if each tried to find out if the others were in love with Mary Feeney.

20   "Oh, well, God is good," said Mrs. Feeney, as she wiped her lips with the tip of her bright, clean, check apron. "What will be must be, and sure there is hope from the sea, but there is no hope from the grave. It is sad and the poor have to suffer, but . . ." Mrs. Feeney stopped suddenly, aware that all these platitudes meant nothing whatsoever. Like her husband she was unable to think intelligently about her two children going away. Whenever the reality of their going away, maybe for ever, three thousand miles into a vast unknown world, came before her mind, it seemed that a thin bar of some hard metal thrust itself forward from her brain and rested behind the wall of her forehead. So that almost immediately she became stupidly conscious of the pain caused by the imaginary bar of metal and she forgot the dread prospect of her children going away. But her mind grappled with the things about her busily and efficiently, with the preparation of food, with the entertaining of her guests, with the numerous little things that have to be done in a house where there is a party and which only a woman can do properly. These little things, in a manner, saved her, for the moment at least, from bursting into tears whenever she looked at her daughter and whenever she thought of her son, whom she loved most of all her children, because perhaps she nearly died giving birth to him and he had been very delicate until he was twelve years old. So she laughed down in her breast a funny laugh she had that made her heave where her check apron rose out from the waist band in a deep curve. "A person begins to talk," she said with a shrug of her shoulders sideways, "and then a person says foolish things."

21   "That's true," said the old peasant, noisily pouring more tea from his cup to his saucer.

22   But Mary knew by her mother laughing that way that she was very near being hysterical. She always laughed that way before she had one of her fits of hysterics. And Mary's heart stopped beating suddenly and then began again at an awful rate as her eyes became acutely conscious of her mother's body, the rotund, short body with the wonderful mass of fair hair growing grey at the temples and the fair face with the soft liquid brown eyes, that grew hard and piercing for a moment as they looked at a thing and then grew soft and liquid again, and the thin-lipped small mouth with the beautiful white teeth and the deep perpendicular grooves in the upper lip and the tremor that always came in the corner of the mouth, with love, when she looked at her children. Mary became acutely conscious of all these little points, as well as of the little black spot that was on her left breast below the nipple and the swelling that came now and again in her legs and caused her to have hysterics and would one day cause her death. And she was stricken with horror at the thought of leaving her mother and at the selfishness of her thoughts. She had never been prone to thinking of anything important but now, somehow for a moment, she had a glimpse of her mother's life that made her shiver and hate herself as a cruel, heartless, lazy, selfish wretch. Her mother's life loomed up before her eyes, a life of continual misery and suffering, hard work, birth pangs, sickness and again hard work and hunger and anxiety. It loomed up and then it fled again, a little mist came before her eyes and she jumped down from the bed, with the jaunty twirl of her head that was her habit when she set her body in motion.

23   "Sit down for a while, mother," she whispered, toying with one of the black ivory buttons on her mother's brown bodice. "I'll look after the table." "No, no," murmured the mother with a shake of her whole body, "I'm not a bit tired. Sit down, my treasure. You have a long way to travel to-day."

24   And Mary sighed and went back to the bed again.

25   At last somebody said: "It's broad daylight." And immediately everybody looked out and said: "So it is, and may God be praised." The change from the starry night to the grey, sharp dawn was hard to notice until it had arrived. People looked out and saw the morning light sneaking over the crags silently, along the ground, pushing the mist banks upwards. The stars were growing dim. A long way off invisible sparrows were chirping in their ivied perch in some distant hill or other. Another day had arrived and even as the people looked at it, yawned and began to search for their hats, caps and shawls preparing to go home, the day grew and spread its light and made things move and give voice. Cocks

crew, blackbirds carolled, a dog let loose from a cabin by an early riser chased madly after an imaginary robber, barking as if his tail were on fire. The people said goodbye and began to stream forth from Feeney's cabin. They were going to their homes to see to the morning's work before going to Kilmurrage to see the emigrants off on the steamer to the mainland. Soon the cabin was empty except for the family.

26   All the family gathered into the kitchen and stood about for some minutes talking sleepily of the dance and of the people who had been present. Mrs. Feeney tried to persuade everybody to go to bed, but everybody refused. It was four o'clock and Michael and Mary would have to set out for Kilmurrage at nine. So tea was made and they all sat about for an hour drinking it and eating raisin cake and talking. They only talked of the dance and of the people who had been present.

27   There were eight of them there, the father and mother and six children. The youngest child was Thomas, a thin boy of twelve, whose lungs made a singing sound every time he breathed. The next was Bridget, a girl of fourteen, with dancing eyes and a habit of shaking her short golden curls every now and then for no apparent reason. Then there were the twins, Julia and Margaret, quiet, rather stupid, flat-faced girls of sixteen. Both their upper front teeth protruded slightly and they were both great workers and very obedient to their mother. They were all sitting at the table, having just finished a third large pot of tea, when suddenly the mother hastily gulped down the remainder of the tea in her cup, dropped the cup with a clatter to her saucer and sobbed once through her nose.

28   "Now mother," said Michael sternly, "what's the good of this work?"

29   "No, you are right, my pulse," she replied quietly. "Only I was just thinking how nice it is to sit here surrounded by all my children, all my little birds in my nest, and then two of them going to fly away made me sad." And she laughed, pretending to treat it as a foolish joke.

30   "Oh, that be damned for a story," said the father, wiping his mouth on his sleeve; "there's work to be done. You Julia, go and get the horse. Margaret, you milk the cow and see that you give enough milk to the calf this morning." And he ordered everybody about as if it were an ordinary day of work.

31   But Michael and Mary had nothing to do and they sat about miserably conscious that they had cut adrift from the routine of their home life. They no longer had any place in it. In a few hours they would be homeless wanderers. Now that they were cut adrift from it, the poverty and sordidness of their home life appeared to them under the aspect of comfort and plenty.

32   So the morning passed until breakfast time at seven o'clock. The morning's work was finished and the family was gathered together

again. The meal passed in a dead silence. Drowsy after the sleepless night and conscious that the parting would come in a few hours, nobody wanted to talk. Everybody had an egg for breakfast in honour of the occasion. Mrs. Feeney, after her usual habit, tried to give her egg first to Michael, then to Mary, and as each refused it, she ate a little herself and gave the remainder to little Thomas who had the singing in his chest. Then the breakfast was cleared away. The father went to put the creels on the mare so as to take the luggage into Kilmurrage. Michael and Mary got the luggage ready and began to get dressed. The mother and the other children tidied up the house. People from the village began to come into the kitchen, as was customary, in order to accompany the emigrants from their home to Kilmurrage.

33   At last everything was ready. Mrs. Feeney had exhausted all excuses for moving about, engaged on trivial tasks. She had to go into the big bedroom where Mary was putting on her new hat. The mother sat on a chair by the window, her face contorting on account of the flood of tears she was keeping back. Michael moved about the room uneasily, his two hands knotting a big red handkerchief behind his back. Mary twisted about in front of the mirror that hung over the black wooden mantelpiece. She was spending a long time with the hat. It was the first one she had ever worn, but it fitted her beautifully, and it was in excellent taste. It was given to her by the schoolmistress, who was very fond of her, and she herself had taken it in a little. She had an instinct for beauty in dress and deportment.

34   But the mother, looking at how well her daughter wore the cheap navy blue costume and the white frilled blouse, and the little round black hat with a fat, fluffy, glossy curl covering each ear, and the black silk stockings with blue clocks in them, and the little black shoes that had laces of three colours in them, got suddenly enraged with . . . She didn't know with what she got enraged. But for the moment she hated her daughter's beauty, and she remembered all the anguish of giving birth to her and nursing her and toiling for her, for no other purpose than to lose her now and let her go away, maybe to be ravished wantonly because of her beauty and her love of gaiety. A cloud of mad jealousy and hatred against this impersonal beauty that she saw in her daughter almost suffocated the mother, and she stretched out her hands in front of her unconsciously and then just as suddenly her anger vanished like a puff of smoke, and she burst into wild tears, wailing: "My children, oh, my children, far over the sea you will be carried from me, your mother." And she began to rock herself and she threw her apron over her head.

35   Immediately the cabin was full of the sound of bitter wailing. A dismal cry rose from the women gathered in the kitchen. "Far over the sea they will be carried," began woman after woman, and they all rocked

themselves and hid their heads in their aprons. Michael's mongrel dog began to howl on the hearth. Little Thomas sat down on the hearth beside the dog and, putting his arms around him, he began to cry, although he didn't know exactly why he was crying, but he felt melancholy on account of the dog howling and so many people being about.

36   In the bedroom the son and daughter, on their knees, clung to their mother, who held their heads between her hands and rained kisses on both heads ravenously. After the first wave of tears she had stopped weeping. The tears still ran down her cheeks, but her eyes gleamed and they were dry. There was a fierce look in them as she searched all over the heads of her two children with them, with her brows contracted, searching with a fierce terror-stricken expression, as if by the intensity of her stare she hoped to keep a living photograph of them before her mind. With her quivering lips she made a queer sound like "im-m-m-m" and she kept kissing. Her right hand clutched at Mary's left shoulder and with her left she fondled the back of Michael's neck. The two children were sobbing freely. They must have stayed that way a quarter of an hour.

37   Then the father came into the room, dressed in his best clothes. He wore a new frieze waistcoat, with a grey and black front and a white back. He held his soft black felt hat in one hand and in the other hand he had a bottle of holy water. He coughed and said in a weak gentle voice that was strange to him, as he touched his son: "Come now, it is time."

38   Mary and Michael got to their feet. The father sprinkled them with holy water and they crossed themselves. Then, without looking at their mother, who lay in the chair with her hands clasped on her lap, looking at the ground in a silent tearless stupor, they left the room. Each hurriedly kissed little Thomas, who was not going to Kilmurrage, and then, hand in hand, they left the house. As Michael was going out the door he picked a piece of loose whitewash from the wall and put it in his pocket. The people filed out after them, down the yard and on to the road, like a funeral procession. The mother was left in the house with little Thomas and two old peasant women from the village. Nobody spoke in the cabin for a long time.

39   Then the mother rose and came into the kitchen. She looked at the two women, at her little son and at the hearth, as if she were looking for something she had lost. Then she threw her hands into the air and ran out into the yard.

40   "Come back," she screamed; "come back to me."

41   She looked wildly down the road with dilated nostrils, her bosom heaving. But there was nobody in sight. Nobody replied. There was a crooked stretch of limestone road, surrounded by crags of grey that

were scorched by the sun. The road ended in a hill and then dropped out of sight. The hot June day was silent. Listening foolishly for an answering cry, the mother imagined she could hear the crags simmering under the hot rays of the sun. It was something in her head that was singing.

42   The two old women led her back into the kitchen. "There is nothing that time will not cure," said one. "Yes. Time and patience," said the other.

WORD FOCUS

VOCABULARY GLOSS

bad cess: *bad will toward someone (19)*

crossed themselves: *made the sign of the cross (38)*

cut adrift: *separated, as in a boat breaking loose from its moorings (31)*

holy water: *water that has been blessed by a priest (37)*

a lump . . . came up his throat: *he felt like crying (3)*

the singing in his chest: *wheezing sounds (32)*

taken it in: *made a garment smaller by sewing (33)*

that be damned for a story: *What's the sense of saying that? (30)*

what's the good of this work?: *What's the point of getting upset? (28)*

VOCABULARY QUESTIONS

1. Note the title of this story, "Going into Exile." Although the following four terms—*displaced person, migrant, outcast,* and *alien*—are listed in *Roget's Thesaurus* (5th ed.) as synonyms for "exile," their meanings are not exactly alike; therefore, they cannot always be used interchangeably. Look up these words in a dictionary and then, in a group, discuss the similarities and differences in their meanings.

2. In a text, a writer frequently defines important words or terms by giving their meanings in the same sentence or in a sentence nearby. Underline the term "three deep" (1) and try to identify other words in the text that explain it. Discuss whether the term "three deep" is explained by definition, examples, or some other means.

3. A "curragh" (13) is a small boat used by Irish fishermen. Using a dictionary or a thesaurus, make a list of some other names for boats, and try to identify what groups of people might use them. Similarly, a "cabin" (1) is a small rustic house. Some other words for house are *hut,*

hovel, mansion, condominium. Look up these words in the dictionary, and briefly discuss their differences in meaning.

ENGLISH CRAFT

1. A subordinating conjunction turns an independent clause, which contains a subject and a verb, into a dependent clause. In academic writing, when a dependent clause is punctuated as if it were a sentence—beginning with a capital letter and ending with a period—it is called a fragment. The phrase "so that" is a subordinating conjunction. Look at the following examples:

Independent Clause

the children would get a proper farewell

Subordinating Conjunctions Two examples are:

so that

because

Dependent Clause

so that the children would get a proper farewell

because the children needed a proper farewell

Complete Sentence

So that the children would get a proper farewell, the Feeneys had a party.

Because the children needed a proper farewell, the Feeneys had a party.

Many academic writers would not accept the following as a complete sentence because (1) it begins with the subordinating words "so that," and (2) it contains no independent clause.

So that she seemed to have been born to be fondled and admired in luxurious surroundings instead of having been born a peasant's daughter, who had to go to the United States that day to work as a servant or maybe in a factory. (15)

Rewrite the sentence as one or more complete sentences. Using an independent clause and a subordinating clause, write two sentences of your own about the story. Remember, a complete sentence must contain an independent clause.

2. The type of verb form that is used in a sentence can make that sentence active or passive. Active and passive sentences emphasize different elements within a sentence. For example, *active sentences* focus on the subject and the subject's actions, whereas *passive sentences* focus on the action rather than the agent or doer of the action. Because of this different emphasis, the meanings and grammatical structures of active and passive verbs and sentences are not identical.

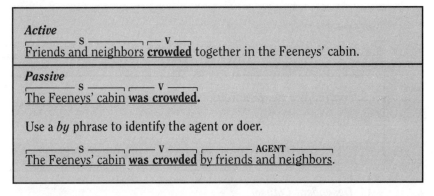

Note in both examples how the verb form shifts in the passive structure. In all passive sentences, a form of the verb *be* becomes part of the verb.

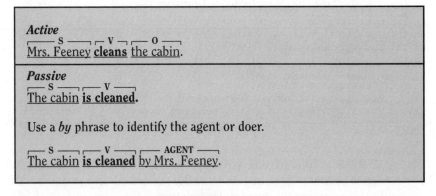

The passive voice must be used carefully, especially when the writer does not want to focus on the doer or agent but on the action or the receiver of the action.

Using the models provided, write a paragraph using active and passive sentences that make statements about the story.

INTERPRETIVE JOURNAL

1. Some of the people at the party seem both happy and sad about the Feeney children's departure for America. Write a brief paragraph connecting these dual feelings shared by the people at the Feeneys' party to mixed feelings you may have had toward a situation. You might want to think about how you felt when entering a new school or coming to a new country.

2. How do Mr. and Mrs. Feeney feel about their children living and working in another country? How do the Feeney children, particularly Michael and Mary, feel about leaving Ireland and going to America?

3. Parents often make sacrifices to give their children a better future. Write about the roles that love and sacrifice may play in a parent's decision to let his or her children go away.

4. When Mary and Michael leave the house, the writer compares their exit to a "funeral procession" (38). Look at the final paragraphs in this short story (35–42), and make a list of any words and phrases that link Mary's and Michael's emigration to a funeral procession. How does this image affect your reaction to the story?

ESSAY QUESTION

It is sometimes said that choice involves *opening one door while closing another.* For example, a major move to another city or country may be thought of as opening a door to adventure and excitement, though the actual departure may bring a sense of finality and loss. Look closely at the Feeneys as a family and their relationship to their land and country. Discuss the risks they are taking and the hopes that are involved in the choices they have made.

Eva Hoffman
Paradise

Preview

Describe in detail a memory you have of a person, place, or event from your childhood. Discuss how this remembrance has influenced you.

Word Preview

You can familiarize yourself with the following words by looking them up in the dictionary. You can broaden your knowledge of these words by pronouncing them and understanding how they are used in context.

annunciation (3)	wiliness (11)	apparition (18)
bunker (3)	poignant (12)	skateboard (18)
lumpen (5)	rake (13)	ado (20)
wizened (8)	pedagogy (14)	surrealism (21)
palpable (10)	Möbius strip (17)	cachet (23)
assuaged (10)	hopscotch (18)	piquantly (24)

1   It is April 1959, I'm standing at the railing of the *Batory*'s upper deck, and I feel that my life is ending. I'm looking out at the crowd that has gathered on the shore to see the ship's departure from Gdynia—a crowd that, all of a sudden, is irrevocably on the other side—and I want to break out, run back, run toward the familiar excitement, the waving hands, the exclamations. We can't be leaving all this behind—but we are. I am thirteen years old, and we are emigrating. It's a notion of such crushing, definitive finality that to me it might as well mean the end of the world.

2   My sister, four years younger than I, is clutching my hand word-lessly; she hardly understands where we are, or what is happening to us. My parents are highly agitated; they had just been put through a body

search by the customs police, probably as the farewell gesture of anti-Jewish harassment. Still, the officials weren't clever enough, or suspicious enough, to check my sister and me—lucky for us, since we are both carrying some silverware we were not allowed to take out of Poland in large pockets sewn onto our skirts especially for this purpose, and hidden under capacious sweaters.

3   When the brass band on the shore strikes up the jaunty mazurka rhythms of the Polish anthem, I am pierced by a youthful sorrow so powerful that I suddenly stop crying and try to hold still against the pain. I desperately want time to stop, to hold the ship still with the force of my will. I am suffering my first, severe attack of nostalgia, or *tęsknota*—a word that adds to nostalgia the tonalities of sadness and longing. It is a feeling whose shades and degrees I'm destined to know intimately, but at this hovering moment, it comes upon me like a visitation from a whole new geography of emotions, an annunciation of how much an absence can hurt. Or a premonition of absence, because at this divide, I'm filled to the brim with what I'm about to lose—images of Cracow, which I loved as one loves a person, of the sun-baked villages where we had taken summer vacations, of the hours I spent poring over passages of music with my piano teacher, of conversations and escapades with friends. Looking ahead, I come across an enormous, cold blankness—a darkening, an erasure, of the imagination, as if a camera eye has snapped shut, or as if a heavy curtain has been pulled over the future. Of the place where we're going—Canada—I know nothing. There are vague outlines of half a continent, a sense of vast spaces and little habitation. When my parents were hiding in a branch-covered forest bunker during the war, my father had a book with him called *Canada Fragrant with Resin* which, in his horrible confinement, spoke to him of majestic wilderness, of animals roaming without being pursued, of freedom. That is partly why we are going there, rather than to Israel, where most of our Jewish friends have gone. But to me, the word "Canada" has ominous echoes of the "Sahara." No, my mind rejects the idea of being taken there, I don't want to be pried out of my childhood, my pleasures, my safety, my hopes for becoming a pianist. The *Batory* pulls away, the foghorn emits its lowing, shofar sound, but my being is engaged in a stubborn refusal to move. My parents put their hands on my shoulders consolingly; for a moment, they allow themselves to acknowledge that there's pain in this departure, much as they wanted it.

4   Many years later, at a stylish party in New York, I met a woman who told me that she had had an enchanted childhood. Her father was a highly positioned diplomat in an Asian country, and she had lived surrounded by sumptuous elegance, the courtesy of servants, and the delicate advances of older men. No wonder, she said, that when this part of

her life came to an end, at age thirteen, she felt she had been exiled from paradise, and had been searching for it ever since.

5   No wonder. But the wonder is what you can make a paradise out of. I told her that I grew up in a lumpen apartment in Cracow, squeezed into three rudimentary rooms with four other people, surrounded by squabbles, dark political rumblings, memories of wartime suffering, and daily struggle for existence. And yet, when it came time to leave, I, too, felt I was being pushed out of the happy, safe enclosures of Eden.

• • • • • • • •

6 I am lying in bed, watching the slowly moving shadows on the ceiling made by the gently blowing curtains, and the lights of an occasional car moving by. I'm trying hard not to fall asleep. Being awake is so sweet that I want to delay the loss of consciousness. I'm snuggled under an enormous goose-feather quilt covered in hand-embroidered silk. Across the room from me is my sister's crib. From the next room, "the first room," I hear my parents' breathing. The maid—one of a succession of country girls who come to work for us—is sleeping in the kitchen. It is Cracow, 1949, I'm four years old, and I don't know that this happiness is taking place in a country recently destroyed by war, a place where my father has to hustle to get us a bit more than our meager ration of meat and sugar. I only know that I'm in my room, which to me is an every-where, and that the patterns on the ceiling are enough to fill me with a feeling of sufficiency because . . . well, just because I'm conscious, be-cause the world exists and it flows so gently into my head. Occasionally, a few blocks away, I hear the hum of the tramway, and I'm filled by a sense of utter contentment. I love riding the tramway, with its bracing but not overly fast swaying, and I love knowing, from my bed, the street over which it is moving; I repeat to myself that I'm in Cracow, Cracow, which to me is both home and the universe. Tomorrow I'll go for a walk with my mother, and I'll know how to get from Kazimierza Wielkiego, the street where we live, to Urzędnicza Street, where I'll visit my friend Krysia—and already the anticipation of the walk, of retracing familiar steps on a route that may yet hold so many surprises, fills me with plea-sure.

7   Slowly, the sights and sounds recede, the words with which I name them in my head become scrambled, and I observe, as long as possible, the delicious process of falling asleep. That awareness of subsiding into a different state is also happiness.

• • • • • • • •

8 Each night, I dream of a tiny old woman—a wizened Baba Yaga, half grandmother, half witch, wearing a black kerchief and sitting shriveled

and hunched on a tiny bench at the bottom of our courtyard, way, way down. She is immeasurably old and immeasurably small, and from the bottom of the courtyard, which has become immeasurably deep, she looks up at me through narrow slits of wise, malicious eyes. Perhaps, though, I am her. Perhaps I have been on the earth a long, long time and that's why I understand the look in her eyes. Perhaps this childish disguise is just a dream. Perhaps I am being dreamt by a Baba Yaga who has been here since the beginning of time and I am seeing from inside her ancient frame and I know that everything is changeless and knowable.

· · · · · · · · ·

9   It's the middle of a sun-filled day, but suddenly, while she's kneading some dough, or perhaps sewing up a hole in my sweater's elbow, my mother begins to weep softly. "This is the day when she died," she says, looking at me with pity, as if I too were included in her sorrow. "I can't stop thinking about her."

10   I know who "she" is; I feel as if I've always known it. She's my mother's younger sister, who was killed during the war. All the other members of my mother's family died as well—her mother, father, cousins, aunts. But it's her sister whose memory arouses my mother's most alive pain. She was so young, eighteen or nineteen—"She hadn't even lived yet," my mother says—and she died in such a horrible way. The man who saw her go into the gas chamber said that she was among those who had to dig their own graves, and that her hair turned gray the day before her death. That strikes me as a fairy tale more cruel, more magical than anything in the Brothers Grimm. Except that this is real. But is it? It doesn't have the same palpable reality as the Cracow tramway. Maybe it didn't happen after all, maybe it's only a story, and a story can be told differently, it can be changed. That man was the only witness to what happened. Perhaps he mistook someone else for my mother's sister. In my head, without telling anyone, I form the resolve that when I grow up, I'll search the world far and wide for this lost aunt. Maybe she lived and emigrated to one of those strange places I've heard about, like New York, or Venezuela. Maybe I'll find her and bring her to my mother, whose suffering will then be assuaged.

11   My own sister is named after this person who exists like an almost concrete shadow in our lives—Alina—and my mother often feels a strange compassion for her younger daughter, as if with the name, she had bestowed on her some of fate's terrible burden. "Sometimes my heart aches for her," she tells me, "I don't know why. I'm afraid for her." I inherit some of this fear, and look on my sister as a fragile, vulnerable creature who needs all my love and protection. But then, my mother too seems breakable to me, as if she had been snatched from death only

provisionally, and might be claimed by it at any moment. The ocean of death is so enormous, and life such a tenuous continent. Everyone I know has lost some relatives during the war, and almost none of my friends have grandparents. On the tramway, I see men with limbs missing—and the thought of how difficult life must be for them terrifies me. To be an adult, I conclude, is to be close to death. Only my father, who saved my parents' lives repeatedly during the war by acts of physical strength and sheer wiliness, seems strong and sturdy enough to resist its ever-present tug.

· · · · · · · ·

12   My father is a short, powerfully built man who, of course, seems very tall to me, and who, in his youth, had a reputation for being "strong as a bull." I am later told that almost the only time he has ever been seen crying was when I was born. But then, my life was claimed from near death too; I came into the world about two months after the end of the war. While my mother was in the advanced stages of pregnancy, my parents made the trek from Lvov—which during the war was unceremoniously switched from Polish to Russian territory—to Cracow, where they were going because it was the nearest large Polish city. They made this journey on a rattling truck filled with potato sacks and other people trying as quickly as possible to cross the new borders so they could remain within their old nationality even at the cost of leaving home. So when I was born after all these travails, in the safety of a city hospital and with some prospect of a normal life resuming after the horror, I must have signified, aside from everything else, a new beginning—and my parents wanted, badly, to begin again, to live. Later, they told me how happy they were to have "all that" behind them, how happy when, on rare occasions, someone they thought was dead reappeared from somewhere or other. But how poignant that happiness must have been! My father— this is one of the few hints I have of the pain of loss he must have felt— asked if I could be named after his mother, even though in the natural course of events, a first daughter would have been named after the nearest dead maternal relative. But my parents have no lack of the dead to honor, and I am named after both my grandmothers—Ewa, Alfreda— two women of whom I have only the dimmest of impressions. There aren't even any photographs which have survived the war: the cut from the past is complete.

13   My parents tell me little about their prewar life in Zalosce, a small town near Lvov, as if the war erased not only the literal world in which they lived but also its relevance to their new conditions. "Well, we were just ordinary mass men," my father once tells me in reply to some question, dismissing the significance of that chunk of their lives. Only

sketchy outlines of a picture emerge. Both of them came from families of respectable merchants. My father was the coddled son and the village rake, who lassoed girls on street corners and didn't finish high school just because he was a ne'er-do-well. My mother's family was the more Orthodox, and even though she was a prize pupil, she was not allowed to go to the university, which she ardently wanted to do, or to study the violin when one of her teachers offered to give her free lessons because he thought she was "musical." She was also not allowed to bare her arms or her legs, or to talk to boys on her own. I don't have a clear notion of how my parents' courtship proceeded, but I know that my mother's decision to marry my father—one of the town's bad boys—was an act of considerable rebellion. Her own history instilled in my mother a determined—and, in someone of her time, surprising—aversion to "feminine" pursuits, and throughout my childhood and youth, she is quite set on not teaching me how to cook or sew, lest such skills prevent me from turning to more interesting things.

14   My father, I think, in his excess of happiness, mistakes his firstborn for a son, and he tends in many ways to treat me like a little boy. He prefers to see me in "sports outfits"—meaning shorts or long pants— and with my hair cropped. Altogether, he wants me to be *sportif*—good at games and all manner of physical endeavor. So in our "first room," he teaches me how to perform "gymnastics"—acrobatic exercises, which are very popular at the time, maybe because of the general call for physical fitness that is part of the new ideology and a feature of the New Man. Outside, he tries to initiate me into as many sports as possible. Sometimes his pedagogy is less than encouraging. When I am five or so, he buys me a boy's bicycle that is too high for me, and once I learn how to keep my balance, he pushes me off, shouting "faster, faster, faster!"—till I rush headlong into a fall. He initiates me into swimming by that time-honored method of dunking me into a river and watching from a nearby bridge, till I nearly go under and come up again with my mouth full of water and a sense of injured dignity. He takes me to Cracow's outdoor skating rink and pulls me around in the freezing cold at fast speeds. One of his happier inspirations for me and my sister is buying a Hula Hoop. This happens when the Hula Hoop craze, imported straight from America, hits Cracow with symbolic force, and he gets this incredibly desirable object by cutting his way into one of the snakelike queues that are ubiquitous on Polish streets. My father is particularly ingenious at making his way into such lines, but in this case the item is so rare that some people have waited through the night for their chance to purchase it, and he is courting mob assault by his bold move. Nevertheless, he brings home an orange plastic wheel that, as far as I am concerned, is worth every risk, for it makes me extremely popular with my friends,

and we spend hours learning how to twirl it around our hips, waists, and necks and holding competitions for who can do it the longest.

15   And then, when I am about eleven years old, my father acquires a motorcycle. Ah, the motorcycle! This pièce de résistance comes from Russia (nobody calls it the Soviet Union in ordinary speech), where my parents take their one and only trip in 1956, for the purpose of purchasing some advanced goods unavailable in postwar Poland—a fridge, a vacuum cleaner, a fur coat for my mother—and this large, ungainly machine, which is the envy of our whole neighborhood. At this point, no one we know owns a motorized vehicle of any kind, not to speak of a car. The traffic on Cracow's cobblestone roads is made up mostly of tramways and horse-drawn *dorozbkas,* although in the busiest parts of the city there are occasionally several cars in a row, which seem to tear by at enormous speeds.

16   Now I get to taste how such speed feels on my body, for as soon as he learns how to operate the motorcycle, my father picks me as his first companion for an outing to the country. Over my mother's worried protestations, I climb on the large seat behind him, the motor starts up with a great drumroll of noise, and then we are off, bumping over the cobblestones, moving smoothly over stretches of asphalt, and then gathering speed as we enter open country roads in the most thrilling, rhythmical momentum. We fall down twice during this first adventure—my father, as usual, is being more reckless than methodical—but somehow we get up with only a scraped knee or two, which I hardly mind. I'm certainly not afraid of a real accident—I have too much confidence in my father for that—and the truth is that I like being treated like my father's buddy, and I come back flushed with wind and triumph.

· · · · · · · ·

17   *"Bramaramaszerymery, rotumotu pulimuli,"* I say in a storytelling voice, as if I were starting out a long tale, even though I know perfectly well that what I am making up are nonsense syllables. "What are you talking about?" my mother asks. "Everything," I say, and then start again: *"Bramarama, szerymery . . ."* I want to tell A Story, Every Story, everything all at once, not anything in particular that might be said through the words I know, and I try to roll all sounds into one, to accumulate more and more syllables, as if they might make a Möbius strip of language in which everything, everything is contained. There is a hidden rule even in this game, though—that the sounds have to resemble real syllables, that they can't disintegrate into brute noise, for then I wouldn't be talking at all. I want articulation—but articulation that says the whole world at once.

• • • • • • • •

18   I'm playing hopscotch or riding a sort of skateboard with handlebars on the street below our building when my mother's face appears at the window, and she shouts, "Ewa, it's time to come in!" After the requisite protest, I run in; the entryway, as usual, is blocked by the Fellini-fat figure of the caretaker, her enormous breasts emerging nearly whole from her sloppy dress. I try to slide by, but she angrily mutters something about "The little Jew, she thinks she's somebody," and I run up the stairs half in fear, half laughing at this dragonlike apparition.

19   Our modest apartment is considered respectable by postwar Polish standards, if only because we have it all to ourselves. The kitchen is usually steamy with large pots of soup cooking on the wood stove for hours, or laundry being boiled in vats for greater whiteness; behind the kitchen, there's a tiny balcony, barely big enough to hold two people, on which we sometimes go out to exchange neighborly gossip with people peeling vegetables, beating carpets, or just standing around on adjoining balconies. Looking down, you see a paved courtyard, in which I spend many hours bouncing a ball against the wall with other kids, and a bit of a garden, where I go to smell the few violets that come up each spring and climb the apple tree, and where my sister gathers the snails that live under the boysenberry bushes, to bring them proudly into the house by the bucketful.

20   Aside from the kitchen, our apartment consists of the "first room," with a large mahogany chifforobe, a blue porcelain-tile stove reaching from floor to ceiling, the table on which we take our meals, and my parents' sofa bed. The "second room" serves as the bedroom for my sister and me. The bathroom has a gas stove to heat up the water, and it's quite an ado to prepare a hot bath. At the beginning of each winter, a man in peasant garb brings us a supply of coal and thin-chopped wood for the whole apartment, and sometimes I'm sent to fetch some from the basement—a dark, damp place into which I peer nervously before plunging in and filling my two buckets with the coal stacked on our pile.

21   The three-story building is always full of talk, visits, and melodrama. The dragon caretaker is married to a thin, forlorn man, at whom she shouts perpetually and whom one day she stabs with a knife. After that, he slumps even more sadly than before, avoids everyone, and takes to breeding chickens in the enormous attic under the roof. Their squawks and flying feathers turn the interior into a place of Bruno Schulz surrealism, and I'm drawn there as if it were inhabited by magic.

22   The other downstairs apartment is occupied by a shoemaker, who, in more classic style, gets drunk and beats his wife. Everyone has heard her cry behind their leathery-smelling shop, and everyone nods in commiseration when the couple is mentioned. But nobody is astonished. Husbands sometimes beat their wives. That's life.

23   Then there are the real neighbors—people between whose apartments there's constant movement of kids, sugar, eggs, and teatime visits. The Czajkowskis, on the second floor, are "better people," meaning that they have some prewar cachet: perhaps they had money, or education, or a prestigious profession. Pan (Mr.) Czajkowski, a gaunt, handsome man, is ill often, and from his bed he speaks intensely about what they did to "our country," as if he is trying to burn some message on my mind. Later, I realize that during the war he fought in the underground resistance. The Rumeks get the first telephone on the block, and from then on, there are often several people in their tiny foyer waiting to avail themselves of this instrument. Across the hall from us are the Twardowskis, who come to our apartment regularly to talk politics and listen to Radio Free Europe—our front door is carefully locked for these occasions—and to discuss what snippets of information can be heard through the static. I particularly like the Twardowskis' daughter, Basia, who is several years older than I and who has the prettiest long braids, which she sometimes coils around her head; she stays with me and my sister when there is no one else to mind us. She wants to study medicine, and she shows me books with horrific drawings of body parts and diseases, and I talk to her about questions that occupy me deeply, such as whether it would be worse to die yourself or to have somebody close to you die first. But then, one day when I go to her apartment to borrow something, I find Basia in the middle of being spanked: she is stretched across her father's lap—she is about sixteen at the time—and he is methodically applying a leather strap to her behind. He doesn't stop when I come in, and, not knowing what to do, I stand there through this humiliation, until Basia is allowed to walk away. After that, she does not talk to me in the old friendly way.

· · · · · · · ·

24   The building where all of this happens, at Kazimierza Wielkiego 79, is situated on the periphery of the city, in an area where urban houses give way to small rural cottages, patches of garden, and weed-covered no-man's-land. And, like the apartment in which we live, we ourselves are located somewhere on the tenuous margins of middle-class society, in an amphibian, betwixt and between position. This, actually, seems just fine with my parents. They are as aware of the nuances of class as anyone, but their pretensions are unaffected. In the melee of postwar Poland, they've done well, and they tackle their lives with great zest. My father prefers the adventurism of independent entrepreneurship—illegal though it is in his society—to the industriousness of everyday routine. Although he has a regular job at an "Import-Export" store, his real resourcefulness and cleverness are deployed in risky money-making schemes—buying forbidden dollars, or smuggling silver from East Germany. He is one of a large number of people who engage in such games—part of the constant, ongoing Game of outwitting the System of which so much Polish life consists, and which, given people's attitude toward that System, is thought to be honorable and piquantly reckless. Everyone—this is the common wisdom—is involved in an illicit activity of some kind: moonlighting, or using the factory equipment to make extra goods for private sale after hours, or going to Hungary to sell some items unavailable there—sheets or plastic combs, for example (for a while, plastic products are all the rage)—in exchange for those forbidden and invaluable dollars. How anyone can get along without such sidelines is a mystery, for the normal job wage is hardly enough to feed a family, never mind to clothe them.

25   So, throughout my childhood, my father vanishes for several days at a time, and reappears just as unexpectedly, bringing into the apartment the invigorating aroma of cigarettes, his capacious leather coat, and the great world. Usually, when he comes back, my mother and he fall into an earnest conversation in Yiddish—the language of money and secrets. But it's only when we are about to leave for Canada that he shows me a jigsaw puzzle he has made within our parquet floor, which opens to expose a little hiding place where, through all these years, he has kept his foreign currency.

26   It's pretty dangerous stuff, as we learn when one of his pals is sentenced to a camp in Siberia—but my father thrives on it, as he thrives on riding his motorcycle at top speed on Poland's bumpy roads. His illicit initiatives are also what keep us within the bounds of the respectable middle class, which means that we go to a restaurant perhaps once a month, take long summer vacations, have a live-in maid and more than one change of clothing, and can occasionally afford to buy an imported item, like spike-heeled shoes for my mother, or a nylon blouse for me.

27   My mother, in a modest way, fashions herself as a lady and leads a pleasantly bustling life. She runs her household with the help of a maid, makes new friends at the park where she takes me and my sister daily, reads her books, takes me for ice cream to one of Cracow's lovely coffeehouses, and counsels my father in his enterprises. We go to the theater, the opera, the movies—all accessible to us at popular prices—and on a constant round of visits. For a while, my parents are satisfied, pleased to be in a big urban center with its culture, its lively talk, its news from other parts of the world.

28   Of course, both my parents want "something better" for their children. In fact, they have great ambitions, particularly for me—the first-born, who turns out to be clever and talented. But neither of them is very clear about how you get to those other things, whatever they may

be—how much work you need to do, how much discipline is required. No matter how many accoutrements of middle-class life they'll later acquire, my parents never quite buy into the work ethic. Life has been irrational enough for them to believe in the power of the gamble—in games of luck and risk—more than in orderly progress. Anyway, there is no such thing as orderly progress in the Socialist People's Republic. It's clear enough to everybody that you don't get anywhere by trying. Working hard in your "chosen profession," when the profession is most often chosen for you, when there's no reward and no possibility of improving your conditions, and when anything may happen tomorrow, is for fools or schlemiels. The System—compounded by the Poles' perennial skepticism about all systems—produces a nation of ironists and gamblers.

WORD FOCUS

VOCABULARY GLOSS

Baba Yaga: *a female supernatural ogre of Russian folklore (8)*

Brothers Grimm: *German authors of famous fairy tales such as "Snow White," "Red Riding Hood," and "Hansel and Gretel"; each of these stories involves cruelty (10)*

camp in Siberia: *prison camp in the snowy wastelands of Siberia (26)*

chifforobe: *a tall piece of furniture with drawers and closet space (20)*

dorozbkas: *(Polish) carriages (15)*

an everywhere: *a place that is complete and has no equal (6)*

exiled from paradise: *a reference to the biblical banishment of Adam and Eve from the Garden of Eden; an ideal and beautiful place (4)*

far and wide: *extensively (10)*

Fellini-fat figure: *a reference to characters in the movies of Italian director Federico Fellini (18)*

mazurka: *a lively dance like the polka (3)*

a ne'er-do-well: *an irresponsible person; a failure (13)*

New Man: *modern person (14)*

no wonder: *a phrase indicating that it is understandable why something occurred (4)*

outwitting the System: *getting around established political authority (24)*

pièce de résistance: *(French) the last and best of something (15)*

Radio Free Europe: *a radio station established in 1950 in Western Europe* to broadcast news and propaganda to Communist Eastern European countries (23)

schlemiels: *(Yiddish) comically foolish people (28)*

shofar: *a trumpet made from a ram's horn used in Jewish religious ceremonies (3)*

underground resistance: *a secret political movement fighting against Hitler's occupation during World War II (23)*

work ethic: *a philosophy that views work as morally good (28)*

VOCABULARY QUESTIONS

1. The Hula Hoop is a plastic toy that is twirled around the hips. It became very popular in the United States and in many parts of the world during the late 1950s. Look up the underlined words in the following passage and discuss the effect that the Hula Hoop had in Poland.

   This happens when the Hula Hoop <u>craze</u>, imported straight from America, <u>hits</u> Cracow with <u>symbolic</u> force, and he gets this incredibly desirable object by <u>cutting</u> his way into one of the <u>snakelike</u> <u>queues</u> that are <u>ubiquitous</u> on Polish streets. (14)

2. *Synonym* is a term for words that have similar meanings. Although synonyms may be alike in meaning, they often cannot replace each other. Look at the following sentence: "In the melee of postwar Poland, they've done well, and they tackle their lives with great zest" (24). Some synonyms for the word "melee" are *riot, rebellion, scuffle, fray, fracas,* and *free-for-all.* How would each of these words change the meaning of the sentence? Which of these words could replace "melee" without changing the meaning of Hoffman's sentence?

3. In describing her pain over leaving Cracow, Hoffman uses the word "nostalgia," although she believes her feelings are better expressed by the Polish word "tesknota" (3). Define the word "nostalgia," and discuss how its meaning differs from synonyms such as *reminiscence, remembrance, longing,* and *yearning.*

ENGLISH CRAFT

1. A *phrasal verb* is a unit consisting of a verb and a preposition or an adverb. For example, *turn on* as in the sentence *Please turn on the light* is a phrasal verb. *Throw away* as in the sentence *Don't throw away any rough drafts of your paper* is also a phrasal verb. As a unit, *turn on* and *throw away* have different meanings from the simple verbs *turn* and *throw.*

The phrasal verb "break out" in Hoffman's sentence "I want to break out" (1) means that she wants to escape. Look at the chart below and note that changing the preposition or adverb alters the meaning of the phrasal verb.

Phrasal Verbs

Verb	Preposition	Adverb	Meaning
break	in		• to train • to soften for use • to enter a place forcibly or illegally
break		away	• to come apart • to escape • to end one's connection to a group

Many English verbs form phrasal units—such as *run out, run across, run up,* and *run down.* Find the meanings of these phrasal verbs, and add other combinations to the list. Write a sentence for each one showing the differences in meaning.

2. Verb tenses are important in English for a number of reasons. The table below contains sample tense forms of "clutch" (2), one of the verbs that Hoffman uses in her essay.

Verb Tenses

Tenses	Base Form	Simple	Progressive	Perfect	Perfect Progressive
	clutch				
PRESENT		clutch	am/is/are clutching	have clutched	has/have been clutching
PAST		clutched	was/were clutching	had clutched	had been clutching
FUTURE		will clutch	will be clutching	will have clutched	will have been clutching

Note: This table does not include irregular verbs or verbs in the passive voice.

a. It is often difficult to decide which tense to choose because English verb tenses signal more than just concepts about time (past, present, future). The verb tense can also signal the relevance of an event, action, or condition such as whether it is immediate or distant, momentary or habitual, ongoing or completed, temporary or permanent.

The *present tense* is conventionally used to write about another text, its author, the main action of a text, and general truths and beliefs. For example, the present tense can signal immediacy, that the events or topics are currently relevant, regardless of whether or not they occurred in the past. The main action of Hoffman's text, for example, is the exploration of her experiences and feelings about moving from Poland to Canada. The following sentence about Hoffman's text is written in the present tense:

In her narrative, Hoffman <u>explores</u> the meaning of belonging to more than one country.

Write a brief paragraph about Hoffman's text using this convention of the present tense.

b. The past tense is used for specific events that are more distant from the observations a writer is making. Look at the following example:

Hoffman <u>talks</u> about the fear and pain her parents <u>experienced</u> when her aunt died.

What is significant here is that the observation begins in the present tense *(talks)* and then moves to the past tense verbs *(experienced* and *died).* Read the following excerpt and write a paragraph exploring what you find most striking about this passage. Use the present tense to make your observations and the past tense when necessary to show distance or something that happened in the past. Be consistent in your use of either tense.

I know who "she" is; I feel as if I've always known it. She's my mother's younger sister, who was killed during the war. All the other members of my mother's family died as well—her mother, father, cousins, aunts. But it's her sister whose memory arouses my mother's most alive pain. She was so young, eighteen or nineteen—"She hadn't even lived yet," my mother says—and she died in such a horrible way. The man who saw her go into the gas chamber said that she was among those who had to dig their own graves, and that her hair turned gray the day before her death. That strikes me as a fairy tale more cruel, more magical than anything in the Brothers Grimm. (10)

3. A claim is an assertion or observation based on evidence or experience; it is made in the form of a statement. There are three basic types of claims that are very important in academic essays:

- **Thesis Claims:** Claims that function as a thesis—the claim made by a writer that provides an overall conceptual point of view and organizes an entire essay.
- **Topic Sentence Claims:** Claims that function as topic sentences of paragraphs—claims that provide the conceptual point of view for an entire paragraph and organize the paragraph in relation to the thesis.
- **Support Claims:** Claims that function as statements in the text that support either the thesis claim, the topic sentence claim, or each other.

a. A reader of Hoffman's text could make the following *thesis claim: Hoffman's portrayal of her life in Poland before she emigrated to Canada reveals feelings of betrayal and isolation.* In an essay written about Hoffman's narrative, this statement could act as a thesis claim for two reasons:

- It is a hypothesis that the writer has arrived at based on an observation of the content of Hoffman's text
- It can be tested—that is, supported, agreed or disagreed with, or reinterpreted by another reader of Hoffman's text

Write two topic sentence claims that support the thesis claim provided in the example above. Discuss the function of these topic sentence claims in terms of how they relate to the thesis claim.

b. *Thesis claims, topic sentence claims,* and *support claims* contain key words. In the thesis claim *Hoffman's portrayal of her life in Poland before she emigrated to Canada reveals feelings of betrayal and isolation,* the words *portrayal, emigrated, reveals, betrayal,* and *isolation* are key terms. These key terms can be used in discussions and analyses of Hoffman's narrative in order to link ideas in the essay, thereby further explaining, supporting, and expanding the thesis claim.

Identify some of the key words in the sentences that follow, and in a group discuss what makes these words important in Hoffman's text. As you do this exercise, you should consider whether either of these statements could be considered as the thesis claim of Hoffman's essay.

i. "[Emigrating is] a notion of such crushing, definitive finality that to me it might as well mean the end of the world" (1).

ii. "[T]he wonder is what you can make a paradise out of" (5).

INTERPRETIVE JOURNAL

1. In thinking about her childhood, Hoffman says "the wonder is what you can make a paradise out of" (5). What is a "paradise," and what is Hoffman making a paradise out of? Describe a place you remember, and explain how that particular place remains important in your memory. Could you describe this place as a "paradise"?

2. Hoffman says that her Aunt Alina's death strikes her as "a fairy tale more cruel, more magical than anything in the Brothers Grimm" (10). What is a fairy tale, and why might it be described as both cruel and magical?

3. Do you think that Hoffman idealizes her homeland? Do you think she remembers Poland as being better than it really was? Or do you think she remembers it the way it was—that is, is she reporting her remembrances accurately?

ESSAY QUESTION

Students are often asked to find the thesis claim or main point of an assigned story or essay and to take a position in relation to that claim. However, sometimes supporting claims (other important statements that the author makes) also reveal valuable aspects of an author's text. In the essay you write, take a position on a supporting claim in Hoffman's text that is not the main point but that interests you and reveals another dimension of her story.

Context and Identity
Sequence of Essay Assignments

READINGS

Sandra Cisneros, "No Speak English," excerpt from *The House on Mango Street*

Liam O'Flaherty, "Going into Exile"

Eva Hoffman, "Paradise," excerpt from *Lost in Translation: A Life in a New Language*

The following assignments form a sequence of interrelated topics. They become progressively more challenging as they ask you to interact with more texts. Assignment 1 asks you to write about a topic in Cisneros's text; Assignment 2 asks you to reconsider your first essay in light of O'Flaherty's text; and Assignment 3 asks you to consider all three texts as you establish your point of view on the assigned topic.

These assignments can be written as a sequence or they can be written individually. However you approach these essays, each one you write should be supported with citations from the text and examples. Whenever possible, include your own experience and knowledge on the subject.

ASSIGNMENT 1

CISNEROS

When families move from one place to another, each family member reacts differently to the new environment and the demands it makes on them. Write an essay in which you discuss the different kinds of adjustments that people must make. Be sure to take into consideration the way age, gender, and economic status affect each individual's reactions to new situations.

ASSIGNMENT 2

O'FLAHERTY AND CISNEROS

A sense of place, particularly the place where a person is born and grows up, involves both location and relationships among family, friends, and neighbors. Analyze how changing one's location affects the relationships of people in Cisneros's and O'Flaherty's short stories.

ASSIGNMENT 3

HOFFMAN, O'FLAHERTY, AND CISNEROS

Like the characters in the short stories "No Speak English" and "Going into Exile," Hoffman sees moving differently from the way she believes her parents see it. Look carefully at Hoffman's and her parents' descriptions of and reactions to Poland and Canada. Analyze how Hoffman's perception of the places she has lived in—the languages she has spoken, the things she has touched and owned—differs from the perceptions of her parents. Compare her situation to Mamacita's in "No Speak English" and Michael's and Mary's in "Going into Exile."

Chapter 2

Environment and Behavior

The place where people live plays a significant role in shaping the rules and conventions that govern their behavior. Sometimes, individuals can choose to accept or challenge these rules and conventions. The choices they make may have consequences for the individual, the community, and the place in which they live. Ignoring the relationship between place and behavior can have surprising consequences.

ABOUT THE AUTHORS

Maya Angelou (b. 1928)

Maya Angelou, an African American writer, narrates incidents from her own life in her autobiography *I Know Why the Caged Bird Sings* (1970). In the excerpt "Mary," the narrator recounts an incident from childhood. Working as a maid, she discovers the public and private significance of her name.

Peter Freuchen (1886–1957)

Peter Freuchen's story "Dead Man's Cache" is an excerpt from *Book of the Eskimos* (1961). This Danish-born author shows his respect for humankind's need to live cooperatively with nature and the community. His first-hand understanding of the Arctic world allows him to emphasize the consequences that occur when people do not interact effectively with their surroundings.

Edward Abbey (1927–1989)

American writer Edward Abbey, in his book *Desert Solitaire: A Season in the Wilderness* (1968), traces the exploitative ruin of nature brought about by mining and drilling for oil, as well as by the tourist industry. In the excerpt "Water," he describes the menacing yet majestic beauty of the southwestern desert, while he seeks an intelligent understanding of nature and its value to the world.

Maya Angelou

Mary

Preview

Think of an incident or a situation in your life when you expressed through gestures or other actions what you could not express in words. Describe the circumstances in detail. What point were you trying to make? What was the outcome?

Word Preview

You can familiarize yourself with the following words by looking them up in the dictionary. You can broaden your knowledge of these words by pronouncing them and understanding how they are used in context.

debutante (1)	embroider (2)	impish (3)
ludicrous (1)	crocheting (2)	elf (3)
waltz (1)	doilies (2)	impudent (4)
ecru (1)	sacheted (2)	barrenness (13)
tatting (1)	perpetually (3)	

1   Recently a white woman from Texas, who would quickly describe herself as a liberal, asked me about my hometown. When I told her that in Stamps my grandmother had owned the only Negro general merchandise store since the turn of the century, she exclaimed, "Why, you were a debutante." Ridiculous and even ludicrous. But Negro girls in small Southern towns, whether poverty-stricken or just munching along on a few of life's necessities, were given as extensive and irrelevant preparations for adulthood as rich white girls shown in magazines. Admittedly the training was not the same. While white girls learned to waltz and sit gracefully with a tea cup balanced on their knees, we were lagging behind, learning the mid-Victorian values with very little money to indulge them. (Come and see Edna Lomax spending the money she made picking cotton on five balls of ecru tatting thread. Her fingers are bound to snag the work and she'll have to repeat the stitches time and time again. But she knows that when she buys the thread.)

2   We were required to embroider and I had trunkfuls of colorful dishtowels, pillowcases, runners, and handkerchiefs to my credit. I mastered the art of crocheting and tatting, and there was a lifetime's supply of dainty doilies that would never be used in sacheted dresser drawers. It went without saying that all girls could iron and wash, but the finer touches around the home, like setting a table with real silver, baking roasts, and cooking vegetables without meat, had to be learned elsewhere. Usually at the source of those habits. During my tenth year, a white woman's kitchen became my finishing school.

3   Mrs. Viola Cullinan was a plump woman who lived in a three-bedroom house somewhere behind the post office. She was singularly unattractive until she smiled, and then the lines around her eyes and mouth which made her look perpetually dirty disappeared, and her face looked like the mask of an impish elf. She usually rested her smile until late afternoon when her women friends dropped in and Miss Glory, the cook, served them cold drinks on the closed-in porch.

4   The exactness of her house was inhuman. This glass went here and only here. That cup had its place and it was an act of impudent rebellion to place it anywhere else. At twelve o'clock the table was set. At 12:15 Mrs. Cullinan sat down to dinner (whether her husband had arrived or not). At 12:16 Miss Glory brought out the food.

5   It took me a week to learn the difference between a salad plate, a bread plate, and a dessert plate.

6   Mrs. Cullinan kept up the tradition of her wealthy parents. She was from Virginia. Miss Glory, who was a descendant of slaves that had worked for the Cullinans, told me her history. She had married beneath her (according to Miss Glory). Her husband's family hadn't had their money very long and what they had "didn't 'mount to much."

7   As ugly as she was, I thought privately, she was lucky to get a husband above or beneath her station. But Miss Glory wouldn't let me say a thing against her mistress. She was very patient with me, however, over the housework. She explained the dishware, silverware, and servants' bells.

8   The large round bowl in which soup was served wasn't a soup bowl,

it was a tureen. There were goblets, sherbet glasses, ice-cream glasses, wine glasses, green glass coffee cups with matching saucers, and water glasses. I had a glass to drink from, and it sat with Miss Glory's on a separate shelf from the others. Soup spoons, gravy boat, butter knives, salad forks, and carving platter were additions to my vocabulary and in fact almost represented a new language. I was fascinated with the novelty, with the fluttering Mrs. Cullinan and her Alice-in-Wonderland house.

9   Her husband remains, in my memory, undefined. I lumped him with all the other white men that I had ever seen and tried not to see.

10   On our way home one evening, Miss Glory told me that Mrs. Cullinan couldn't have children. She said that she was too delicate-boned. It was hard to imagine bones at all under those layers of fat. Miss Glory went on to say that the doctor had taken out all her lady organs. I reasoned that a pig's organs included the lungs, heart, and liver, so if Mrs. Cullinan was walking around without those essentials, it explained why she drank alcohol out of unmarked bottles. She was keeping herself embalmed.

11   When I spoke to Bailey[1] about it, he agreed that I was right, but he also informed me that Mr. Cullinan had two daughters by a colored lady and that I knew them very well. He added that the girls were the spitting image of their father. I was unable to remember what he looked like, although I had just left him a few hours before, but I thought of the Coleman girls. They were very light-skinned and certainly didn't look very much like their mother (no one ever mentioned Mr. Coleman).

12   My pity for Mrs. Cullinan preceded me the next morning like the Cheshire cat's smile. Those girls, who could have been her daughters, were beautiful. They didn't have to straighten their hair. Even when they were caught in the rain, their braids still hung down straight like tamed snakes. Their mouths were pouty little cupid's bows. Mrs. Cullinan didn't know what she missed. Or maybe she did. Poor Mrs. Cullinan.

13   For weeks after, I arrived early, left late, and tried very hard to make up for her barrenness. If she had had her own children, she wouldn't have had to ask me to run a thousand errands from her back door to the back door of her friends. Poor old Mrs. Cullinan.

14   Then one evening Miss Glory told me to serve the ladies on the porch. After I set the tray down and turned toward the kitchen, one of the women asked, "What's your name, girl?" It was the speckled-faced one. Mrs. Cullinan said, "She doesn't talk much. Her name's Margaret."

15   "Is she dumb?"

16   "No. As I understand it, she can talk when she wants to but she's usually quiet as a little mouse. Aren't you, Margaret?"

---

1. The author's brother.—ED.

17   I smiled at her. Poor thing. No organs and couldn't even pronounce my name correctly.

18   "She's a sweet little thing, though."

19   "Well, that may be, but the name's too long. I'd never bother myself. I'd call her Mary if I was you."

20   I fumed into the kitchen. That horrible woman would never have the chance to call me Mary because if I was starving I'd never work for her. I decided I wouldn't pee on her if her heart was on fire. Giggles drifted in off the porch and into Miss Glory's pots. I wondered what they could be laughing about.

21   Whitefolks were so strange. Could they be talking about me? Everybody knew that they stuck together better than the Negroes did. It was possible that Mrs. Cullinan had friends in St. Louis who heard about a girl from Stamps being in court and wrote to tell her. Maybe she knew about Mr. Freeman.

22   My lunch was in my mouth a second time and I went outside and relieved myself on the bed of four-o'clocks. Miss Glory thought I might be coming down with something and told me to go on home, that Momma would give me some herb tea, and she'd explain to her mistress.

23   I realized how foolish I was being before I reached the pond. Of course Mrs. Cullinan didn't know. Otherwise she wouldn't have given me the two nice dresses that Momma cut down, and she certainly wouldn't have called me a "sweet little thing." My stomach felt fine, and I didn't mention anything to Momma.

24   That evening I decided to write a poem on being white, fat, old, and without children. It was going to be a tragic ballad. I would have to watch her carefully to capture the essence of her loneliness and pain.

25   The very next day, she called me by the wrong name. Miss Glory and I were washing up the lunch dishes when Mrs. Cullinan came to the doorway. "Mary?"

26   Miss Glory asked, "Who?"

27   Mrs. Cullinan, sagging a little, knew and I knew. "I want Mary to go down to Mrs. Randall's and take her some soup. She's not been feeling well for a few days."

28   Miss Glory's face was a wonder to see. "You mean Margaret, ma'am. Her name's Margaret."

29   "That's too long. She's Mary from now on. Heat that soup from last night and put it in the china tureen and, Mary, I want you to carry it carefully."

30   Every person I knew had a hellish horror of being "called out of his name." It was a dangerous practice to call a Negro anything that could be loosely construed as insulting because of the centuries of their having been called niggers, jigs, dinges, blackbirds, crows, boots, and spooks.

31   Miss Glory had a fleeting second of feeling sorry for me. Then as she handed me the hot tureen she said, "Don't mind, don't pay that no mind. Sticks and stones may break your bones, but words . . . You know, I been working for her for twenty years."

32   She held the back door open for me. "Twenty years. I wasn't much older than you. My name used to be Hallelujah. That's what Ma named me, but my mistress give me 'Glory,' and it stuck. I likes it better too."

33   I was in the little path that ran behind the houses when Miss Glory shouted, "It's shorter too."

34   For a few seconds it was a tossup over whether I would laugh (imagine being named Hallelujah) or cry (imagine letting some white woman rename you for her convenience). My anger saved me from either outburst. I had to quit the job, but the problem was going to be how to do it. Momma wouldn't allow me to quit for just any reason.

35   "She's a peach. That woman is a real peach." Mrs. Randall's maid was talking as she took the soup from me, and I wondered what her name used to be and what she answered to now.

36   For a week I looked into Mrs. Cullinan's face as she called me Mary. She ignored my coming late and leaving early. Miss Glory was a little annoyed because I had begun to leave egg yolk on the dishes and wasn't putting much heart in polishing the silver. I hoped that she would complain to our boss, but she didn't.

37   Then Bailey solved my dilemma. He had me describe the contents of the cupboard and the particular plates she liked best. Her favorite piece was a casserole shaped like a fish and the green glass coffee cups. I kept his instructions in mind, so on the next day when Miss Glory was hanging out clothes and I had again been told to serve the old biddies on the porch, I dropped the empty serving tray. When I heard Mrs. Cullinan scream, "Mary!" I picked up the casserole and two of the green glass cups in readiness. As she rounded the kitchen door I let them fall on the tiled floor.

38   I could never absolutely describe to Bailey what happened next, because each time I got to the part where she fell on the floor and screwed up her ugly face to cry, we burst out laughing. She actually wobbled around on the floor and picked up shards of the cups and cried, "Oh, Momma. Oh, dear Gawd. It's Momma's china from Virginia. Oh, Momma, I sorry."

39   Miss Glory came running in from the yard and the women from the porch crowded around. Miss Glory was almost as broken up as her mistress. "You mean to say she broke our Virginia dishes? What we gone do?"

40   Mrs. Cullinan cried louder, "That clumsy nigger. Clumsy little black nigger."

41   Old speckled-face leaned down and asked, "Who did it, Viola? Was it Mary? Who did it?"

42   Everything was happening so fast I can't remember whether her action preceded her words, but I know that Mrs. Cullinan said, "Her name's Margaret, goddamn it, her name's Margaret!" And she threw a wedge of the broken plate at me. It could have been the hysteria which put her aim off, but the flying crockery caught Miss Glory right over her ear and she started screaming.

43   I left the front door wide open so all the neighbors could hear.

44   Mrs. Cullinan was right about one thing. My name wasn't Mary.

WORD FOCUS

VOCABULARY GLOSS

bed of four o'clocks: *planted flowers (22)*

beneath her station: *below her social class (7)*

broken up: *devastated (39)*

Cheshire cat's smile: *a reference to the mysterious smiling cat in Lewis Carroll's* Alice's Adventures in Wonderland; *the cat disappears, leaving only its grin behind (12)*

didn't 'mount to much: *was of little consequence (6)*

finishing school: *a school where girls are taught proper manners (2)*

impish elf: *a mischievous little creature (3)*

lunch was in my mouth: *I was feeling nauseated, sick (22)*

mid-Victorian values: *a strict sense of ethics and morality that was typical of English society during the reign of Queen Victoria (1)*

munching along on a few of life's necessities: *getting by in life with just the basics (1)*

niggers, jigs, dinges, blackbirds, crows, boots, and spooks: *derogatory names for African Americans (30)*

old biddies: *a belittling term for old women (37)*

pay that no mind: *disregard it (31)*

pouty little cupid's bows: *lips pursed in the form of a kiss (12)*

relieved myself: *vomited (22)*

speckled-face: *someone with freckles (14)*

spitting image: *looking exactly alike; identical (11)*

Sticks and stones may break your bones, but words [will never hurt you]: *a saying that people's unkind words cannot hurt you (31)*

taken out all her lady organs: *performed a hysterectomy (10)*

tossup: *a decision based on chance; a decision made by throwing a coin in the air (34)*

tragic ballad: *a sad song (24)*

went without saying: *was understood (2)*

VOCABULARY QUESTIONS

1. *Antonyms* are words or phrases that generally have opposite meanings. *Synonyms* are words or phrases that have similar meanings. For example, an antonym of *happy* is *sad,* and an antonym of *pleasure* is *pain.* In the first sentence of the story, Margaret refers to "a white woman from Texas, who would quickly describe herself as a liberal" (1). Some synonyms for "liberal" are *broad-minded, tolerant,* and *generous.* Some antonyms are *conservative, traditional,* and *conventional.* Look up these words in the dictionary, and use both synonyms and antonyms to describe different points of view about Mrs. Cullinan.

2. In describing her employer's drinking habits, the narrator says that Mrs. Cullinan was "keeping herself embalmed" (10). Look up the dictionary definition of "embalm," and explain how it is being used to describe Mrs. Cullinan's drinking habits.

3. Words have *denotative* and *connotative* meanings. The denotation of a word is its central meaning and is directly related to objects or concepts. For example, the word "hometown" denotes the place where someone grows up. The connotation adds to the central meaning of "hometown," referring to associations and feelings that people have when the word is used. For example, "hometown" could be associated with love, childhood, or safety.

    At one point in the story the narrator says, "I fumed into the kitchen" (20). Make a list of some denotative and connotative meanings for the word "kitchen."

ENGLISH CRAFT

1. One student wrote the following journal response to "Mary":

   Maya Angelou's descriptions of Mrs. Cullinan are vivid. They depict her as a Southern society woman who appears gentle and isolated. Angelou says that Mrs. Cullinan is the fluttering type and lives in an Alice-in-Wonderland house.

   This student writer demonstrates two conventions of academic writing by: (1) using the author's full name (Maya Angelou) the first time she is mentioned and, thereafter, her last name only; and (2) making observations about the story in the present tense. Write a paragraph of your own using these two conventions to analyze two characters in the story.

2. A list is a powerful way to organize information. Each item in a list contributes to an overall impression. In her description of Mrs. Cullinan's house, Margaret remarks, "Soup spoons, gravy boat, butter knives, salad forks, and carving platter were additions to my vocabulary and in fact almost represented a new language" (8). Discuss the impression that this list creates.

3. The text of "Mary" is autobiographical. That is, it is about the author's life. Other words used to talk about a text are *story, essay,* and *report.* Define each of these terms, and discuss what would be confusing about referring to "Mary" as an essay or report.

    The following are some other words used in talking or writing about a text: *author, narrator, speaker, character.* Look up these terms in a dictionary, and discuss which of them applies to "Mary."

INTERPRETIVE JOURNAL

1. The narrator ends her description of Mrs. Cullinan's home by calling it an "Alice-in-Wonderland house" (8). Referring to the narrator's descriptions throughout the story, identify what some of the characteristics of an "Alice-in-Wonderland house" may be. Check your definition in a dictionary, and show how these features exist in Mrs. Cullinan's house.

2. At the end of the story, after she sees her broken dishes, Mrs. Cullinan shouts, "Her name's Margaret, goddamn it, her name's Margaret!" (42). What does Mrs. Cullinan's use of the word "goddamn" reveal about her?

3. When the narrator says, "Every person I know had a hellish horror of being 'called out of his name'" (30), she associates it with a familiar childhood saying, "Sticks and stones may break [my] bones, but words [will never hurt me]" (31). In what ways can names hurt? Does this saying offer protection against the hurt that Angelou describes in her story, or against any hurt?

ESSAY QUESTION

The story "Mary" is an excerpt from the author's autobiography, *I Know Why the Caged Bird Sings.* Discuss how the words "caged" and "sings" may illustrate Margaret's attitude toward her situation and identity. You might want to explore whether or not she breaks out of her cage.

Peter Freuchen
Dead Man's Cache

Preview

Think about some of the different rules that you need to learn when you enter a new situation—such as a new community, a new job, or even a new country. Discuss two problems that you may encounter in learning the rules. How does past experience help you to deal with these problems?

Word Preview

You can familiarize yourself with the following words by looking them up in the dictionary. You can broaden your knowledge of these words by pronouncing them and understanding how they are used in context.

ordeal (1)	mangled (31)	whelp (62)
cloister (13)	menial (33)	festering (63)
disillusion (15)	boisterous (38)	dub (63)
jagged (18)	tempest (43)	unabated (65)
tundra (20)	igloo (52)	promontory (66)
mending (24)	bevel (53)	suppressed (66)
shirked (26)	rousted (55)	vanished (76)
pelts (27)	buffeted (56)	stupor (76)
tormentors (29)	agony (59)	incredulously (82)
lust (30)	daze (60)	hideous (88)
strenuous (30)		

1   Elmer is dead. Old Tulimak brought me the news and we sat for a long time without talking, reaching out once in a while for the coffee pot on the stove, mourning a man who was a good friend to me and a good friend to all the Eskimos. It is hard to think of him as dead and even harder to think what an ordeal he survived, only to lose out to common

influenza. After a while Tulimak and I talked, and it was decided that now I am released from my old promise. Now at last I am free to tell the strange story of Elmer Boyle and Gotthart Snider, though I've not used their right names for fear of hurting someone even yet.

2   It began a long way from the Arctic, in a little town in New England where both boys were born and grew up. They were about the same age but different in every way. Elmer never had the breaks. His trouble started before he was born, when his mother was a pretty nurse in the local hospital and got too interested in a sailor patient with good looks and a smooth line.

3   When the sailor got well he took the nurse out a few times and the sailor did what a lot of sailors do and then went away to sea and probably never gave her another thought. Pretty soon she had to give up nursing and go away somewhere for a year. When she came back she had Elmer and, of course, no reputation left at all. A thing like that will set tongues to wagging anywhere, but they wag worst in a New England town.

4   Naturally nobody would hire a nurse who got into that kind of trouble, so Elmer's mother took up dressmaking. She did pretty well, because she had to work cheap. Nobody would think of paying her the same price a decent woman would charge, any more than they would think of saying "Good morning" to her on the street or of asking her into their homes.

5   Elmer grew up under that cloud, without any friends or any other clothes except mostly cast-offs, and no spending money. The kids made life hell for him all the time, so he took to hiding out in the woods. He built himself a secret hut and spent most of his time there, filling up the emptiness inside him by getting acquainted with the birds and animals and all outdoor life. It was the one place he felt happy and like a whole person.

6   Then times got tougher and he had to quit school and take a job in a local factory, and that was pure misery. He didn't dare complain, though, because everybody said what a fine Christian man the owner was to give a good job to someone like Elmer. The real reason was he could make Elmer work longer and for less money than boys who just wanted spending money.

7   There was only one good part about that job: the night watchman was an old Hudson Bay man, and sometimes Elmer would sit around half the night listening to stories of bear hunts and dog sledge runs under the Northern Lights. Elmer made up his mind that some day he was going to do those things himself. His mother had been withering away for a long time, like a flower cut off from water. When she died, mostly of pure loneliness, Elmer just boarded up the house and

disappeared. Nobody knew where he went and nobody much cared, least of all Gotthart Snider.

8   Gotthart was a big, mean, overgrown bully, the son of a German butcher and always a troublemaker in school and out. His favorite sport was picking on smaller kids and beating them up, and of course picking on Elmer was the most fun of all, because Elmer had nobody to stand up for him. Gotthart knew the old Hudson Bay man, too, and in a way that's how this story all came to happen.

9   Somehow the stories he heard gave Gotthart the idea that the Arctic was a great place for excitement and adventure and easy money without much effort, which suited him just fine. Still, until he got into the Big Trouble, he never really figured on going north.

10   He was running around with Mabel Greencut, the daughter of the factory owner, and in no time his money was used up, but not his passion. He needed more money, so he just helped himself to some that belonged to, of all people, Mabel's own father. He got caught, because along with everything else, Gotthart wasn't very bright. He got a good, stiff prison term, and when he got out he had a sneaking hunch he wouldn't be welcome in his home town.

11   Some of the crowd he met in jail were going north to work in a mine up around the Cobbermine River, where they looked more at a man's muscles than they did at his past. Gotthart remembered how the old Hudson Bay stories used to fire him up, so he decided to go along.

12   In no time he found out that toiling in a mine with clouds of mosquitoes so thick he couldn't breathe wasn't his idea of adventure. By that time the mine bosses had found out that having muscles didn't make Gotthart any bargain, either. He complained so much and so loud about everything that he was getting the rest of the men dissatisfied and cutting down on work, and he was always whining about having a stomachache or a lame back so he couldn't work. They were trying to figure out how to get rid of Gotthart, short of kicking him out into the wilderness with winter coming on, when he settled it for himself.

13   Six men came along in a big canoe, heading north for a winter of hunting and trapping in the real Arctic. Seven men had started, but one took sick and had to be left behind with some holy brothers in a cloister hospital. Now they were short-handed and willing to offer a share in the expedition to another man.

14   "I'll go," Gotthart said. He figured anything was better than mining.

15   They looked at his muscles and accepted. The mine crowd was too glad to be rid of him to disillusion them, so off they went.

16   At first it was easy, just Gotthart's style, sitting in the canoe while wind and current did all the work. Then they came to a wild rapids where all their heavy stuff had to be portaged while the steersman ran

the canoe through almost empty. "I should have a man in the bow," the steersman told them, "to fend us off the big rocks. Somebody with experience."

17   The other men looked at the white, thundering rapids and shook their heads. Gotthart looked at the heavy packs that had to be lugged a mile or more and spoke up fast. "I'll handle the bow pole. I'm an old man at it."

18   When the rapids caught hold and they began racing and whirling and bouncing, with jagged black teeth of rocks reaching out on all sides, he almost wished he had taken the portage. He was half blind and dizzy from the speed and the spume, but for once he was too scared to fold up. He yelled his panic into the roar of the rapids and jabbed crazily at the hurtling rocks, but by a miracle they got through without a scrape. Gotthart was shaking all over and sick with his fright until the steersman said, "You did a mighty fine job there, fellow. You're a real boatman."

19   Gotthart stopped shaking and started bragging. After that he rode every rapids and missed all the carry work, but before long the others began to see what kind of companion they had picked up and they weren't too happy. An arctic winter is bad enough to take without being cooped up with somebody like Gotthart. But they had him, and they couldn't get rid of him now.

20   The expedition was to split up, part of them staying in the lower Arctic and the rest going on far up into the real barren tundra beyond the tree line. When they reached the first company post it didn't look too bad. The company hut was sound and comfortable, there were plenty of provisions and at least a scattering of stunted trees. Gotthart looked it over and wanted to know which bunk was his.

21   "Huh-uh," the boss said. "We stay here. You go on north with Ralph and Billy to the other post."

22   Gotthart wasn't happy, but he couldn't do anything about it. He got more unhappy when he saw his winter home up in the bleakest tundra, without trees or grass.

23   The hut was there, but some Eskimos had helped themselves to a couple of siding boards to fix a sledge runner or something, and there was no wood to patch it with. All they could do was tear the whole hut down and rebuild it smaller to eliminate the hole, and that was mighty hard work. Ralph and Billy were hard workers themselves, and they expected as much or more out of Gotthart. He whined and complained and that didn't help relations, either.

24   With that job done, they set him to mending nets while they began storing up whitefish for winter food. The nets were always getting ripped on rocks, so his job was never finished. With winter coming on, the other two couldn't wait around for Gotthart to take his time. They gave

him a couple of warnings and then they took him out and gave him the beating of his life.

25   "We took you on because you said you'd work," Ralph told him grimly. "Now you're going to work and do your share, or you don't eat or sleep inside. There's no time to coddle slackers in the Arctic."

26   Gotthart sobbed and whined, but after he missed a meal and found himself locked outside with a cold night wind coming up, he howled his surrender. For a while he really did work, because he was afraid not to. As long as he did his job, they were easy and friendly. When he shirked, like the day he failed to bring in a full supply of firewood, he got the same treatment, only worse.

27   He thought he would die then, but that was only the beginning. When they started setting traplines for muskrats and martens and foxes, they made him go along to learn the job because he was expected to run his share of line and produce his share of pelts.

28   By noon of his first day with Ralph, Gotthart was so tired he lay down and cried, but there was no rest for him. "Get going or stay here and die," Ralph told him bluntly. "We're stuck with you, so we mean to make a man of you or kill you trying. This is nothing. Wait until snow comes and you have to stay out alone from Monday to Friday running your set."

29   Somehow Gotthart made it back. Then he had to chop ice and get water as well as work on frames for stretching skins before they let him fall into his bunk. His last thought was a fierce determination to kill his tormentors. He would shoot them the moment the first snowstorm came and then report that they were lost in the storm.

30   With every day of added hell, Gotthart's lust for murder grew in him. They drove him unmercifully, day after day, and while Gotthart was still convinced he was being worked to death, he was actually getting hardened so the work was not nearly as strenuous as he still imagined. For a while he nourished himself on his dream of freedom.

31   Then the wolves began to come down with winter. He heard them howling outside at night and the bloodthirsty sound filled him with trembling terror. Billy and Ralph talked of experienced arctic trappers killed and mangled by the brutes. Gotthart suddenly realized how helpless he would be alone. To paddle back up that wild river unaided was impossible, and he knew no trail and had no dog sledge to carry provisions. With that realization, his dream of murder evaporated, and he began to feel like a rat caught in one of his own traps. When he wasn't too weary to think at all, he lay in his bunk and wept tears of self-pity each night.

32   Day by day the work speeded up and the men drove him more mercilessly. Then came the snow, endless and terrible and frightening, and

the fresh agony of learning to use snowshoes. It was like running up-stairs all day, until his legs wanted to break off at the knees and the agony of cramped muscles made him howl. "You'll get the knack," they told him without sympathy. "In a month you'll walk as naturally as you did without them." Gotthart began to yearn for the comparative ease of life in prison.

33   He proved such a poor trapper that in disgust they left him at home to prepare skins, cut firewood, and do other menial jobs to pay for his grub. When he tried to shirk even those duties, he was beaten harder and warned with frightening grimness of even worse penalties. The Arctic lays its terrible weight on all and there is no place for weaklings or non-producers. Gotthart looked ahead at five more months of agony and burst into tears.

34   Then one day he peered across the snow and saw a dog team approaching with two muffled figures trotting easily behind the sledge. They swung up and halted. The taller man threw back his parka.

35   "Well, I'll be damned! Gotthart Snider."

36   It was Elmer Boyle, of all the people on earth. Elmer had followed his dreams to the Arctic long before and found his world in the frozen wastes. Tall and husky and bronzed, he was working for the Canadian government, delivering mail and messages to remote Eskimo tribes and isolated trappers. With him was a young man named Ryan, a *chechako,* a newcomer in his first year north but already making a place for himself with his enthusiasm and his eagerness to learn.

37   After that first startled greeting, Elmer was no more than cool to his old schoolmate. He knew Gotthart too well from personal experience and knew of his prison record. Gotthart, on his part, was cautious. This rugged, confident giant bore little resemblance to the helpless boy he had picked on remorselessly at home. He measured the muscular frame, gauged the steady gray eyes, and shivered.

38   Ralph and Billy returned to give the newcomers a boisterous welcome. They knew Elmer well and liked Ryan on sight as much as they despised Gotthart. After the first shock of amazement at finding that two such opposites had been boyhood neighbors, they excluded him from the conversation for a long time. It was not until the next day that he learned what was on their minds.

39   "Ryan wants to join our crew and we want him, Elmer," Ralph said. "You can probably guess what a worthless burden Gotthart has been to us. If you'll take him off our hands, back to the nearest post, and leave Ryan, we'll be everlastingly grateful. If he stays here any longer, we won't be responsible for what might happen to him. You look like a person who could handle him for a short trip."

40   Elmer turned those cold gray eyes on Gotthart for a penetrating moment. "I can handle him."

41   "Now, wait," Gotthart yelled, frightened at the look and at his own memories. "I'm not going off into the wilderness with him. I can't stand such a journey in this cold. I won't go."

42   "Gotthart." Billy said softly, caressing his rifle. "Maybe you don't know that a trapper always checks his supply of sugar and tobacco. Ours has been disappearing too fast. Robbing supplies in the Arctic is a major crime. You could be shot for it, and nobody in the Arctic would blame the man who did it."

43   Gotthart subsided, blubbering and shaking. Elmer faced him grimly. "I'll take you, on one condition. You do your full share of the labor and you'll get your full share of food. Do less and you'll get less. Lag behind and you'll be left behind." Gotthart could only remain silent, but in his heart raged a new tempest of murderous hatred and all of it was suddenly directed at Elmer Boyle.

44   From the start, the journey into the sub-zero cold of full Arctic winter was ten times worse than Gotthart's imaginings. It was bad enough to learn that he must run on snowshoes instead of riding the sledge runners. Luckily, he was hardened enough by then to keep up, but he wailed steadily. Elmer ignored him. By night they pitched a thin tent and, if they found a few sticks, had a brief fire for warmth. Otherwise they cooked on a kerosene primus stove and had no heat.

45   The gale hit them without warning, coming in the night. Gotthart awoke as the tent whipped away, and with it his boots and mittens. Dogs and sledge were lost somewhere behind a white wall of screaming torment that engulfed them.

46   Somehow Elmer got his own spare boots and mittens, got his companion dressed and dragged him to the poor shelter of the river bank. Gotthart howled and cursed all the way. "You're dragging me somewhere to die."

47   "Don't be a fool," Elmer shouted above the wind. "Why should I do that? I promised to get you out and I will."

· · · · · · · ·

48   The gale howled on without letup while they huddled and felt the numbness creep over them. By the next day they were half frozen. Elmer stood up with a struggle. "Come on. We can't keep this up much longer. Follow me and don't get lost."

49   "I can't," Gotthart wailed. "I won't. You can't make me."

50   He tried to fight back, and suddenly he was being jerked up with amazing strength, then hurled to the snow with stunning force. Again

and again Elmer lifted him and threw him down, smiling as Gotthart cursed and cried and pawed at him.

51   Suddenly Gotthart realized that he was getting warm, that blood was once more coursing through his body. Elmer grinned at him then and stopped. "It was the best way to get us warm. Now we can huddle down again with our sleeping bags and last out the day."

52   That night the wind died. Elmer dragged the cursing Gotthart up and forced him to stumble around until they found the half-buried sledge, its cargo intact, the dogs snugly curled nearby. Their tent was gone, with the caribou skins they put under sleeping bags for warmth, but Elmer was optimistic. "The snow is packed now so we can make ourselves an igloo each night. It's warmer, anyhow, and there's no frozen canvas to struggle with."

53   The big snowknife carved out heavy blocks. These were set in a circle and gradually built into a solid dome. Gotthart momentarily forgot his hate in admiration as Elmer cut his way out after placing the last block. When he would have dived inside, Elmer caught him back. "Not yet. Take a knife and help bevel the cracks between all the blocks. They have to be packed with snow like mortar to keep out the wind."

54   Finally the job was done, the corn meal and seal oil cooked for the seven dogs, and then their own slim supper. "The dogs are fed first," Elmer explained, not unkindly, "because they haven't the resistance we have and our lives depend upon them. We'll all be on short rations until we reach my big cache on the coast, unless by luck we sight a bear or caribou. I only hope the dogs' strength holds out until we make it."

55   Gotthart was silent, hating Elmer for his logic and his knowledge, hating him for feeding dogs ahead of men. Still he was forced to admit that their snug night in the igloo was the pleasantest so far, although much too short. Elmer rousted him out long before light to take full advantage of the packed snow. With luck, they could make the cache in five days, eat their fill and rest a day or two before pushing on to civilization. But in the Arctic man could rarely trust in his luck to hold. Theirs ran out in a day and a half.

56   The second gale hit them a little past noon, more savage than the first had been. The howling wind buffeted them and slashed their faces with a million knives. A white wall hid the dogs. In that screaming, agonizing tumult there was no sense of direction.

57   Gotthart stumbled and fell and huddled there, sobbing wild curses, his face whitening with frostbite. Elmer caught hold of his arm and struggled to drag him to his feet. "We've got to go on as long as we can. Every inch we make it toward the cache is another chance to survive. Get up."

58   "I won't!" the other screamed. "I won't move. I can't."

59   Elmer stepped back, his face grim, and swung the long dog-whip. Gotthart screamed again as the lashes stung him mercilessly, over and over, until the pain was greater than the agony of exhaustion. Somehow he got to his feet and they stumbled on.

60   They endured that nightmare journey almost two hours before Elmer was willing to give in. The moment they stopped, the dogs simply curled up in their tracks and vanished under a blanket of sheltering snow. For the two men there was no such easy rest. Gotthart stumbled in a daze of exhaustion while Elmer found packed snow, cut the blocks and began their igloo. In the teeth of the terrible wind, Gotthart had to brace the walls with his body to keep the blocks from being hurled down before the lower rounds were finished.

61   When Gotthart howled and protested that he could not breathe in the storm, Elmer, too tired to argue, did the job himself. He came back to find Gotthart dozing on the floor. Nothing had been done. No hard-packed snow was melting for water. The snow had not been brushed from their sleeping bags nor the ice beaten out of the mattress skins.

62   "You damned, worthless, no-good whelp," Elmer roared, and his fist lashed out. Gotthart fell back, blood streaming from his nose. He struggled to get up and Elmer knocked him down again and again until exhaustion had replaced rage. "Get the hell out and cut blocks for drinking water, damn you. And none of this loose snow, either. Find packed stuff so we'll be sure of plenty."

63   Gotthart stumbled out into the terrible storm with a new and deeper rage festering in his mind. He had wanted to destroy his tormentors before, but those feelings had been mild compared to this new fierce longing to kill Elmer Boyle. Suddenly it came to him that soon he could enjoy that pleasure without any fear. This storm was really his ally. When it ended and they were close to the precious cache, so close that not even a dub could miss, the deed could be done. A shot in the back, a body left for the wolves, and Gotthart would have everything to himself. He could invent any of a dozen fatal accidents blamed on the storm and no one could doubt or disprove him. When he returned to the igloo he was almost happy in his new-found hope.

64   All that night the storm blew in savage gusts and by morning there was no sign of letup. Gotthart was hungry and said so. Elmer shook his head. "Sorry, but I'm afraid you'll get a lot hungrier. This storm might last for days, but our food supply won't. One of the first rules in the Arctic is to fast the first three days of storm. That still leaves you enough food and strength to go on again. Otherwise we might eat everything and die of starvation waiting for it to clear, or be too weak to travel when we could."

65   Gotthart made so little protest that Elmer gave him a look of sharp

surprise. They settled down with their pipes and their thoughts. The storm raged unabated through the day, and eventually the weight of solitude and the pangs of hunger drove them to talking. They avoided childhood and the immediate past and for a time were almost friendly.

66 Elmer estimated, he told his companion, that two to three days of clear travel would see them at the cache, where a generous supply of food for men and dogs had been stored for just such emergencies. They were following the river which emptied into the sea. A scant twenty miles west of its mouth was a tiny promontory with a slight rise at its tip, too small to be called a hill but easy to identify. Here was his cache, raised on a high pole out of reach of marauding bears and clearly visible. Gotthart listened and suppressed a smile of triumph. Elmer, the fool, was making his plan childishly simple.

67 At last the storm began to wane. They set out before it was over, because now every minute was precious. Gotthart did his full share of packing for once, telling himself that he was preparing his own survival after Elmer's death.

68 They made the coast at last, only to find the shore piled high with ice. They had to stay inland over rough ground and inch their way, but at last there came the moment when Elmer saw a landmark. "We're ten miles from the cache, Gotthart. Ten miles west along the shore and we're saved. We'll camp now and finish in the morning when we're fresher."

69 That night the third gale hit them and pinned them down for a day of torture. Gotthart was sure he was dying of hunger, but Elmer laughed at him. "You'd be surprised how much you can take. A fast like this is good for you. Stop whining and think of the feast we'll have at the cache."

70 The next day the wind was down enough to travel and they set out in new high spirits. Presently Elmer went on ahead to get his bearings from a high ice peak. Gotthart and the dogs dropped in their tracks. He was too tired even to unlash the rifle on the sled. That could come later. The moment Elmer reported the cache in sight, he would find the strength to complete his plan of murder.

71 Gotthart awoke to see Elmer stumbling toward him, his whole figure glistening with ice. "Hurry!" Elmer yelled. "I'm drenched and freezing. I fell into a crack where two floes had parted and had to swim to solid ice. Get an igloo built quick and get my sleeping bag beaten out. If I don't get a change fast, I'm done for. Get moving, man."

• • • • • • • •

72 Gotthart gaped at him stupidly. "Igloo? But . . . but you never taught me how to build one."

73   "Then I'll build it," Elmer panted, "but get my sleeping bag beaten out and my change of clothes. Hurry, you fool."

74   He worked furiously, cutting and setting the blocks. Gotthart did as he was told, but his mind was whirling with this unexpected good fortune. Now there was no risk at all, no rifle slug to be found, no possible question of accidental death.

75   With the house done, Elmer swiftly undressed and crawled into the sleeping bag. "Take my clothes outside. As soon as the water freezes you can beat it out of them as ice. It won't be warm but at least it will be dry and we can make the cache before dark."

76   Gotthart took the clothes and vanished outside. Elmer fell into a stupor of exhaustion, cold and shock. At last, after an endless time, he aroused himself and yelled for Gotthart. There was no answer. He called again and again and at last forced himself to brave the savage cold long enough to peer outside.

77   A deep, terrible curse burst from his lips. There was no one outside, no frozen clothing, nothing but a fresh trail and at the end of it, far to the west, the tiny figure of Gotthart clumsily driving the dogs toward the cache.

78   For a time Elmer's rage bordered close to madness. He was left without food or clothing, to die here so near his cache. At last, back in his sleeping bag for protection, the rage wore itself out and with the creeping cold came a dreamy sense of well-being.

79   The day dragged on and the cold bit deeper and in time Elmer knew that Gotthart was not coming back. By then he was too far gone to care. . . .

80   On the ice, Gotthart was alternately jubilant and frightened. His hated enemy was dead or dying, and no one on earth could blame Gotthart. They might even hail him as a hero and reward him for his courage in trying to get help in time.

81   When he finally saw the little unmistakable promontory with the hillock at its tip it took him moments to realize he had found his goal. Then the knowledge struck him and he forgot the dogs, forgot everything, to stumble crazily out over the ice toward the haven of promised food and fuel.

82   He reached the hummock and climbed and stared wildly, incredulously around. Here was the exact spot Elmer had described. Every landmark was clear and unmistakable. Everything was in its place . . . except the pole that held the cache.

83   He ran wildly, he cried and sobbed and blubbered, he cursed and called and even prayed, but nowhere was there a sign of the pole above the broken expanse of snow and ice. He climbed onto the highest jumble of rocks and ice chunks to see if perhaps another point might be the

right one. He could see nothing and he was too utterly weary to hunt further.

84   He must have sleep first. He thought of the sleeping bag back on the sled and cursed his foolishness in abandoning it. Now he lacked the strength to go back and get it. He had to sleep a little first. Then he would be stronger.

· · · · · · · ·

85   Three Eskimos, Tulimak, Papeek, and a friend, came to their cache of caribou and stared with rage. A bear had been at it, only hours before to judge by the tracks. The meat was devoured, the cache stones scattered. This was serious and infuriating. In the code of the Arctic, the robber of a cache deserves to die. Besides, this particular robber could supply his own flesh in place of what he had stolen.

86   They set out grimly to track down the bear, and that is how they came upon a hastily made igloo and a man without clothing or food and almost dead from the cold. But the Eskimos are wise in the ways of the North. They cared for Elmer and brought the blood back to his veins. Then, warmly wrapped in skins, they took him to their village and nursed him back to strength.

87   In the spring, when the ice broke, Elmer and his saviors set out by kayak for the post. On the way they passed the little point where the cache was stored, and Elmer asked that they go ashore to see if, by chance, Gotthart had reached the cache and revived himself enough to escape.

88   With the snow gone, the cache was plain to see, the stout boxes of food for man and dogs, the spare skins and clothing, the fuel for the stove. They were there, scratched and marked by a prowling bear, but safely closed. On top of the little mound they made on the hummock, the highest point anywhere near, the place a dying man would climb for his last despairing search of the horizon, they found a hideous thing.

89   It lay sprawled across the little artificial hill. Foxes and ravens and gulls had been at it, but there was enough of the clothing left to identify the body.

90   Gotthart had lain down for his last sleep on top of the very snow-buried cache that could have saved his life.

91   They found the pole down by the shore. Some bad-tempered bear, irritated at this man-thing poking up above his familiar world of snow and ice, had batted it down and eaten the fresh meat tied to its top. The snow had quickly hidden the pole.

92   But any man who knows the Arctic knows a thing like that happens all the time in the North.

WORD FOCUS

VOCABULARY GLOSS

the breaks: *the opportunities (2)*

cast-offs: *clothes discarded by others (5)*

coddle slackers: *pamper lazy people (25)*

fire him up: *get him excited (11)*

fold up: *lose courage; give up (18)*

helped himself to: *took without permission; stole (10)*

inch their way: *move very slowly and cautiously (68)*

kayak: *a light, narrow boat (87)*

kerosene primus stove: *a stove used while camping outdoors (44)*

Northern Lights: *a display of lights in the night sky; also known as aurora borealis (7)*

set tongues to wagging: *start gossip (3)*

a smooth line: *glib talk (2)*

sneaking hunch: *a suspicion (10)*

spume: *foamy water (18)*

stand up for: *support or defend (8)*

too far gone: *completely exhausted; close to death (79)*

took sick: *became ill (13)*

tree line: *a point beyond which trees do not grow (20)*

under that cloud: *bearing that stigma or shame (5)*

VOCABULARY QUESTIONS

1. The word *cash* is a term for money, whereas the word "cache" (pronounced in the same way as *cash*), is a hiding place for valuable items. Such pairs of words are called *homonyms* because they are identical in sound and sometimes even in spelling but different in meaning. Look up the following homonyms in the dictionary and use them in sentences:

rain	reign	rein
bank	bank	
their	there	they're

2. Since "chechako" may be an unfamiliar word to his audience, the author signals its meaning through his choice of other words nearby. Freuchen

writes that Ryan is "a *chechako,* a newcomer in his first year north but already making a place for himself with his enthusiasm and his eagerness to learn" (36). Underline the words and phrases that define "chechako," and find other words in a dictionary or thesaurus that can be used as synonyms.

3. Some phrases are difficult to understand even if you know the meanings of each word in the phrase. Look at the following phrases used in this text, and propose a meaning for each one. Refer to your dictionary, and examine the context in which the phrase is used in "Dead Man's Cache." Rewrite Freuchen's sentences, substituting other words while keeping the original meaning.

hiding out (5)   cooped up with (19)
picking on (8)   get rid of (19)
stand up for (8)   lashed out (62)
figured on (9)   pinned down (69)
running around with (10)

ENGLISH CRAFT

1. A writer connects ideas throughout a text not only by repeating important key words, but also by using words that provide different perspectives of a core idea. For example, Freuchen repeats the following verbs in order to create a picture of Gotthart's actions: "whined" (23), "complained" (23), and "protest" (65). Look through the text and make a list of other verbs that contribute to creating a picture of the way Gotthart acts. Do the same for Elmer and the men with whom he works.

2. The narrator describes Elmer's mother as someone who has been "withering away for a long time, like a flower cut off from water" (7). Note that the narrator compares Elmer's mother to a flower by using the word "like." This kind of comparison is called a *simile.* By comparing Mrs. Boyle to a flower, we picture her in a certain way. Discuss this picture we get of Mrs. Boyle's attributes. Write three similes to create a broader picture of three other characters in the story.

3. People communicate with each other for many different reasons: for example, to exchange information, to manipulate or deceive, to persuade, and to teach. Describe two incidents when Elmer and Gotthart communicate with each other, and discuss the purpose of their communication.

INTERPRETIVE JOURNAL

1. The narrator claims that Elmer Boyle's "trouble started before he was born" (2). What trouble did Elmer face at birth and during his childhood? How do you think these troubles influenced his adult personality? Use this information to write a brief character sketch of Elmer Boyle.

2. Gotthart Snider is described as a "big, mean, overgrown bully" (8). How do these personality traits get in the way of his understanding the communities in which he lives? Provide a brief character sketch of Gotthart Snider, and compare it with your description of Elmer Boyle.

3. Pay particular attention to the title of this story, "Dead Man's Cache." Write a paragraph explaining the meaning of the title, and relate it to specific parts of the story.

4. Discuss the interactions of the group of men at the first Arctic camp, and point out what creates a bond among them (23–27). Describe the nature of this type of bonding among men (and women) in other situations.

5. Freuchen says, "In the code of the Arctic, the robber . . . deserves to die" (85). Why might a man or woman like Elmer Boyle consider such punishment harsh in the United States but necessary in the Arctic?

ESSAY QUESTION

Discuss the relationship between Elmer Boyle and Gotthart Snider, which started when they were boys, and show what aspects of their backgrounds made them incompatible teammates. In this analysis, describe in detail how the shifts of environment contribute to the tension between these two men.

Edward Abbey

Water

Preview

Discuss a place you have visited where you had to behave differently in order to protect yourself. Write in detail about the changes you made and your reaction to them.

Word Preview

You can familiarize yourself with the following words by looking them up in the dictionary. You can broaden your knowledge of these words by pronouncing them and understanding how they are used in context.

barren (3)	brim (38)	menace (63)
desolate (6)	transfixed (39)	slickrock (65)
aridity (10)	deluge (40)	slake (66)
dome (11)	turrets (40)	gourd (66)
perennial (13)	pellucid (41)	summit (66)
fens (14)	scuds (44)	devoid (67)
potable (17)	amoeba (45)	counterpoint (68)
enervates (20)	forelip (45)	perseverance (69)
prostrates (20)	spoor (45)	metamorphosis (71)
quenched (23)	dun (46)	trivial (71)
mirage (23)	avalanche (49)	illusory (71)
maze (24)	contours (50)	austerely (72)
guise (27)	quicksand (50)	interminably (75)
colander (28)	extricate (52)	schemes (75)
exasperation (29)	defile (53)	diverting (75)
transfigured (30)	ghastly (54)	monomania (76)
monolith (34)	abysmal (54)	obsession (76)
pinnacles (35)	caterwauling (54)	

1   "This would be good country," a tourist says to me, "if only you had some water."

2   He's from Cleveland, Ohio.

3   "If we had water here," I reply, "this country would not be what it is. It would be like Ohio, wet and humid and hydrological, all covered with cabbage farms and golf courses. Instead of this lovely barren desert we would have only another blooming garden state, like New Jersey. You see what I mean?"

4   "If you had more water more people could live here."

5   "Yes sir. And where then would people go when they wanted to see something besides people?"

6   "I see what you mean. Still, I wouldn't want to live here. So dry and desolate. Nice for pictures but my God I'm glad I don't have to live here."

7   "I'm glad too, sir. We're in perfect agreement. You wouldn't want to live here, I wouldn't want to live in Cleveland. We're both satisfied with the arrangement as it is. Why change it?"

8   "Agreed."

9   We shake hands and the tourist from Ohio goes away pleased, as I am pleased, each of us thinking he has taught the other something new.

10   The air is so dry here I can hardly shave in the mornings. The water and soap dry on my face as I reach for the razor: aridity. It is the driest season of a dry country. In the afternoons of July and August we may get thundershowers but an hour after the storms pass the surface of the desert is again bone dry.

11   It seldom rains. The geography books credit this part of Utah with an annual precipitation of five to nine inches but that is merely a statistical average. Low enough, to be sure. And in fact the rainfall and snowfall vary widely from year to year and from place to place even within the Arches region. When a cloud bursts open above the Devil's Garden the sun is blazing down on my ramada. And wherever it rains in this land of unclothed rock the run off is rapid down cliff and dome through the canyons to the Colorado.

12   Sometimes it rains and still fails to moisten the desert—the falling water evaporates halfway down between cloud and earth. Then you see curtains of blue rain dangling out of reach in the sky while the living things wither below for want of water. Torture by tantalizing, hope without fulfillment. And the clouds disperse and dissipate into nothingness.

13   Streambeds are usually dry. The dry wash, dry gulch, *arroyo seco*. Only after a storm do they carry water and then but briefly—a few minutes, a couple of hours. The spring-fed perennial stream is a rarity. In this area we have only two of them, Salt Creek and Onion Creek, the first too salty to drink and the second laced with arsenic and sulfur.

14   Permanent springs or waterholes are likewise few and far between though not so rare as the streams. They are secret places deep in the canyons, known only to the deer and the coyotes and the dragonflies and a few others. Water rises slowly from these springs and flows in little rills over bare rock, over and under sand, into miniature fens of wire grass, rushes, willow and tamarisk. The water does not flow very far before disappearing into the air and under the ground. The flow may reappear farther down the canyon, surfacing briefly for a second time, a third time, diminishing in force until it vanishes completely and for good.

15   Another type of spring may be found on canyon walls where water seeps out between horizontal formations through cracks thinner than paper to support small hanging gardens of orchids, monkeyflower, maidenhair fern, and ivy. In most of these places the water is so sparingly measured that it never reaches the canyon floor at all but is taken up entirely by the thirsty plant life and transformed into living tissue.

16   Long enough in the desert a man like other animals can learn to smell water. Can learn, at least, the smell of things associated with water—the unique and heartening odor of the cottonwood tree, for example, which in the canyonlands is the tree of life. In this wilderness of naked rock burnt to auburn or buff or red by ancient fires there is no vision more pleasing to the eyes and more gratifying to the heart than the translucent acid green (bright gold in autumn) of this venerable tree. It signifies water, and not only water but also shade, in a country where shelter from the sun is sometimes almost as precious as water.

17   *Signifies* water, which may or may not be on the surface, visible and available. If you have what is called a survival problem and try to dig for this water during the heat of the day, the effort may cost you more in sweat than you will find to drink. A bad deal. Better to wait for nightfall when the cottonwoods and other plants along the streambed will release some of the water which they have absorbed during the day, perhaps enough to allow a potable trickle to rise to the surface of the sand. If the water still does not appear you may then wish to attempt to dig for it. Or you might do better by marching farther up the canyon. Sooner or later you should find a spring or at least a little seep on the canyon wall. On the other hand you could possibly find no water at all, anywhere. The desert is a land of surprises, some of them terrible surprises. Terrible as derived from terror.

18   When out for a walk carry water; not less than a gallon a day per person.

19   More surprises. In places you will find clear-flowing streams, such as Salt Creek near Turnbow Cabin, where the water looks beautifully drinkable but tastes like brine.

20   You might think, beginning to die of thirst, that any water however

salty would be better than none at all. Not true. Small doses will not keep you going or alive and a deep drink will force your body to expend water in getting rid of the excess salt. This results in a net loss of bodily moisture and a hastening of the process of dehydration. Dehydration first enervates, then prostrates, then kills.

21   Nor is blood, your own or a companion's, any adequate substitute for water; blood is too salty. The same is true of urine.

22   If it's your truck or car which has failed you, you'd be advised to tap the radiator, unless it's full of Prestone. If this resource is not available and water cannot be found in the rocks or under the sand and you find yourself too tired and discouraged to go on, crawl into the shade and wait for help to find you. If no one is looking for you write your will in the sand and let the wind carry your last words and signature east to the borders of Colorado and south to the pillars of Monument Valley— someday, never fear, your bare elegant bones will be discovered and wondered and marveled at.

23   A great thirst is a great joy when quenched in time. On my first walk down into Havasupai Canyon, which is a branch of the Grand Canyon, never mind exactly where, I took with me only a quart of water, thinking that would be enough for a mere fourteen-mile downhill hike on a warm day in August. At Topocoba on the rim of the canyon the temperature was a tolerable ninety-six degrees but it rose about one degree for each mile on and downward. Like a fool I rationed my water, drank frugally, and could have died of the heatstroke. When late in the afternoon I finally stumbled—sun-dazed, blear-eyed, parched as an old bacon rind—upon that blue stream which flows like a miraculous mirage down the floor of the canyon I was too exhausted to pause and drink soberly from the bank. Dreamily, deliriously, I waded into the waist-deep water and fell on my face. Like a sponge I soaked up moisture through every pore, letting the current bear me along beneath a canopy of overhanging willow trees. I had no fear of drowning in the water—I intended to drink it all.

24   In the Needles country high above the inaccessible Colorado River there is a small spring hidden at the heart of a maze of fearfully arid grabens and crevasses. A very small spring: the water oozes from the grasp of moss to fall one drop at a time, one drop per second, over a lip of stone. One afternoon in June I squatted there for an hour—two hours? three?—filling my canteen. No other water within miles, the local gnat population fought me for every drop. To keep them out of the canteen I had to place a handkerchief over the opening as I filled it. Then they attacked my eyes, drawn irresistibly by the liquid shine of the human eyeball. Embittered little bastards. Never have I tasted better water.

25   Other springs, more surprises. Northeast of Moab in a region of gargoyles and hobgoblins, a landscape left over from the late Jurassic, is a peculiar little waterhole named Onion Spring. A few wild onions grow in the vicinity but more striking, in season, is the golden princess plume, an indicator of selenium, a mild poison often found in association with uranium, a poison not so mild. Approaching the spring you notice a sulfurous stink in the air though the water itself, neither warm nor cold, looks clear and drinkable.

26   Unlike most desert waterholes you will find around Onion Spring few traces of animal life. Nobody comes to drink. The reason is the very good one that the water of Onion Spring contains not only sulfur, and perhaps selenium, but also arsenic. When I was there I looked at the water and smelled it and ran my hands through it and after a while, since the sampling of desert water is in my line, I tasted it, carefully, and spat it out. Afterwards I rinsed my mouth with water from my canteen.

27   This poison spring is quite clear. The water is sterile, lifeless. There are no bugs, which in itself is a warning sign, in case the smell were not sufficient. When in doubt about drinking from an unknown spring look for life. If the water is scummed with algae, crawling with worms, grubs, larvae, spiders and liver flukes, be reassured, drink hearty, you'll get nothing worse than dysentery. But if it appears innocent and pure, beware. Onion Spring wears such a deceitful guise. Out of a tangle of poison-tolerant weeds the water drips into a basin of mud and sand, flows from there over sandstone and carries its potent solutions into the otherwise harmless waters of the creek.

28   There are a number of springs similar to this one in the American desert. Badwater pool in Death Valley, for example. And a few others in the canyonlands, usually in or below the Moenkopi and Shinarump formations—mudstone and shales. The prospector Vernon Pick found a poison spring at the source of the well-named Dirty Devil River, when he was searching for uranium over in the San Rafael Swell a few years ago. At the time he needed water; he *had* to have water; and in order to get a decent drink he made something like a colander out of his canteen, punching it full of nail holes, filling it with charcoal from his campfire and straining the water through the charcoal. How much this purified the water he had no means of measuring but he drank it anyway and although it made him sick he survived, and is still alive today to tell about it.

29   There are rumors that when dying of the thirst you can save your soul *and* body by extracting water from the barrel cactus. This is a dubious proposition and I don't know anyone who has made the experiment. It might be possible in the Sonoran desert where the barrel cactus grows tall as a man and fat as a keg of beer. In Utah, however, its

nearest relative stands no more than a foot high and bristles with nee-dles curved like fishhooks. To get even close to this devilish vegetable you need leather gloves and a machete. Slice off the top and you find in-side not water but only the green pulpy core of the living plant. Carv-ing the core into manageable chunks you might be able to wring a few drops of bitter liquid into your cup. The labor and the exasperation will make you sweat, will cost you dearly.

30   When you reach this point you are doomed. Far better to have stayed at home with the TV and a case of beer. If the happy thought ar-rives too late, crawl into the shade and contemplate the lonely sky. See those big black scrawny wings far above, waiting? Comfort yourself with the reflection that within a few hours, if all goes as planned, your human flesh will be working its way through the gizzard of a buzzard, your essence transfigured into the fierce greedy eyes and unimaginable con-sciousness of a turkey vulture. Whereupon you, too, will soar on mo-tionless wings high over the ruck and rack of human suffering. For most of us a promotion in grade, for some the realization of an ideal.

31   In July and August on the high desert the thunderstorms come. Mornings begin clear and dazzling bright, the sky as blue as the Virgin's cloak, unflawed by a trace of cloud in all that emptiness bounded on the north by the Book Cliffs, on the east by Grand Mesa and the La Sal Mountains, on the south by the Blue Mountains and on the west by the dragon-tooth reef of the San Rafael. By noon, however, clouds begin to form over the mountains, coming it seems out of nowhere, out of noth-ing, a special creation.

32   The clouds multiply and merge, cumuli-nimbi piling up like whipped cream, like mashed potatoes, like sea foam, building upon one another into a second mountain range greater in magnitude than the terrestrial range below.

33   The massive forms jostle and grate, ions collide, and the sound of thunder is heard over the sun-drenched land. More clouds emerge from empty sky, anvil-headed giants with glints of lightning in their depths. An armada assembles and advances, floating on a plane of air that makes it appear, from below, as a fleet of ships must look to the fish in the sea.

34   At my observation point on a sandstone monolith the sun is blazing down as intensely as ever, the air crackling with dry heat. But the storm clouds continue to spread, gradually taking over more and more of the sky, and as they approach the battle breaks out.

35   Lightning streaks like gunfire through the clouds, volleys of thun-der shake the air. A smell of ozone. While the clouds exchange their bolts with one another no rain falls, but now they begin bombarding the buttes and pinnacles below. Forks of lightning—illuminated nerves—join heaven and earth.

36   The wind is rising. For anyone with sense enough to get out of the rain now is the time to seek shelter. A lash of lightning flickers over Wilson Mesa, scorching the brush, splitting a pine tree. Northeast over the Yellowcat area rain is already sweeping down, falling not vertically but in a graceful curve, like a beaded curtain drawn lightly across the desert. Between the rain and the mountains, among the tumbled masses of vapor, floats a segment of a rainbow—sunlight divided. But where I stand the storm is only beginning.

37   Above me the clouds roll in, unfurling and smoking billows in malignant violet, dense as wool. Most of the sky is lidded over but the sun remains clear halfway down the west, shining in under the storm. Overhead the clouds thicken, then crack and split with a roar like that of cannonballs tumbling down a marble staircase; their bellies open—too late to run now—and the rain comes down.

38   *Comes down:* not softly not gently, with no quality of mercy but like heavy water in buckets, raindrops like pellets splattering on the rock, knocking the berries off the junipers, plastering my shirt to my back, drumming on my hat like hailstones and running in a waterfall off the brim.

39   The pinnacles, arches, balanced rocks, fins and elephant-backs of sandstone, glazed with water but still in sunlight, gleam like old gray silver and everything appears transfixed in the strange wild unholy light of the moment. The light that never was.

40   For five minutes the deluge continues under the barrage of thunder and lightning, then trails off quickly, diminishing to a shower, to a sprinkling, to nothing at all. The clouds move off and rumble for a while in the distance. A fresh golden light breaks through and now in the east, over the turrets and domes, stands the rainbow sign, a double rainbow with one foot in the canyon of the Colorado and the other far north in Salt Wash. Beyond the rainbow and framed within it I can see jags of lightning still playing in the stormy sky over Castle Valley.

41   The afternoon sun falls lower; above the mountains and the ragged black clouds hangs the new moon, pale fragment of what is to come; in another hour, at sundown, Venus too will be there, planet of love, to glow bright as chromium down on the western sky. The desert storm is over and through the pure sweet pellucid air the cliff swallows and the nighthawks plunge and swerve, making cries of hunger and warning and—who knows?—maybe of exultation.

42   Stranger than the storms, though not so grand and symphonic, are the flash floods that follow them, bursting with little warning out of the hills and canyons, sometimes an hour or more after the rain has stopped.

43   I have stood in the middle of a broad sandy wash with not a trickle

of moisture to be seen anywhere, sunlight pouring down on me and on the flies and ants and lizards, the sky above perfectly clear, listening to a queer vibration in the air and in the ground under my feet—like a freight train coming down the grade, very fast—and looked up to see a wall of water tumble around a bend and surge toward me.

44   A wall of water. A poor image. For the flash flood of the desert poorly resembles water. It looks rather like a loose pudding or a thick dense soup, thick as gravy, dense with mud and sand, lathered with scuds of bloody froth, loaded on its crest with a tangle of weeds and shrubs and small trees ripped from their roots.

45   Surprised by delight, I stood there in the heat, the bright sun, the quiet afternoon, and watched the monster roll and roar toward me. It advanced in crescent shape with a sort of forelip about a foot high streaming in front, making hissing sucking noises like a giant amoeba, nosing to the right and nosing to the left as if on the spoor of something good to eat. Red as tomato soup or blood it came down on me about as fast as a man could run. I moved aside and watched it go by.

46   A flick of lightning to the north
where dun clouds grumble—
while here in the middle of the wash
black beetles tumble
and horned toads fumble
over sand as dry as bone
and hard-baked mud and glaring stone.

47   Nothing here suggests disaster
for the ants' shrewd play;
their busy commerce for tomorrow
shows no care for today;
but a mile away
and rolling closer in a scum of mud
comes the hissing lapping blind mouth of the flood.

48   Through the tamarisk whine the flies
in pure fat units of conceit
as if the sun and the afternoon
and blood and the smells and the heat
and something to eat
would be available forever, never die
beyond the fixed imagination of a fly.

49   The flood comes, crawls thickly by, roaring
with self-applause, a brown
spongy smothering liquid avalanche:
great ant-civilizations drown,

worlds go down,
trees go under, the mud bank breaks
and deep down underneath the bedrock shakes.

50   A few hours later the bulk of the flood was past and gone. The flow dwindled to a trickle over bars of quicksand. New swarms of insect life would soon come to recover the provinces of those swept away. Nothing had changed but the personnel, a normal turnover, and the contours of the watercourse, that not much.

51   Now we've mentioned quicksand. What is quicksand anyway? First of all, quicksand is *not* as many think a queer kind of sand which has the hideous power to draw men and animals down and down into a bottomless pit. There can be no quicksand without water. The scene of the sand-drowned camel boy in the movie *Lawrence of Arabia* is pure fakery. The truth about quicksand is that it is simply a combination of sand and water in which the upward force of the water is sufficient to neutralize the frictional strength of the particles of sand. The greater the force and saturation, the less weight the sand can bear.

52   Ordinarily it is possible for a man to walk across quicksand, if he keeps moving. But if he stops, funny things begin to happen. The surface of the quicksand, which may look as firm as the wet sand on an ocean beach, begins to liquefy beneath his feet. He finds himself sinking slowly into a jelly-like substance, soft and quivering, which clasps itself around his ankles with the suction power of any viscous fluid. Pulling out one foot, the other foot necessarily goes down deeper, and if a man waits too long, or cannot reach something solid beyond the quicksand, he may soon find himself trapped. The depth to which he finally sinks depends upon the depth and the fluidity of the quicksand, upon the nature of his efforts to extricate himself, and upon the ratio of body weight to volume of quicksand. Unless a man is extremely talented, he cannot work himself in more than waist-deep. The quicksand will not *pull* him down. But it will not let him go either. Therefore the conclusion is that while quicksand cannot drown its captive, it could possibly starve him to death. Whatever finally happens, the immediate effects are always interesting.

53   My friend Newcomb, for instance. He has only one good leg, had an accident with the other, can't hike very well in rough country, tends to lag behind. We were exploring a deep dungeon-like defile off Glen Canyon one time (before the dam). The defile turned and twisted like a snake under overhanging and interlocking walls so high, so close, that for most of the way I could not see the sky. The floor of this cleft was irregular, wet, sandy, in places rather soupy, and I was soon far ahead and out of sight of Newcomb.

54   Finally I came to a place in the canyon so narrow and dark and wet and ghastly that I had no heart to go farther. Retracing my steps I heard, now and then, a faint and mournful wail, not human, which seemed to come from abysmal depths far back in the bowels of the plateau, from the underworld, from subterranean passageways better left forever unseen and unknown. I hurried on, the cries faded away. I was glad to be getting out of there. Then they came again, louder and as it seemed from all sides, out of the rock itself, surrounding me. A terrifying caterwauling it was, multiplied and amplified by echoes piled on echoes, overlapping and reinforcing one another. I looked back to see what was hunting me but there was only the naked canyon in the dim, bluish light that filtered down from far above. I thought of the Minotaur. Then I thought of Newcomb and began to run.

55   It wasn't bad. He was in only a little above the knees and sinking very slowly. As soon as he saw me he stopped hollering and relit his pipe. Help, he said, simply and quietly.

56   What was all the bellowing about? I wanted to know. I'm sorry, he said, but it's a horrible way to die. Get out of that mud, I said, and let's get out of here. It ain't just mud, he said. I don't care what it is, get out of there; you look like an idiot. I'm sinking, he said.

57   And he was. The stuff was now halfway up his thighs.

58   Don't you ever read any books? I said. Don't you have sense enough to know that when you get in quicksand you have to lie down flat? Why? he asked. So you'll live longer, I explained. Face down or face up? he asked next.

59   That stumped me. I couldn't remember the answer to that one. You wait here, I said, while I go back to Albuquerque and get the book.

60   He looked down for a moment. Still sinking, he said; please help?

61   I stepped as close to him as I could without getting bogged down myself but our extended hands did not quite meet. Lean forward, I said. I am, he said. All the way, I said; fall forward.

62   He did that and then I could reach him. He gripped my wrist and I gripped his and with a slow steady pull I got him out of there. The quicksand gurgled a little and made funny, gasping noises, reluctant to let him go, but when he was free the holes filled up at once, the liquid sand oozing into place, and everything looked as it had before, smooth and sleek and innocent as the surface of a pudding. It was in fact the same pool of quicksand that I had walked over myself only about an hour earlier.

63   Quicksand is more of a menace to cattle and horses, with their greater weight and smaller feet, than it is to men, and the four-legged beasts generally avoid it when they can. Sometimes, however, they are forced to cross quicksand to reach water, or are driven across, and then

the cattleman may have an unpleasant chore on his hands. Motor vehicles, of course, cannot negotiate quicksand; even a four-wheel-drive jeep will bog down as hopelessly as anything else.

64   Although I hesitate to deprive quicksand of its sinister glamour I must confess that I have not yet heard of a case where a machine, an animal or a man has actually sunk *completely* out of sight in the stuff. But it may have happened; it may be happening to somebody at this very moment. I sometimes regret that I was unable to perform a satisfactory experiment with my friend Newcomb when the chance presented itself; such opportunities come but rarely. But I needed him; he was among other things a good camp cook.

65   After the storms pass and the flash floods have dumped their loads of silt into the Colorado, leaving the streambeds as arid as they were before, it is still possible to find rainwater in the desert. All over the slickrock country there are natural cisterns or potholes, tubs, tanks and basins sculptured in the soft sandstone by the erosive force of weathering, wind and sand. Many of them serve as little catchment basins during rain and a few may contain water for days or even weeks after a storm, the length of time depending on the shape and depth of the hole and the consequent rate of evaporation.

66   Often far from any spring, these temporary pools attract doves, ravens and other birds, and deer and coyotes; you, too, if you know where to look or find one by luck, can slake your thirst and fill your water gourd. Such pools may be found in what seem like the most improbable places: out on the desolate White Rim below Grandview Point, for example, or on top of the elephant-back dome above the Double Arch. At Toroweap in Grand Canyon I found a deep tank of clear sweet water almost over my head, countersunk in the summit of a sandstone bluff which overhung my campsite by a hundred feet. A week after rain there was still enough water there to fill my needs; hard to reach, it was well worth the effort. The Bedouin know what I mean.

67   The rain-filled potholes, set in naked rock, are usually devoid of visible plant life but not of animal life. In addition to the inevitable microscopic creatures there may be certain amphibians like the spadefoot toad. This little animal lives through dry spells in a state of estivation under the dried-up sediment in the bottom of a hole. When the rain comes, if it comes, he emerges from the mud singing madly in his fashion, mates with the handiest female and fills the pool with a swarm of tadpoles, most of them doomed to a most ephemeral existence. But a few survive, mature, become real toads, and when the pool dries up they dig into the sediment as their parents did before, making burrows which they seal with mucus in order to preserve that moisture necessary to life. There they wait, day after day, week after week, in patient

spadefoot torpor, perhaps listening—we can imagine—for the sound of raindrops pattering at last on the earthen crust above their heads. If it comes in time the glorious cycle is repeated; if not, this particular colony of *Bufonidae* is reduced eventually to dust, a burden on the wind.

68   Rain and puddles bring out other amphibia, even in the desert. It's a strange, stirring, but not uncommon thing to come on a pool at night, after an evening of thunder and lightning and a bit of rainfall, and see the frogs clinging to the edge of their impermanent pond, bodies immersed in water but heads out, all croaking away in tricky counterpoint. They are windbags: with each croak the pouch under the frog's chin swells like a bubble, then collapses.

69   Why do they sing? What do they have to sing about? Somewhat apart from one another, separated by roughly equal distances, facing outward from the water, they clank and croak all through the night with tireless perseverance. To human ears their music has a bleak, dismal, tragic quality, dirgelike rather than jubilant. It may nevertheless be the case that these small beings are singing not only to claim their stake in the pond, not only to attract a mate, but also out of spontaneous love and joy, a contrapuntal choral celebration of the coolness and wetness after weeks of desert fire, for love of their own existence, however brief it may be, and for joy in the common life.

70   Has joy any survival value in the operations of evolution? I suspect that it does; I suspect that the morose and fearful are doomed to quick extinction. Where there is no joy there can be no courage; and without courage all other virtues are useless. Therefore the frogs, the toads, keep on singing even though we know, if they don't, that the sound of their uproar must surely be luring all the snakes and ringtail cats and kit foxes and coyotes and great horned owls toward the scene of their happiness.

71   What then? A few of the little amphibians will continue their metamorphosis by way of the nerves and tissues of one of the higher animals, in which process the joy of one becomes the contentment of the second. Nothing is lost, except an individual consciousness here and there, a trivial perhaps even illusory phenomenon. The rest survive, mate, multiply, burrow, estivate, dream, and rise again. The rains will come, the potholes shall be filled. Again. And again. And again.

72   More secure are those who live in and around the desert's few perennial waterholes, those magical hidden springs that are scattered so austerely through the barren vastness of the canyon country. Of these only a rare few are too hot or too briny or too poisonous to support life—the great majority of them swarm with living things. Here you will see the rushes and willows and cottonwoods, and four-winged dragonflies in green, blue, scarlet and gold, and schools of minnows in the water, moving from sunlight to shadow and back again. At night the mammals

come—deer, bobcat, cougar, coyote, fox, jackrabbit, bighorn sheep, wild horse and feral burro—each in his turn and in unvarying order, under the declaration of a truce. They come to drink, not to kill or be killed.

73   Finally, in this discussion of water in the desert, I should make note of a distinctive human contribution, one which has become a part of the Southwestern landscape no less typical than the giant cactus, the juniper growing out of solid rock or the red walls of a Navajo canyon. I refer to the tiny oasis formed by the drilled well, its windmill and storage tank. The windmill with its skeleton tower and creaking vanes is an object of beauty as significant in its way as the cottonwood tree, and the open tank at its foot, big enough to swim in, is a thing of joy to man and beast, no less worthy of praise than the desert spring.

74   Water, water, water. . . . There is no shortage of water in the desert but exactly the right amount, a perfect ratio of water to rock, of water to sand, insuring that wide, free, open, generous spacing among plants and animals, homes and towns and cities, which makes the arid West so different from any other part of the nation. There is no lack of water here, unless you try to establish a city where no city should be.

75   The Developers, of course—the politicians, businessmen, bankers, administrators, engineers—they see it somewhat otherwise and complain most bitterly and interminably of a desperate water shortage, especially in the Southwest. They propose schemes of inspiring proportions for diverting water by the damful from the Columbia River, or even from the Yukon River, and channeling it overland down into Utah, Colorado, Arizona and New Mexico.

76   What for? "In anticipation of future needs, in order to provide for the continued industrial and population growth of the Southwest." And in such an answer we see that it's only the old numbers game again, the monomania of small and very simple minds in the grip of an obsession. They cannot see that growth for the sake of growth is a cancerous madness, that Phoenix and Albuquerque will not be better cities to live in when their populations are doubled again and again. They would never understand that an economic system which can only expand or expire must be false to all that is human.

77   So much by way of futile digression: the pattern is fixed and protest alone will not halt the iron glacier moving upon us.

78   No matter, it's of slight importance. Time and the winds will sooner or later bury the Seven Cities of Cibola—Phoenix, Tucson, Albuquerque, all of them—under dunes of glowing sand, over which blue-eyed Navajo bedouin will herd their sheep and horses, following the river in winter, the mountains in summer, and sometimes striking off across the desert toward the red canyons of Utah where great waterfalls plunge over silt-filled, ancient, mysterious dams.

79   Only the boldest among them, seeking visions, will camp for long in the strange country of the standing rock, far out where the spadefoot toads bellow madly in the moonlight on the edge of doomed rainpools, where the arsenic-selenium spring waits for the thirst-crazed wanderer, where the thunderstorms blast the pinnacles and cliffs, where the rust-brown floods roll down the barren washes, and where the community of the quiet deer walk at evening up glens of sandstone through tamarisk and sage toward the hidden springs of sweet, cool, still, clear, unfailing water.

WORD FOCUS

VOCABULARY GLOSS

armada: *a fleet of ships (33)*

Bedouin: *nomadic Arab tribes who roam the desert (66)*

bogged down: *weighed down or stuck in a situation (61)*

bone dry: *dry like a bone stripped of its meat (10)*

Bufonidae: *(Latin) frog species (67)*

buzzard: *a large scavenger bird of North America (30)*

canteen: *a small container for carrying water (26)*

cisterns: *containers in which water is stored (65)*

contrapuntal: *harmonizing melodies in different scales (69)*

dirgelike: *like funeral chants (69)*

dragon-tooth reef: *a sharp-edged rock formation (31)*

dry gulch, arroyo seco: *a dried-up creek or streambed (13)*

dry wash: *a creek without any water in it (13)*

feral burro: *a wild donkey (72)*

flash floods: *sudden and unexpected floods (42)*

freight train: *a train that carries products instead of people (43)*

gargoyles and hobgoblins: *fearsome and devilish creatures (25)*

gizzard: *a bird's digestive pouch located near the stomach (30)*

grabens and crevasses: *deep cracks in the earth (24)*

iron glacier: *a metaphor for the "continued industrial and population growth" of modern civilization and all that it entails (77)*

late Jurassic: *the geological era when dinosaurs lived (25)*

lidded over: *closed, like eyelids (37)*

Prestone: *a brand of engine coolant (22)*

ramada: *a shelter with a roof built for shade (11)*

ruck and rack: *limits (30)*

run off: *rainfall that flows away because it cannot be absorbed by the ground (11)*

seven cities of Cibola: *imaginary cities believed to be in the American Southwest; sought by early Spanish explorers for their presumed gold and riches (78)*

to lag behind: *to be unable to keep up with someone or something (53)*

unclothed rock: *bare stone (11)*

Virgin's cloak: *a reference to religious paintings in which the Virgin Mary wears a blue cloak (31)*

wash: *a dry streambed (43)*

windbags: *air-filled chambers that produce sound (68)*

with no quality of mercy: *a reference to lines from Shakespeare's* The Merchant of Venice *in which a plea for mercy is compared to soothing rain (38)*

VOCABULARY QUESTIONS

1. This essay contains a number of technical words from the physical sciences: "hydrological" (3), "selenium" (25), "cumuli-nimbi" (32), "buttes" (35), "viscous" (52), and "estivation" (67) are some examples. Look up these words in a general or technical dictionary. Then provide a definition for each word as it is used in this text, and suggest contexts other than the desert in which these words might be used.

2. Many English speakers say "a fork of lightning" (35) and *a clap of thunder.* The habitual association of *fork* with *lightning* and *clap* with *thunder* is called *collocation.* It is important for every speaker and writer of English to learn collocations. Following is a list of other collocations about nature. Match them by drawing a line from Column A to Column B. There may be more than one possibility.

COLUMN A		*COLUMN B*
rays		lightning
flash		water
trickle	of	light
flakes		sunshine
beam		snow

3. Abbey ends his essay about water with the words "hidden springs of sweet, cool, still, clear, unfailing water" (79). What does each word in this list of adjectives convey about something so common as water? Would changing the order of adjectives also change Abbey's description?

ENGLISH CRAFT

1. Note that Abbey uses the first person pronoun *I* in this essay. In much academic writing, the pronoun *I* is often omitted, because the emphasis is on the idea that the writer is trying to get across and not on the writer. Look at the following example, which appeared in a student essay about the importance of Watson and Crick's discovery of the double helix.

I believe that Watson and Crick discovered the double helix.

The use of the pronoun *I* in this sentence weakens the strength of the statement and calls unnecessary attention to the writer, when the focus of the sentence should actually be on the discoverers and their discovery. The pronoun *I* is also inappropriate here because the statement is not a matter of opinion but of documentation. Look at the following student writing:

Through "Mary" and "Water," I see the question of fairness as an issue of culture. Fair does not necessarily mean to be right. . . . To be fair means to be just toward a group of people, a society, and living things.

Is the pronoun *I* being used effectively here? Could it be used effectively elsewhere? Could the excerpt be written without the pronoun *I* and still maintain the writer's intent?

2. An *allusion* is an indirect reference to events, places, or someone else's words or ideas. Allusions come from many sources—such as art, religion, and sports—that reflect important elements in a particular culture. Allusions allow writers to make new connections. For example, Abbey alludes to "the Virgin's cloak" (31). The allusion connects the color blue, which refers to the color of the Virgin Mary's cloak in European painting, to the color of the desert sky described by Abbey.

Look at the following allusions in "Water," and identify the meanings and connections that the author is trying to make for the reader. You may have to consult both a dictionary and an encyclopedia.

Allusion	*Reference*
late Jurassic (25)	_____
the Minotaur (54)	_____
the Bedouin (66)	_____

3. Writers sometimes begin their essays with conflicting statements in order to lead into their thesis claim. A *thesis claim* is a statement that establishes a writer's point of view on a particular subject. This type of introduction, which is designed to attract the readers' attention, is called the *hook*. Just as a fishhook is designed to catch and hold a fish, an essay hook is designed to catch and hold a reader's interest. Abbey attracts our attention to his essay by reporting a dialogue with a tourist. A conclusion not only ends a piece of writing but also may refer back to specific words or ideas in the introduction.

   Look at the following two excerpts from "Water," and answer the questions associated with each excerpt.

Introduction

"This would be good country," a tourist says to me, "if only you had some water." (1)

"If we had water here," I reply, "this country would not be what it is." (3)

"If you had more water more people could live here." (4)

"Yes sir. And where then would people go when they wanted to see something besides people?" (5)

Conclusion

Water, water, water. . . . There is no shortage of water in the desert but exactly the right amount, a perfect ratio of water to rock, of water to sand, insuring that wide, free, open, generous spacing among plants and animals, homes and towns and cities, which makes the arid West so different from any other part of the nation. There is no lack of water here, unless you try to establish a city where no city should be. (74)

---

   a. How effective is the introduction of Abbey's essay as a hook to attract the reader's attention? Rewrite this introduction, using a hook that you create to attract the reader.

b. A reader normally expects the conclusion to be in the final para-
    graph. Do you think Abbey's claims in this paragraph represent the
    thesis claim, the conclusion, or both?

c. Discuss how the conclusion connects to words or ideas in the in-
    troduction.

INTERPRETIVE JOURNAL

1. Consider your ideas about any form of water—for example, ice, snow, a
    river, a lake, or even a swimming pool—and write a sentence for each,
    explaining your associations with each word.

2. Abbey goes into great detail when he talks about quicksand. What sci-
    entific facts does he give us about quicksand, and what false beliefs
    about quicksand does he try to dispel?

3. Study the following sentence, which compares clouds to other objects
    by using the word "like": "The clouds multiply and merge, cumuli-nimbi
    piling up like whipped cream, like mashed potatoes, like sea foam, build-
    ing upon one another into a second mountain range . . ." (32). What
    meaning of clouds emerges from this comparison?

4. Discuss how poetry fits (46–49), if it does, into an essay that is basically
    a scientific description of the desert.

5. The title of Abbey's book is *Desert Solitaire: A Season in the Wilderness.*
    What images can you associate with the word "solitaire"?

ESSAY QUESTION

Abbey looks upon both tourists, who arrive in the desert with scant knowledge of day-to-day survival requirements, and developers, who want to ex-
ploit the desert's resources for "industrial and population growth" (76) with
scorn. Select a natural resource or environment, and write an essay applying the arguments of Abbey, the tourist, or the developer to indicate your
own position about how that land should be used.

Environment and Behavior
Sequence of Essay Assignments

READINGS

Maya Angelou, "Mary," excerpt from *I Know Why the Caged Bird Sings*

Peter Freuchen, "Dead Man's Cache," excerpt from *Book of the Eskimos*

Edward Abbey, "Water," excerpt from *Desert Solitaire: A Season in the Wilderness*

The following assignments form a sequence of interrelated topics. They become progressively more challenging as they ask you to interact with more texts. Assignment 1 asks you to write about a topic in Angelou's story; Assignment 2 asks you to reconsider your first essay in light of Freuchen's text; and Assignment 3 asks you to consider all three texts as you establish your point of view on the assigned topic.

These assignments can be written as a sequence or they can be written individually. However you approach these essays, each one you write should be supported with citations from the text and examples. Whenever possible, include your own experience and knowledge on the subject.

ASSIGNMENT 1

ANGELOU

The story "Mary" describes a young African American's experience as a maid in the South during the 1930s, the difficulties she encounters, and her responses to them. Study the following two incidents in the story: Mrs. Cullinan changing Margaret's name; and Margaret, in turn, breaking Mrs. Cullinan's dishes. What do these incidents reveal about Margaret's and Mrs. Cullinan's values?

ASSIGNMENT 2

FREUCHEN AND ANGELOU

Both Margaret in "Mary" and Gotthart in "Dead Man's Cache" enter new environments that require them to change their ways of thinking and behaving. Yet both deliberately rebel rather than submit to the rules of these new environments. Analyze this rebellion for each individual, and discuss whether or not their actions can be justified.

ASSIGNMENT 3

ABBEY, FREUCHEN, AND ANGELOU

In order to survive emotionally, socially, and physically in any new place, people have to know and evaluate the rules of the environment. Identify some of the rules implicit in the texts by Angelou, Freuchen, and Abbey, and then discuss what people need to know about how environments shape rules for survival.

Chapter 3

Individuality and Acceptance

The needs of the individual and the needs of the group are sometimes at cross-purposes. Frequently the greater burden of adjustment is placed on the individual. When the individual is singled out from the dominant group in any way, the individual's acceptance by the group becomes an issue. The group must maintain its unity; the individual must remain part of the group and be unique as well. Both the group and the individual are vulnerable.

ABOUT THE AUTHORS

Bharati Mukherjee (b. 1942)

Bharati Mukherjee was born in Calcutta, India. She earned a master's degree and a doctorate in the United States. This excerpt from *The Tiger's Daughter* (1987) illustrates the effect of her experience in two cultures—India and the United States. Language acts as both a barrier and a bridge in her attempts to reconcile these two worlds.

Nawal El Saadawi (b. 1931)

Egyptian author Nawal El Saadawi's book *Woman at Point Zero* (1989) focuses on injustices that are inflicted on women. This excerpt looks at how male-dominated traditions cause pain and numbness in certain members of that group.

Nancy Mairs (b. 1943)

In "Challenge: An Exploration," from the book *Carnal Acts* (1990), California-born Nancy Mairs discusses her attempt to live fully with multiple sclerosis. This autobiographical essay looks closely at what euphemisms reveal about America's attitude toward the "handicapped."

Bharati Mukherjee
Excerpt from *The Tiger's Daughter*

Preview

Think of a place or an incident that you observed or experienced with a group. Describe the incident as each member of the group perceived it, and try to give reasons for the different responses.

Word Preview

You can familiarize yourself with the following words by looking them up in the dictionary. You can broaden your knowledge of these words by pronouncing them and understanding how they are used in context.

proprietor (2)
showdowns (15)
unions (25)
conspiratorial (28)
lecherous (29)
paroxysms (35)
hysterical (38)
impregnable (51)
ulcerous (54)
pruned (64)
hasten (68)
puns (69)
conspired (72)
placidity (74)
sporting (80)
jitters (83)
compound (83)
squatters (83)

scion (88)
preliminaries (89)
cocky (91)
procrastinated (94)
partition (94)
hardtopped (95)
tubercular (95)
slogans (95)
Semitic (97)
detours (99)
hovels (100)
stalls (100)
corrugated (104)
spout (105)
paraphernalia (108)
eviction (110)
lapel (110)

blazer (110)
obsessive (111)
manicured (114)
mutilation (115)
relentless (123)
anticlimaxes (123)
procured (128)
instinct (131)
penance (131)
confrontations (131)
sightseers (133)
dilapidated (133)
demolition (133)
stunted (141)
leprosy (141)
chronology (143)
maniac (143)

1   "Eesh!" said Reena. "How the Catelli has changed!"

2   The statement was unfair. Very little had changed at the Catelli-Continental in the last fifteen years. The last European proprietor had added a thin band of national orange and green to the white turbans on the waiters. And in 1953, when a Marwari millionaire had bought the Catelli, the Prince Albert Room had been renamed the Ashoka Banquet *Ghar.*

3   "Goodness gracious!" said Reena. "The flowerpots have been re-arranged."

4   "So what!" said Tara.

5   "Am I right in thinking you are being rude to me?"

6   "Yes."

7   "Such rudeness! It is not like you at all. Gosh! That's what happens when Bengali girls go to America."

8   Though Tara did not believe in intense friendships, she wanted Reena to understand her need for rest. She wanted to tell her friend that little things had begun to upset her, that of late she had been outraged by Calcutta, that there were too many people sprawled in alleys and storefronts and staircases. She longed for the Bengal of Satyajit Ray, children running through cool green spaces, aristocrats despairing in music rooms of empty palaces. She hated Calcutta because it had given her kids eating yoghurt off dirty sidewalks.

9   "How is it you've changed too much, Tara?" Reena asked. "I mean this is no moral judgment or anything, but you've become too self-centered and European."

10   So it had to come at last, thought Tara. A quarrel was about to occur. And over such an issue, imagine calling her of all people a European!

11   "That's a goddamn lie!"

12   "Goddamn?" asked Reena. "I've never heard of that one. I know damn by itself. Goddamn is worse?"

13   "It's a lie. You are lying about me right to my face. How can you do that? How dare you?"

14   Such passion did not frighten Reena. The nuns had certified her as a "thoroughly sensible girl." She was ready to cope with Tara's outrage. She wondered if "goddamn" was spelled with one *d* or two. "You see, how you always make things too personal? I was just making an objective analysis of you and you get all het up."

15   Tara felt painfully misunderstood. Her education had ruined her for quarrels and showdowns. No one, it was assumed, would dare to argue with a St. Blaise's girl. Now she was ready to retreat into grudges that would ferment over the years. "But it *is* personal! You're calling me mean and selfish. How can you expect me to be perfectly calm?"

16   "Well, you *are* a goddamn egoist. Don't you remember the way you

reacted to those children on Park Street? They were just sitting and eating and you had the goddamn cheek to turn it into something personal."

17   "Don't *you* think of beggars as your responsibility?"

18   "Why should I, you silly-billy? They're paid professionals, probably paid by a big, fat goddamn Marwari."

19   "Doesn't it bother you that someone's hired these children to beg?"

20   "It doesn't bother me *personally*, no. I always give alms."

21   Tara wanted to go on with the argument, she felt she owed it to herself and to David to go on, but she was alarmed by Reena's distortions.

22   "Why are you always thinking about yourself?" continued Reena. "Why don't you worry about the suffering of your friends, for instance?"

23   "My friends suffer?"

24   "What do you think? Of course they do. As proof I'll tell you a secret about Pronob."

25   On this trip Tara had discovered moods in Pronob that were quite out of keeping with the moods of the group. He was angry quite often or impatient with the endless coffee sessions at Moonlight, Venetia or Kapoor's. He fumed at having to accept the existence of workers' unions. He said things had been much easier for businessmen when his father was young.

26   "I think Pronob is in love with Nilima," said Reena. "I've seen him eye-make at her on several occasions."

27   Tara had not been prepared for this secret.

28   "That's all?" she asked, deflating the conspiratorial look on Reena's face.

29   "You are not satisfied with Pronob's eye-making? You want him to be downright lecherous. My God! You are a real fusspot."

30   It was the word "fusspot" that calmed Tara. What a curious tie language was! She had forgotten so many Indian-English words she had once used with her friends. It would have been treacherous to quarrel with Reena after that.

31   And so they spoke of Pronob's meetings with the Jaycees and hoped the guest list for American exchange students had been finalized for the year. And they recalled other foreign houseguests Pronob had billeted with them in the past.

32   "Do you remember when we took the whole Australian bunch to Kolaghat?"

33   "The toilet paper incident?"

34   "That was really priceless! Wow! Those Australian boys shouting 'Paper! Paper!' and our village servants chasing them in the woods with 'No paper, no paper, only water, sir.' "

35   The plight of the Australians had seemed uncontrollably funny to

the girls at the time. But, in between paroxysms now, she thought of her panic at having to open a milk carton at Horn and Hardart her first night in America. What terror she had felt when faced by machines containing food, machines she was sure she could not operate, or worse still did not dare!

36   "Serves them right for wanting to see the *real* India," giggled Reena. "These foreigners just want to take snaps of bullock carts and garbage dumps. They're not satisfied with modern people like us."

37   Tara wondered what David would do if he ever came to India. He was not like her. Would he sling his camera like other Americans and photograph beggars in Shambazar, squatters in Tollygunge, prostitutes in Free School Street, would he try to capture in color the pain of Calcutta? She thought he would pass over the obvious. Instead he would analyze her life and her friends in the lens of his Minolta. He would group the family carefully, Mummy in new cotton sari on cane chair, Daddy in "bush coat" beside her, she herself on a *morah* in dead center, with servants, maids, and chauffeur in the background smiling fixedly at the camera. He would go with her to the Calcutta Club, take pictures of doctors and lawyers playing canasta. He would explode his flash bulbs at Pronob's parties, and regret he did not own a tape recorder. No, she feared, he was wiser than she cared to admit to herself. Perhaps he would not do these things either. He would land unannounced at Howrah Station and say to the coolie wearing a number, I'd like to see the real India. None of this, of course, helped her relations with Reena.

38   Afraid she might become hysterical at the Catelli or that she might resort to bitter remarks about friends who loved her, Tara returned to the problems of Pronob and the Jaycees, who had to find homes for eighteen teen-age guests from America. I must get busy, she told herself. I must try to care.

39   "I'd be very happy to help you in any way I can when your guest is here. Do you know where he's from?"

40   "Los Angeles. He has a nice Irish name. McDowell."

41   "In the States you can't always tell. It's not like here."

42   There it was again, the envy for Reena's world that was more stable, more predictable than hers. A Banerjee in that world could only be a Bengali Brahmin, no room for nasty surprises. Her instinct was to say something mean that would ruin Reena's confidence in herself, that would make her see that Calcutta could no longer support girls like her.

43   "I'm sure he's Irish. How can a McDowell be anything else? In any case, I'm willing to take my chances with this boy rather than two girls from Columbus, Ohio."

44   "What does your mother feel about all this?"

45   "Come on, you know her. Of course, she expects disaster. She thinks I'll follow your example and marry an American *mleccha.*"

46   And again that bitterness, that instinct for destruction of smug people like Reena. She had never thought of David as a *mleccha,* an outcaste, not good enough for girls like Reena. She was numb with anger against Reena's mother.

47   "I don't like that last remark. Look, Reena—how *dare* you call David a *mleccha?* How dare your mother of all people talk like that about something that does not concern her?"

48   "What are you talking about? Of course my marriage concerns my mother."

49   "But how dare you call my husband a *mleccha?*"

50   "Don't get so excited, my dear. We are very modernized Indians, we don't give two hoots about caste. You should learn to face facts, that's all."

51   It was useless to pursue this anger. Reena and the others were surrounded by an impregnable wall of self-confidence. Through some weakness or fault, Tara had slipped outside. And reentry was barred.

52   "Would *you* marry a non-Brahmin?"

53   "Don't be silly. It's unthinkable that I should break my parents' hearts."

54   Amusing stories about Reena's mother helped to revive Tara. The poor woman was trying out stews and roasts on her family for fear McDowell would find curries uncivilized or ulcerous. She had stocked up on imported canned pork sausages, soups, packaged jelly crystal desserts. She had drawn a line only at beef; she was a good Hindu after all. Reena laughed louder than Tara, repeating details about her mother's efforts that she considered particularly foolish or extreme. The girls laughed with the relief of men who have just escaped disaster. While they laughed, clutching their stomachs, heaving masses of black hair, an elderly gentleman in a blazer touched Tara's shoulder.

55   "Jolly good, Mrs. Cartwright," said the man. "Jolly good to see you again. I was afraid you had disappeared."

56   "Hello, Mr. Roy Chowdhury. I was so worried about *you.* Reena, I'd like you to meet Mr. Roy Chowdhury, who knows Daddy. This is Reena Mukherjee."

57   "How do you do, Miss Mukherjee. Do I know your father?"

58   "I haven't the slightest. It doesn't really matter."

59   After Reena had made her report, Tara knew Pronob and his group would say of her that she was crazy to talk to weird men in the Catelli-Continental. They would say to her wisely, Calcutta has changed, my girl; it's not safe to talk to any strangers, not even at a place as decent as the Continental. They would tell her violent stories of pickpockets and

rape, and remind her again of poor Mrs. General Pumps Gupta at the Metro Cinema.

60   "I thought you would never come back to the Catelli. I thought, Mrs. Cartwright, you had perhaps disappeared."

61   "What a strange word to use. I don't think I like it at all. Tara, we really should be going now. We are supposed to join the rest of the crowd."

62   "It *is* a strange word," agreed Tara. "Sort of chilling, you know."

63   "Mysteries and death. Dear Mrs. Cartwright, do they excite you?"

64   Tara had no idea what the old man meant by his question. She looked to Reena for help but the girl was cleaning her thumbnails, her pruned eyebrows locked in an expression of ill humor.

65   "Are you too one of us?" he asked.

66   "One of you?"

67   "He means are you also a weirdo," whispered Reena.

68   "Yes, one of us, Mrs. Cartwright. An addict of violence and murder, in fiction I hasten to add."

69   Tara felt he was probably speaking in puns, her need to complicate was so great each time the old man appeared. The old man wearing a blazer in the summer heat harassed her notions of the plausible. He spoke knowledgeably of Hercule Poirot and Perry Mason, while Tara recalled a *tantric* singer near funeral pyres and a snake in Barrackpore swimming in the guest house waters.

70   "I'm sorry I left in such a hurry that day," she said. "I don't know what came over me."

71   "No need to apologize. You did the only sensible thing if you know what I mean."

72   "What's all this?" interrupted Reena. And Tara, noting the girl's sudden interest, foresaw stories and misunderstandings that would surround this encounter. There was no way she could explain that a quiet hour by the funeral *ghat* had conspired with the pain within her till she had been forced to exclaim that it was no use, that it was hopeless, that things in Calcutta would never get any better.

73   "For today, ladies," Tara heard the absurdly dapper man declare, "I have a very simple plan in mind."

74   "We don't have time for plans today, I'm afraid," said Tara. "But if we did, what had you in mind?" She herself did not like adventures, especially if they came to a bad end as they always seemed to in Calcutta. But she needed incidents to make much of in letters to David. David was painfully western; he still complained of her placidity. Things "happened" only when they began and ended. He wrote her that he worried she wasn't doing anything. He didn't mean working on Katherine Mansfield, but just reading and thinking and getting the most out of

her vacation. He said he thought she spent too much time talking to bigots, why didn't she write him of things that really mattered?

75   "I'd like to take you to my place in Tollygunge."

76   "Mr. Roy Chowdhury, really!"

77   "What a lot of cheek he has!"

78   "What kind of girls do you take us for?" Reena confessed later that she had assumed at once the old man intended improper designs on them. After all they were both reasonably good-looking, almost beautiful if one overlooked small imperfections of teeth and ear.

79   "No, no, ladies. I'm gravely misunderstood. I mean no evil by my invitation."

80   Tara admitted in her letter to David that if she had been in New York and the old man an American, his invitation would have been merely sporting. But, at the Catelli-Continental, she shared the outrage that inflamed her companion.

81   "It's your fault," whispered Reena. "With your American husband, this chap thinks he can make these horrible proposals to us."

82   "It's *not* my fault. You're insulting my husband. You're insulting me."

83   "Ladies, ladies, please. Your whispering's giving me the jitters. I meant no harm at all." He explained he had a house and large compound in Tollygunge. He did not live there because it had been taken over by refugees and squatters. In any case, he had a roomy flat on Park Street, close to Kapoor's Restaurant. He thought it might amuse Mrs. Cartwright to drive with him across town to see his squatters. The other young lady, of course, was also most welcome.

84   "Is it a *bustee?*" asked Tara. She recalled frustrating moments at Vassar, when idealistic dormitory neighbors had asked her to describe the slums of India. "Are you taking us to see a *real bustee?*"

85   "It's a *bustee* of a sort."

86   "Do the squatters pay you rent?"

87   "Certainly not. I, dear lady, do not take from the poor."

88   Tara realized her last question had wounded the old man far more than her earlier suspicions about his honor. He stood in his sockless oxfords, the last insulted scion of a *zamindar* family, owner of tea estates in Assam, and he quivered. "To give, Mrs. Cartwright, is more pleasing than to receive."

89   He was pompous, of course. Besides, Reena and the others were quite right, Tara knew; Calcutta had become more dangerous than she remembered. It would be stupid to ride through the city with Mr. Roy Chowdhury to look at insolent strangers. But she wanted to trust the eccentric old man, who had without preliminaries shown her the funeral pyres.

90   "We've got to get going now," said Reena. "Really, my dear, don't you have any sense of time? We've got to rest for Sanjay's party tonight."

91   Tara's wish to trust the old man doubled with every obstacle offered by Reena. If Mr. Roy Chowdhury had been a little more cocky she might have responded differently. But she thought she could defend herself against any threat from a sockless man in a blazer. So she whispered to Reena that they had done the man an injustice, that good manners demanded they accompany him to Tollygunge.

92   "I want to go on record," Reena objected loudly, "as being totally opposed to this trip. It'll come to a bad end. I'm going for the sole purpose of protecting my friend here." Then she went to telephone Tara's and her own mother with invented excuses about going to the movies with an old St. Blaise's girl.

93   The trip to Tollygunge was preceded by the usual confusion about which car or cars to take. Tara was no longer bothered by such confusion. She had come to expect it; she assumed that even a phone call meant several bad connections in Calcutta. This, she guessed, was an extraordinary trip worthy of several arguments and false starts. In the end they agreed that they would all travel in Tara's Rover, while Joyonto's chauffeur would run an errand for the widowed Roy Chowdhury aunt, then go to his own *bustee* for lunch.

94   Tollygunge had once promised to be a splendid residential area, smarter than Ballygunge and without the upstart snobbery of New Alipore. The land had stretched for miles, unmarked by factory chimneys or swamps, broken only by groups of coconut trees. Friends of Tara's parents had bought land there in the forties. You should look into it, Banerjee-*babu,* they had advised, land is best investment, buy now before it all disappears. But the Bengal Tiger had procrastinated. Then had come the partition, and squatters, and finally riots.

95   The road to Tollygunge was circuitous. At first it was *pukka,* black and hardtopped, though very uneven, full of cracks and bumps. It crossed tramlines and railway tracks. It edged half-finished apartment houses where tubercular men shouted slogans from verandahs. Then, as it neared Joyonto's compound, the road was *kutcha,* dry, brown and dusty before the monsoons. It was flanked by huts, cow sheds and stalls. The dust and squalor forced the young ladies from Camac Street to roll up their windows.

96   Had Tara visualized at the start of the journey this exposure to ugliness and danger, to viruses that stalked the street, to dogs and cows scrapping in garbage dumps, she would have refused Joyonto's invitation. She would have remained at the Catelli, sipping espresso and reading old issues of *The New Yorker.* Now she wondered what had made it so easy to come.

97   Finally when the vast compound of Joyonto Roy Chowdhury came into view, Tara thought her chauffeur had made a mistake, it seemed to her so dreary, a wall overgrown with weeds and grass. The opposite side of the street was more interesting. There was a movie house there, two bicycle shops hung with chains and wheels, and a teashop combined with medical clinic. Reena stared at the long line of moviegoers sitting on the sidewalk, and refused to get out of the car at first. Above the squatting moviegoers were giant posters of Hindi film stars, all looking sadly Jewish, Tara noticed; New York had tamed the fierce Semitic charms of Raj Kapoor and Waheeda Rehman. In India, Susie Goldberg would be a goddess. She slid out of her car and saw a very black man near her feet throwing kisses at a gigantic picture of Saira Banu in miniskirt. Then she heard Reena announce she would be sick if they did not go home at once.

98   Mr. Roy Chowdhury tried to head off Reena's sickness by offering to take the young women to the little teashop. Customers sat on uncomfortable wooden chairs, staring at a blackboard on which the proprietor had scrawled: *Try our Vegitable patty (Finest in World) . . . 4as. pr. pc. and Mutton Kofta Curry (Extra Hot) . . . 12as. per odr.* But Tara, who would have liked to say yes to show her friends she was sporting, feared the large flies clinging to tea rings on tables and found herself declining Joyonto's offer. Reena, who had not entertained the lunch invitation seriously, did not bother to answer at all. Only the chauffeur, who had been given lunch *baksheesh* by Tara, was anxious to taste the extra hot curry of mutton.

99   "Enough of detours then," snapped the old man. "Let's get to my squatters."

• • • • • • • •

100 There were no formal gates, only a gap in the wall; also several holes in the wall, jagged and varied openings, where bricks had obviously been pried loose to build hovels or stalls.

101   "I'm sorry there isn't a gate," apologized the host. "The refugees arrived before the construction men had a chance to really get started."

102   Tara was bewildered by her first view of the large and dusty compound. She thought if she had been David she would have taken out notebook and pen and entered important little observations. All she saw was the obvious. Goats and cows grazing in the dust, dogs chasing the friskier children, men sleeping on string beds under a banyan tree. Children playing with mud beside a cracked tube well. Rows of hovels and huts.

103   "This was to have been my rose garden," Joyonto said.

104   The huts were made of canvas cloth, corrugated tin, asbestos sheets, bamboo poles, cardboard pieces and occasional bricks torn loose from compound walls. Posters were used as building material by the more desperate squatters. Saira Banu in ski slacks hung upside down on one wall. DEEPAK GHOSE LIBERATES, CAPITALISM ENSLAVES, announced handbills on many other walls. There were no doors to these hovels. Tara could imagine David asking quite naturally if he might go inside and take a look. But she did not dare look too closely at them herself. Though they were open, these homes seemed to her secretive, almost evil.

105   Tara concentrated on the children playing near a tube well. Most of them were naked. They threw themselves on the tube well's rusty arm, then ran to sit under its spout before the water trickled down. Some of them were holding bananas black with flies. Sometimes they put them down in the mud so they could play with the tube well. She saw a pretty girl in torn bloomers giggle as water sprayed her. She thought the girl would be perfect for adoption ads in western periodicals: *For only a dollar fifty a day you can make this beautiful Indian girl happy. She has no mother or father* . . . She wanted to adopt all the children playing with water.

106   "This is criminal!" said Reena. "What is this? How is it they do this to your private personal property?"

107   "I'm afraid there's nothing I can do about this," answered Joyonto.

108   Now Tara thought she was beginning to understand what Pronob had once called a pain in his stomach. She thought she now knew the meaning of Camac Street and its paraphernalia of spacious lawns, padlocks, chains and triple bolts.

109   "This is too much! Can't you throw them out? I mean bodily throw them out?"

110   "Eviction notices get torn up the moment they are served." Joyonto Roy Chowdhury seemed interested in other dramas. He nibbled the lapel of his blazer and walked ahead of the girls. "Come, Mrs. Cartwright. Come let me show you what should have been my vegetable garden."

111   Tara and Reena followed the goatlike old man past the tube well. *Bustee*-dwellers stared at them. Tara thought they had sly eyes and impudent ears. She thought she saw obsessive distrust on their faces—anger against people who were obviously not squatters.

112   "I told you we shouldn't have come, Tara. I told you it was dangerous to talk to strangers."

113   The young men of the *bustee* closed around the little party. They were shirtless and muscular. They had sun-bleached matted hair. They spat on the ground as they stared at the girls.

114   "Ladies, let me handle this my own way if you please," said Joyonto. Then he raised his manicured fingernails in an exaggerated show of despair. "The weather is unbearable, isn't it, sirs? I wish the rains would come."

115   It occurred to Tara that the next moment could very likely involve her in some tragedy or violence. She did not want to die, though getting hurt by vulgar hands and being left to bleed on the dusty yard would be much worse. She thought she loved David very much, and death or mutilation before she had told him that would be unbearable. If she died in the *bustee* she knew her parents would blame David. They would say that he was not like "us people," that he let his wife wander into danger. She thought again how much she loved David and how impossible it was to tell him that in the aerogrammes bought by the *durwans* of the Bengal Tiger.

116   "Are you the rent collector? Mister, just tell your boss we want to spit on his face," shouted a young man with a scar.

117   "Deepak Ghose liberates, capitalism enslaves," choroused the others.

118   "No," said the old man. "I am not the rent collector. Would I bring these two nice ladies with me to collect rent?"

119   Then the young men accused Joyonto of being a reporter. They struck matches to light their *biris* (Tara noticed the matches had been manufactured by Pronob's company), and they threatened to burn Calcutta. But Joyonto told them quietly that they were not reporters.

120   "How is that?" asked the young men. "You are really just looking around?" They offered, like tourist guides at official ruins, to show their *bustee* to the old man. They sang film songs as they led the way, even imitated love scenes between Raj Kapoor and Vijayantimala. They pushed aside children playing with a bucket of water. A naked ugly girl threw water on Tara and ran away giggling to the door of her hut.

121   "Chase her! Chase the *pugli!*" shouted the young men. "One *lakh* pardons. She's a *pugli,* she's mad."

122   "Don't worry," assured Joyonto. "It's nothing serious."

123   But Tara could not dismiss the incident as casually as the old man. There was to be no major drama, no sensational excitement, she understood that now. No big crises that she could later point to and say: that was when I became a totally different person. She would only suffer relentless anticlimaxes, which Joyonto would dismiss as nothing at all.

124   "I want to go back," said Tara. "I'm afraid I might catch a cold from this damp sari."

125   "But we have just begun, big sister," said the muscular young men. "You haven't yet seen the *pukka* house. The bathing area for ladies. The temple."

126   "I've seen enough, thank you," said Tara. "It's been a most unusual trip. Thank you very much."

127   Joyonto Roy Chowdhury, however, refused to let her go. He discarded

good manners. "You can't leave," he insisted. "I'm not worried about my transportation back home. It is you I'm worried about."

128   Reena was a few feet ahead of them, notebook in hand, entering names and details she procured cunningly from the *bustee* children. She looked efficient and self-confident, an old man's secretary doing routine jobs for her boss.

129   "This compound, Mrs. Cartwright, was meant for eight separate mansions." Joyonto's voice was louder now, the English accent less pronounced. He was like a guide at some obscure, vastly sacred shrine, as if he were recounting history and not the failure of his own fortune. "There was to be a house for me, all on one floor, you understand. A museum, you understand, for all the things I bought in auctions."

130   Reena, still ahead, notebook in hand, had not missed the explanations of her host. "What about the other seven?" she asked.

131   Tara attributed Reena's new energy to her instinct for self-protection; it could not possibly be penance. Perhaps Reena felt if she could write it all down, she would calculate and avoid future confrontations.

132   "I'm partial to family compounds," Joyonto cried, yet louder. "The others were to be for my nephews and nephews-in-law."

133   Then the young men led the sightseers to a brick house. It was still incomplete. A hundred bamboo poles supported the second floor. But already the house looked dilapidated, fit for a demolition crew. A rusty cement mixer lay on its side before the house. Here too the walls were pocked with holes where loose bricks had been pulled away by other *bustee*-dwellers. The young men said that they would be honored to have the guests inspect this house.

134   The house was shaking with voices: of mothers scolding children, women fighting in the kitchen, young men wrestling in tiny rooms and old men smoking in open hallways. There must have been two families to each room. Others spilled out into the courtyard and the porches. The men and women who lived in this decaying brick house had more confidence than the inhabitants of huts and hovels. Some of their young men had enrolled in and dropped out of evening college. Some were businessmen who hawked safety pins and hair ribbons all day. They made the rules of the *bustee* and they enforced them.

135   "I was going to build a swimming pool right in front of this house," Joyonto said, now calmly.

136   "You were wise not to," said Tara.

137   Reena kicked the rusty cement mixer. Perhaps it confirmed to her that Joyonto was prodigal and a danger to her class. Perhaps she saw in that decaying machinery the end of her own dreams of technological progress. "It's criminal," she said. "If we start giving in to these people once there'll be no way to stop them."

138   Joyonto waited for her to finish, then turned to the rough young men. "It's been a satisfactory trip," he said, tipping them lavishly.

139   Though there was a note of finality in Joyonto's voice, the drama of the day had not been completed. It was time for the little party to leave. They had made excursions to the ladies' bathing area and the temple, and now they were going through the motions of farewell.

140   "We'll be late for Sanjay's party if we don't hurry," Reena said.

141   The squatters and their children were walking back with the visitors. For them, too, it had been a satisfactory day. Suddenly a little girl in faded party dress, her arms covered with muddy bandages, detached herself from the other children. She blocked Tara's way. Except for its size there was nothing childish in the little girl's face. It had already assumed the lines of disappointment that it would retain. The body, rectangular and skinny under the party dress, would no doubt thicken a little with unlovely handling but it was already the body of a stunted young woman. She came forward, shrill and angry, circling the visitors like a bird of prey till they responded with embarrassed endearments and nods of the head. The little girl raised her arms, making exit impossible for Tara and her friends. The arms quivered with hatred and Tara, who was only inches away, saw blood spreading on the bandage. There were sores on the little girl's legs, sores that oozed bloody pus with each shiver of hatred. How horrible, thought Tara, the kid's got leprosy, she's being eaten away!

142   "I want that!" screamed the little girl. "I want a sari just like that! I want that! I want that!"

143   It is harder to damage others than to damage oneself. Tara, who had been carefully trained to discipline mind and body by the nuns at St. Blaise's, lost her composure at that moment, and had to be dragged quickly to the Rover. No one was sure what exactly had happened. On going over the incident in Camac Street or at the Catelli-Continental the girls remembered outstanding details, but with each telling the chronology changed. Had Tara fallen on the child in order to beat her to silence? Or had the child thrown herself on Tara and tugged at her *dhakai* sari with bloody, poisonous hands? Reena insisted she had heard Tara scream, *Don't touch me, don't touch me!* She said that she had seen Tara claw like a maniac at the spot that the girl had soiled with her bandages. Tara only knew she had seen the muscular men pin down the offensive girl and fling her out of the room. A pail of water had been brought to Tara as a token of amendment. The mother of the little girl had threatened to beat her daughter. A five-rupee note had been offered guiltily to the child, and the money accepted on her behalf by two virile young men.

144   In the car, revived by smelling salts the faithful chauffeur kept in the glove compartment for just such emergencies, Tara had worried about

making a fool of herself. "I'm sorry I ruined the trip for you people. I don't know what came over me. I saw that girl with leprosy and I just lost my head."

145   Reena had tried to comfort her friend. "It probably wasn't leprosy! Don't worry about it. It's infectious only if you have an open wound. I've heard from my medical-college uncle leprosy is a very hard disease to catch."

146   Joyonto alone had maintained an indifferent silence.

147   Tara remembered being grateful to the chauffeur for taking charge of the situation. "I go straight to Camac Street double fast," the man had said. He had deposited the girls on the steps of the Bengal Tiger's house so that they could gaze at the deserted lawns, wander through the empty marble rooms, linger on the spacious verandahs, bathe themselves in the "English" style bathroom, and regain their composure before the maid brought them tea and sandwiches.

148   But more than anything else Tara remembered Reena just before they had parted from Joyonto in the car. Reena had drawn herself up like a tremulous Brahminical Joan of Arc. "Here are the names I took down, Mr. Roy Chowdhury. It's your duty to serve them new eviction notices. Good-bye."

WORD FOCUS

VOCABULARY GLOSS

aerogrammes: *airmail letters like the kind sold at post offices (115)*

babu: *a colloquial way of saying Mister (94)*

baksheesh: *money offered as a tip (98)*

Banerjee: *a person's last name, indicative of the Brahmin—priestly—caste (42)*

banyan: *a type of tree whose roots grow downward from its branches; symbolic of continuity and rejuvenation (102)*

Bengal Tiger: *the royal Bengal Tiger considered king of the jungle in India; honorary title given to Tara's father to denote his power and position in Bengali society (94)*

Bengali Brahmin: *a person of the highest social class or caste in India (42)*

billeted: *stationed in temporary quarters (31)*

bird of prey: *a large bird like a hawk or eagle that kills smaller creatures for food (141)*

bullock carts: *animal-drawn wooden vehicles used in farm work (36)*

bush coat: *a cotton jacket for casual wear (37)*

bustee: *a slum; dwellings of the very poor (84)*

canasta: *a card game (37)*

cheek: *nerve; audacity (16)*

dapper: *neatly and fashionably dressed (73)*

dhakai sari: *an expensive cotton sari woven in Bangladesh (143)*

don't give two hoots: *do not care; are not interested (50)*

durwans: *doormen who keep guard (115)*

Eesh!: *an exclamatory sound expressing surprise or disgust (1)*

eye-make: *English slang: flirt with; American slang: make eyes at (26)*

face facts: *confront issues that are often unpleasant (50)*

funeral pyres: *wooden platforms for cremation in Hindu last rites (69)*

fusspot: *one who is fussy or picky; one who looks for flaws (29)*

Ghar: *a room or house (2)*

ghat: *banks of a river where the dead are cremated (72)*

giving in: *conceding; accepting someone else's point (137)*

go on record: *to make something official (92)*

handbills: *paper notices or handouts that contain information about political meetings; advertisements (104)*

Horn and Hardart: *a famous automated restaurant in New York that is no longer in existence (35)*

Jaycees: *a social service organization (31)*

kutcha: *literally "unripe"; an unfinished road not laid with concrete and tar (95)*

lost my head: *lost control (144)*

Marwari: *a wealthy businessman from Marwar (18)*

mleccha: *outcaste or untouchable; one who doesn't belong (45)*

morah: *a stool to sit on made of cane, stuffed plastic, or leather (37)*

pugli: *a madwoman (121)*

pukka: *absolute; pure; concrete (95)*

silly-billy: *an affectionate term used in teasing (18)*

smelling salts: *a compound used to revive a person who has fainted (144)*

take my chances: *take a risk (43)*

tantric: *relating to religious meditations that test the concentration of holy men (69)*

tea estates: *plantations where tea is grown (88)*
tramlines: *tracks for trams or streetcars (95)*
turbans: *long cloth strips wrapped around men's heads (2)*
workers' unions: *associations that defend workers' rights (25)*

VOCABULARY QUESTIONS

1. *Antonyms* are words or phrases with opposite meanings—such as *delighted* and *disappointed,* and *enormous* and *insignificant.* The context in which the word appears in a sentence determines the meaning of the word and its opposite. Look at the following list of words from Mukherjee's story, and find antonyms for each word. Use the antonyms to make a statement about the text.

   distortions (21)   circuitous (95)
   predictable (42)   obsessive (111)
   placidity (74)   sacred (129)
   squalor (95)   lavishly (138)

2. The word *bigot,* like many words in the English language, has different forms to represent different uses in a sentence: *bigot, bigoted, bigotry.* Look at the following sentences:

   A <u>bigot</u> accepts only one view of the world as correct—his or her own.

   She detected <u>bigotry</u> in his actions toward other ethnic groups.

   His <u>bigoted</u> views about marrying Europeans offended her.

   Look up the following words, and provide alternate forms of each. Use each form in a sentence that comments on the text. Note that some words might not have forms for all categories.

Noun	*Verb*	*Adjective*	*Adverb*
chronology (143)			
		conspiratorial (28)	
		hysterical (38)	
	procrastinated (94)		
	procured (128)		

3. What does "prodigal" (137) mean? Why does Reena use the word "prodi-
    gal" to describe Joyonto? Could another word or words be used effec-
    tively to portray this meaning?

ENGLISH CRAFT

1. In written English *the apostrophe:* (1) shows possession; and (2) shows
    contractions. In *possession,* the apostrophe signals ownership or be-
    longing, as in *Tara's feelings about her friend Reena were mixed.* Pos-
    session is also signaled by possessive pronouns and adjectives:

	Possessive Pronouns	*Possessive Adjectives*
First person		
singular	mine	my
plural	ours	our
Second person		
singular/plural	yours	your
Third person		
singular	hers, his	her, his, its
plural	theirs	their

In *contractions,* the apostrophe replaces missing letters. A *contraction*
typically represents two words that are joined together to make one word.
Two types of commonly used contractions appear in the following table:

Contractions of the Auxiliary **have**		*Contractions of the Auxiliary* **be**	
I've	I have	I'm	I am
you've	you have	you're	you are
he's	he has	he's	he is
she's	she has	she's	she is
it's	it has	it's	it is
we've	we have	we're	we are
they've	they have	they're	they are

The words *its* and *it's* have different meanings and uses. <u>Its</u> without the apostrophe is a possessive pronoun.

The new car lost <u>its</u> shine quickly.

<u>It's</u> with the apostrophe is a contraction of the pronoun *it* and either *has* or *is*. <u>It's</u> means either *it has* or *it is*.

<u>It's</u> unusual for a new car to lose its shine quickly.

<u>It's</u> been a typically durable paint job.

Refer to the reading, and write three sentences that reflect the distinction between possessive pronouns, adjectives, and contractions.

2. An important group of auxiliary (helping) verbs in English are *modal verbs,* which have many uses: to make predictions; to express uncertainty; to indicate habits; to show ability; to give permission; to make inferences. Modal verbs, like other auxiliary verbs, have tense forms. However, unlike other auxiliary verbs, they are always followed by the base verb, the simplest form of the verb.

Auxiliary Verb + Participle

Mukherjee <u>has written</u> a culturally rich story about India.

Mukherjee <u>has been writing</u> a culturally rich story about India for several years.

Modal + Base

Mukherjee <u>can write</u> interesting stories about India.

Mukherjee <u>should write</u> interesting stories about India.

The following is a list of some modals.

Modals	
will/would	may/might
shall/should	must
can/could	

Look through the text, and make a list of three modals and the base forms that go with each modal. Make three statements about Mukherjee's text using a modal and the base form of a verb.

INTERPRETIVE JOURNAL

1. Reena says to Tara, "I mean this is no moral judgment or anything, but you've become too self-centered and European" (9). Discuss what the pairing of the terms "self-centered" and "European" implies.

2. In a conversation about the Australian boys shouting for "paper," Reena says, "Serves them right for wanting to see the *real* India" (36). What does Reena mean by the "real" India? What does her comment reveal about her attitude toward the boys from Australia? What does it reveal about her attitude toward her own country?

3. Tara and Reena react differently to their visit to the *bustee* (84). Describe the *bustee,* and discuss their individual reactions to it. Analyze why they have such different reactions.

4. Tara talks about the terror she felt during her first night in America. Discuss an incident that made you or someone you know feel frightened when encountering a new place or situation.

ESSAY QUESTION

This excerpt shows a strong contrast between action (doing something) and inaction (doing nothing at all). Look at some of the scenes, descriptions of characters, and choices of particular words, and discuss the ways in which Mukherjee creates this impression of action versus inaction.

Nawal El Saadawi
Excerpt from *Woman at Point Zero*

Preview

Think about a time when you experienced the importance of being a man or a woman. Did gender make a difference in this situation? Describe this experience and how it affected you.

Word Preview

You can familiarize yourself with the following words by looking them up in the dictionary. You can broaden your knowledge of these words by pronouncing them and understanding how they are used in context.

hunched over (3)	restored (51)	rasping (64)
warder (3)	probing (52)	servile (64)
psychiatrist (5)	prostitute (60)	stealthy (64)
commuted (5)	accentuated (60)	maize (66)
emitted (30)	seductiveness (60)	nudge (67)
indifference (33)	eloquent (62)	glimpse (68)
myriads (45)	nod (63)	clamber (73)
gasps (49)	guttural (63)	buffeted by (80)
pace (50)	subdued (63)	prolonged (87)
composure (51)	invoked (64)	resonate (87)

1   This is the story of a real woman. I met her in the Qanatir Prison a few years ago. I was doing research on the personalities of a group of women prisoners and detainees convicted or accused of various offences.

2   The prison doctor told me that this woman had been sentenced to death for killing a man. Yet she was not like the other female murderers held in the prison.

3   'You will never meet anyone like her in or out of prison. She refuses all visitors, and won't speak to anyone. She usually leaves her food untouched, and remains wide awake until dawn. Sometimes the prison warder observes her as she sits staring vacantly into space for hours. One day she asked for pen and paper, then spent hours hunched over them without moving. The warder could not tell whether she was writing a letter or something else. Perhaps she was not writing anything at all.'

4   I asked the prison doctor, 'Will she see me?'

5   'I shall try to persuade her to speak to you for a while,' he said. 'She might agree if I explain you are a psychiatrist, and not one of the Public Prosecutor's assistants. She refuses to answer my questions. She even refused to sign an appeal to the President so that her sentence could be commuted to imprisonment for life.'

6   'Who made out the appeal for her?' I asked.

7   'I did,' he said. 'To be quite honest, I do not really feel she is a murderer. If you look into her face, her eyes, you will never believe that so gentle a woman can commit murder.'

8   'Who says murder does not require that a person be gentle?'

9   He stared at me in surprise for a brief moment, and then laughed nervously.

10   'Have you ever killed anybody?'

11   'Am I a gentle woman?' I replied.

12   He turned his head to one side, pointed to a tiny window, and said, 'That's her cell. I'll go and persuade her to come down and meet you.'

13   After a while he came back without her. Firdaus had refused to see me.

14   I was supposed to examine some other women prisoners that day, but instead I got into my car and drove away.

15   Back home I could not do anything. I had to revise the draft of my latest book, but I was incapable of concentrating. I could think of nothing but the woman called Firdaus who, in ten days' time, would be led to the gallows.

16   Early next morning I found myself at the prison gates again. I asked the warder to let me see Firdaus, but she said: 'It's no use, Doctor. She will never agree to see you.'

17   'Why?'

Editor's note: El Saadawi uses British conventions in spelling and punctuation.

18   'They're going to hang her in a few days' time. What use are you, or anybody else to her? Leave her alone!'

19   There was a note of anger in her voice. She gave me a look charged with wrath, as though I was the one who would hang Firdaus in a few days' time.

20   'I have nothing to do with the authorities either here or any other place,' I said.

21   'That's what they all say,' she said angrily.

22   'Why are you so worked up?' I asked. 'Do you think Firdaus is innocent, that she didn't kill him?'

23   She replied with an added fury, 'Murderer or not, she's an innocent woman and does not deserve to be hanged. They are the ones that ought to hang.'

24   'They? Who are *they?*'

25   She looked at me with suspicion and said, 'Tell me rather, who are you? Did they send you to her?'

26   'Whom do you mean by "they"?' I asked again.

27   She looked around cautiously, almost with fear, and stepped back away from me.

28   ' "They" . . . You mean to say you don't know them?'

29   'No,' I said.

30   She emitted a short, sarcastic laugh and walked off. I heard her muttering to herself:

31   'How can she be the only one who does not know them?'

• • • • • • • •

32   I returned to the prison several times, but all my attempts to see Firdaus were of no avail. I felt somehow that my research was now in jeopardy. As a matter of fact, my whole life seemed to be threatened with failure. My self-confidence began to be badly shaken, and I went through difficult moments. It looked to me as though this woman who had killed a human being, and was shortly to be killed herself, was a much better person than I. Compared to her, I was nothing but a small insect crawling upon the land amidst millions of other insects.

33   Whenever I remembered the expression in the eyes of the warder, or the prison doctor, as they spoke of her complete indifference to everything, her attitude of total rejection, and above all her refusal to see me, the feeling that I was helpless, and of no significance grew on me. A question kept turning round and round in my mind increasingly: 'What sort of woman was she? Since she had rejected me, did that mean she was a better person than me? But then, she had also refused to send an appeal to the President asking him to protect her from the gallows. Could that signify that she was better than the Head of State?'

34   I was seized by a feeling very close to certainty, yet difficult to ex-plain, that she was, in fact, better than all the men and women we nor-mally hear about, or see, or know.

35   I tried to overcome my inability to sleep, but another thought started to occupy my mind and keep me awake. When she refused to see me did she know who I was, or had she rejected me without knowing?

36   The following morning, I found myself back once more in the prison. I had no intention of trying to meet Firdaus, for I had given up all hope. I was looking for the warder, or the prison doctor. The doctor had not yet arrived but I found the warder.

37   'Did Firdaus tell you she knew me?' I asked her.

38   'No, she did not tell me anything,' the warder replied. 'But she does know you.'

39   'How do you know that she knows me?'

40   'I can sense her.'

41   I just stood there as though turned to stone. The warder left me to get on with her work. I tried to move, to go towards my car and leave, but in vain. A strange feeling of heaviness weighed down my heart, my body, drained my legs of their power. A feeling heavier than the weight of the whole earth, as though instead of standing above its surface, I was now lying somewhere beneath it. The sky also had undergone a change; its colour had turned to black, like that of the earth, and it was press-ing down upon me with its added load.

42   It was a feeling I had known only once before, many years ago. I had fallen in love with a man who did not love me. I felt rejected, not only by him, not only by one person amongst the millions that peopled the vast world, but by every living being or thing on earth, by the vast world itself.

43   I straightened my shoulders, stood as upright as I could, and took a deep breath. The weight on my head lifted a little. I began to look around me and to feel amazed at finding myself in the prison at this early hour. The warder was bent double, scrubbing the tiled floor of the corridor. I was overcome by an unusual contempt towards her. She was no more than a woman cleaning the prison floor. She could not read or write and knew nothing about psychology, so how was it that I had so easily believed her feelings could be true?

44   Firdaus did not actually say she knew me. The warder merely sensed it. Why should that indicate that Firdaus really knew me? If she had re-jected me without knowing who I was there was no reason for me to feel hurt. Her refusal to see me was not directed against me personally, but against the world and everybody in it.

45   I started to walk towards my car with the intention of leaving. Subjective feelings such as those that had taken hold of me were not worthy of a researcher in science. I almost smiled at myself as I opened the door of the car. The touch of its surface helped to restore my identity, my self-esteem as a doctor. Whatever the circumstances, a doctor was surely to be preferred to a woman condemned to death for murder. My normal attitude towards myself (an attitude which rarely deserts me) gradually returned. I turned the ignition key and pressed my foot down on the accelerator, firmly stamping out the sudden feeling (which occasionally haunts me in moments of failure) of merely being an insignificant insect, crawling on the earth amidst myriads of other similar insects. I heard a voice behind me, rising over the sound of the engine.

46   'Doctor! Doctor!'

47   It was the warder. She ran up to me panting heavily. Her gasping voice reminded me of the voices I often heard in my dreams. Her mouth had grown bigger, and so had her lips, which kept opening and closing with a mechanical movement, like a swing door.

48   I heard her say, 'Firdaus, Doctor! Firdaus wants to see you!'

49   Her breast was heaving up and down, her breathing had become a series of rapid gasps, and her eyes and face reflected a violent emotion. If the President of the Republic in person had asked to see me, she could not have been swept by such an overpowering emotion.

50   My breathing in turn quickened, as though by infection, or to be more precise, I felt out of breath, for my heart was beating more strongly than it had ever done before. I do not know how I climbed out of the car, nor how I followed so closely behind the warder that I sometimes overtook her, or moved ahead. I walked with a rapid, effortless pace, as though my legs were no longer carrying a body. I was full of a wonderful feeling, proud, elated, happy. The sky was blue with a blueness I could capture in my eyes. I held the whole world in my hands; it was mine. It was a feeling I had known only once before, many years ago. I was on my way to meet the first man I loved for the first time.

51   I stopped for a moment in front of Firdaus' cell to catch my breath and adjust the collar of my dress. But I was trying to regain my composure, to return to my normal state, to the realization that I was a researcher in science, a psychiatrist, or something of the kind. I heard the key grind in the lock, brutal, screeching. The sound restored me to myself. My hand tightened its grasp on the leather bag, and a voice within me said, 'Who is this woman called Firdaus? She is only . . .'

52   But the words within me stopped short. Suddenly we were face to face. I stood rooted to the ground, silent, motionless. I did not hear the beat of my heart, nor the key as it turned in the lock, closing the heavy door behind me. It was as though I died the moment her eyes looked into mine. They were eyes that killed, like a knife, probing, cutting deep

down inside, their look steady, unwavering. Not the slightest movement of a lid. Not the smallest twitch of a muscle in the face.

53   I was brought back suddenly by a voice. The voice was hers, steady, cutting deep down inside, cold as a knife. Not the slightest wavering in its tone. Not the smallest shiver of a note. I heard her say:

54   'Close the window.'

55   I moved up to the window blindly and closed it, then cast a bemused look around. There was nothing in the cell. Not a bed, or a chair, or anything on which I could sit down. I heard her say:

56   'Sit down on the ground.'

57   My body bent down and sat on the ground. It was January and the ground was bare, but I felt no cold. Like walking in one's sleep. The ground under me was cold. The same touch, the same consistency, the same naked cold. Yet the cold did not touch me, did not reach me. It was the cold of the sea in a dream. I swam through its waters. I was naked and knew not how to swim. But I neither felt its cold, nor drowned in its waters. Her voice too was like the voices one hears in a dream. It was close to me, yet seemed to come from afar, spoke from a distance and seemed to arise from nearby. For we do not know from where these voices arise: from above or below, to our left or our right. We might even think they come from the depths of the earth, drop from the rooftops, or fall from the heavens. Or they might even flow from all directions, like air moving in space reaches the ears.

58   But this was no dream. This was not air flowing into my ears. The woman sitting on the ground in front of me was a real woman, and the voice filling my ears with its sound, echoing in a cell where the window and door were tightly shut, could only be her voice, the voice of Firdaus.

· · · · · · · ·

59   Let me speak. Do not interrupt me. I have no time to listen to you. They are coming to take me at six o'clock this evening. Tomorrow morning I shall no longer be here. Nor will I be in any place known to man. This journey to a place unknown to everybody on this earth fills me with pride. All my life I have been searching for something that would fill me with pride, make me feel superior to everyone else, including kings, princes and rulers. Each time I picked up a newspaper and found the picture of a man who was one of them, I would spit on it. I knew I was only spitting on a piece of newspaper which I needed for covering the kitchen shelves. Nevertheless I spat, and then left the spit where it was to dry.

60   Anyone who saw me spitting on the picture might think I knew that particular man personally. But I did not. I am just one woman. And there is no single woman who could possibly know all the men who get their

pictures published in the newspapers. For after all, I was only a successful prostitute. And no matter how successful a prostitute is, she cannot
get to know all the men. However, all the men I did get to know, every
single man of them, has filled me with but one desire: to lift my hand and
bring it smashing down on his face. But because I am a woman I have
never had the courage to lift my hand. And because I am a prostitute, I
hid my fear under layers of make-up. Since I was successful, my make-
up was always of the best and most expensive kind, just like the make-
up of respectable upper-class women. I always had my hair done by styl-
ists who tendered their services only to upper-class society women. The
colour I chose for lipstick was always 'natural and serious' so that it neither disguised, nor accentuated the seductiveness of my lips. The skilful
lines pencilled around my eyes hinted at just the right combination of at-
traction and rejection favoured by the wives of men in high positions of
authority. Only my make-up, my hair and my expensive shoes were
'upper class'. With my secondary school certificate and suppressed desires I belonged to the 'middle class'. By birth I was lower class.

• • • • • • • •

61   My father, a poor peasant farmer, who could neither read, nor write,
knew very few things in life. How to grow crops, how to sell a buffalo
poisoned by his enemy before it died, how to exchange his virgin daughter for a dowry when there was still time, how to be quicker than his
neighbour in stealing from the fields once the crop was ripe. How to
bend over the headman's hand and pretend to kiss it, how to beat his
wife and make her bite the dust each night.

62   Every Friday morning he would put on a clean *galabeya* and head
for the mosque to attend the weekly prayer. The prayer over, I would see
him walking with the other men like himself as they commented on the
Friday sermon, on how convincing and eloquent the *imam* had been to
a degree that he had surpassed the unsurpassable. For was it not ver-
ily true that stealing was a sin, and killing was a sin, and defaming the
honour of a woman was a sin, and injustice was a sin, and beating another human being was a sin . . .? Moreover, who could deny that to be
obedient was a duty, and to love one's country too. That love of the ruler
and love of Allah were one and indivisible. Allah protect our ruler for
many long years and may he remain a source of inspiration and
strength to our country, the Arab Nation and all Mankind.

63   I could see them walking through the narrow winding lanes, nodding their heads in admiration, and in approval of everything his Holi-
ness the *Imam* had said. I would watch them as they continued to nod
their heads, rub their hands one against the other, wipe their brows
while all the time invoking Allah's name, calling upon his blessings,

repeating His holy words in a guttural, subdued tone, muttering and whispering without a moment's respite.

64   On my head I carried a heavy earthenware jar, full of water. Under its weight my neck would sometimes jerk backwards, or to the left or to the right. I had to exert myself to maintain it balanced on my head, and keep it from falling. I kept my legs moving in the way my mother had taught me, so that my neck remained upright. I was still young at the time, and my breasts were not yet rounded. I knew nothing about men. But I could hear them as they invoked Allah's name and called upon His blessings, or repeated His holy words in a subdued guttural tone. I would observe them nodding their heads, or rubbing their hands one against the other, or coughing, or clearing their throats with a rasping noise, or constantly scratching under the armpits and between the thighs. I saw them as they watched what went on around them with wary, doubting, stealthy eyes, eyes ready to pounce, full of an aggressiveness that seemed strangely servile.

65   Sometimes I could not distinguish which one of them was my father. He resembled them so closely that it was difficult to tell. So one day I asked my mother about him. How was it that she had given birth to me without a father? First she beat me. Then she brought a woman who was carrying a small knife or maybe a razor blade. They cut off a piece of flesh from between my thighs.

66   I cried all night. Next morning my mother did not send me to the fields. She usually made me carry a load of manure on my head and take it to the fields. I preferred to go to the fields rather than stay in our hut. There, I could play with the goats, climb over the water-wheel, and swim with the boys in the stream. A little boy called Mohammadain used to pinch me under water and follow me into the small shelter made of maize stalks. He would make me lie down beneath a pile of straw, and lift up my *galabeya*. We played at 'bride and bridegroom'. From some part in my body, where, exactly I did not know, would come a sensation of sharp pleasure. Later I would close my eyes and feel with my hand for the exact spot. The moment I touched it, I would realize that I had felt the sensation before. Then we would start to play again until the sun went down, and we could hear his father's voice calling to him from the neighbouring field. I would try to hold him back, but he would run off, promising to come the next day.

67   But my mother no longer sent me to the fields. Before the sun had started to appear in the sky, she would nudge me in the shoulder with her fist so that I would awaken, pick up the earthenware jar and go off to fill it with water. Once back, I would sweep under the animals and then make rows of dung cakes which I left in the sun to dry. On baking day I would knead dough and make bread.

68   To knead the dough I squatted on the ground with the trough between my legs. At regular intervals I lifted the elastic mass up into the air and let it fall back into the trough. The heat of the oven was full on my face, singeing the edges of my hair. My *galabeya* often slipped up my thighs, but I paid no attention until the moment when I would glimpse my uncle's hand moving slowly from behind the book he was reading to touch my leg. The next moment I could feel it travelling up my thigh with a cautious, stealthy, trembling movement. Every time there was the sound of a footstep at the entrance to our house, his hand would withdraw quickly. But whenever everything around us lapsed into silence, broken only every now and then by the snap of dry twigs between my fingers as I fed the oven, and the sound of his regular breathing reaching me from behind the book so that I could not tell whether he was snoring quietly in his sleep or wide awake and panting, his hand would continue to press against my thigh with a grasping, almost brutal insistence.

69   He was doing to me what Mohammadain had done to me before. In fact, he was doing even more, but I no longer felt the strong sensation of pleasure that radiated from an unknown and yet familiar part of my body. I closed my eyes and tried to reach the pleasure I had known before but in vain. It was as if I could no longer recall the exact spot from which it used to arise, or as though a part of me, of my being, was gone and would never return.

· · · · · · · ·

70   My uncle was not young. He was much older than I was. He used to travel to Cairo alone, attend classes in El Azhar, and study at a time when I was still a child and had not yet learned to read or write. My uncle would put a chalk pencil between my fingers and make me write on a slate: *Alif, Ba, Gim, Dal* . . . Sometimes he made me repeat after him: 'Alif has nothing on her, Ba's got one dot underneath, Gim's got a dot in the middle, Dal has nothing at all.' He would nod his head as he recited from the thousand verse poem of Ibn Malik, just as though he was reciting from the Koran, and I would repeat each letter after him, and nod my head in the same way.

71   Once the holidays were over, my uncle would climb on the back of the donkey, and set off for the Delta Railway Station. I followed close behind carrying his big basket, packed full of eggs, cheese and bread cakes, topped with his books and clothes. All along the way, until we got to the station, my uncle would not cease talking to me about his room at the end of Mohammad Ali Street near the Citadel, about El Azhar, Ataba Square, the trams, the people who lived in Cairo. At moments he would

sing in a sweet voice, his body swaying rhythmically with the movement of the donkey.

72   'I abandoned ye not on the high seas
Yet on the dry land thou hast left me.
I bartered thee not for shining gold
Yet for worthless straw thou didst sell me
O my long night
O mine eyes. Oh.'

73   When my uncle would clamber into the train, and bid me farewell, I would cry and beg him to take me with him to Cairo. But my uncle would ask,

74   'What will you do in Cairo, Firdaus?'

75   And I would reply: 'I will go to El Azhar and study like you.'

76   Then he would laugh and explain that El Azhar was only for men. And I would cry, and hold on to his hand, as the train started to move. But he would pull it away with a force and suddenness that made me fall flat on my face.

77   So I would retrace my steps with bent head, pondering the shape of my toes, as I walked along the country road, wondering about myself, as the questions went round in my mind. Who was I? Who was my father? Was I going to spend my life sweeping the dung out from under the animals, carrying manure on my head, kneading dough, and baking bread?

78   Back in my father's house I stared at the mud walls like a stranger who had never entered it before. I looked around almost in surprise, as though I had not been born here, but had suddenly dropped from the skies, or emerged from somewhere deep down in the earth, to find myself in a place where I did not belong, in a home which was not mine, born from a father who was not my father, and from a mother who was not my mother. Was it my uncle's talk of Cairo, and the people who lived there that had changed me? Was I really the daughter of my mother, or was my mother someone else? Or was I born the daughter of my mother and later changed into someone else? Or had my mother been transformed into another woman who resembled her so closely that I could not tell the difference?

79   I tried to recall what my mother had looked like the first time I saw her. I can remember two eyes. I can remember her eyes in particular. I cannot describe their colour, or their shape. They were eyes that I watched. They were eyes that watched me. Even if I disappeared from their view, they could see me, and follow me wherever I went, so that if I faltered while learning to walk they would hold me up.

80   Every time I tried to walk, I fell. A force seemed to push me from

behind, so that I fell forwards, or a weight from in front seemed to lean on me so that I fell backwards. It was something like a pressure of the air wanting to crush me; something like the pull of the earth trying to suck me down into its depths. And in the midst of it all there I was, struggling, straining my arms and legs in an attempt to stand up. But I kept falling, buffeted by the contradictory forces that kept pulling me in different directions, like an object thrown into a limitless sea, without shores and without a bed, slashed by the waters when it starts to sink, and by the wind if it starts to float. Forever sinking and rising, sinking and rising between the sea and the sky, with nothing to hold on to except the two eyes. Two eyes to which I clung with all my might. Two eyes that alone seemed to hold me up. To this very moment I do not know whether they were wide or narrow, nor can I recall if they were surrounded by lashes or not. All I can remember are two rings of intense white around two circles of intense black. I only had to look into them for the white to become whiter and the black even blacker, as though sunlight was pouring into them from some magical source neither on earth, nor in the sky, for the earth was pitch black, and the sky dark as night, with no sun and no moon.

81   I could tell she was my mother, how I do not know. So I crawled up to her seeking warmth from her body. Our hut was cold, yet in winter my father used to shift my straw mat and my pillow to the small room facing north, and occupy my corner in the oven room. And instead of staying by my side to keep me warm, my mother used to abandon me alone and go to my father to keep him warm. In summer I would see her sitting at his feet with a tin mug in her hand as she washed his legs with cold water.

82   When I grew a little older my father put the mug in my hand and taught me how to wash his legs with water. I had now replaced my mother and did the things she used to do. My mother was no longer there, but instead there was another woman who hit me on my hand and took the mug away from me. My father told me she was my mother. In fact, she looked exactly like my mother; the same long garments, the same face, and the same way of moving. But when I used to look into her eyes I could feel she was not my mother. They were not the eyes that held me up each time I was on the point of falling. They were not two rings of pure white surrounding two circles of intense black, where the white would become even whiter, and the black even blacker every time I looked into them, as though the light of the sun or the moon kept flowing through them.

83   No light seemed ever to touch the eyes of this woman, even when the day was radiant and the sun at its very brightest. One day I took her head between my hands and turned it so that the sun fell directly on her face, but her eyes remained dull, impervious to its light, like two extinguished lamps. I stayed awake all night weeping alone, trying to muffle my sobs so that they would not disturb my little brothers and sisters sleeping on the floor beside me. For, like most people, I had many brothers and sisters. They were like chicks that multiply in spring, shiver in winter and lose their feathers, and then in summer are stricken with diarrhoea, waste away quickly and one by one creep into a corner and die.

• • • • • • • •

84   When one of his female children died, my father would eat his supper, my mother would wash his legs, and then he would go to sleep, just as he did every night. When the child that died was a boy, he would beat my mother, then have his supper and lie down to sleep.

85   My father never went to bed without supper, no matter what happened. Sometimes when there was no food at home we would all go to bed with empty stomachs. But he would never fail to have a meal. My mother would hide his food from us at the bottom of one of the holes in the oven. He would sit eating alone while we watched him. One evening I dared to stretch out my hand to his plate, but he struck me a sharp blow over the back of my fingers.

86   I was so hungry that I could not cry. I sat in front of him watching as he ate, my eyes following his hand from the moment his fingers plunged into the bowl until it rose into the air, and carried the food into his mouth. His mouth was like that of a camel, with a big opening and wide jaws. His upper jaw kept clamping down on his lower jaw with a loud grinding noise, and chewed through each morsel so thoroughly that we could hear his teeth striking against each other. His tongue kept rolling round and round in his mouth as though it also was chewing, darting out every now and then to lick off some particle of food that had stuck to his lips, or dropped on his chin.

87   At the end of his meal my mother would bring him a glass of water. He drank it, then belched loudly, expelling the air from the mouth or belly with a prolonged noise. After that he smoked his water pipe, filling the room around him with thick clouds of smoke, coughing, snorting and inhaling deeply through his mouth and nose. Once over with his pipe he lay down, and a moment later the hut would resonate with his loud snoring.

88   I sensed he was not my father. Nobody told me, and I was not really aware of the fact. I could just feel it deep down inside me. I did not whisper the secret to anyone but kept it to myself. Every time my uncle came back for the summer holidays, I would hang on to his *galabeya* when the time came for him to leave, and ask that he take me with him. My uncle was closer to me than my father. He was not so old, and he

allowed me to sit beside him and look at his books. He taught me the alphabet, and after my father died he sent me to elementary school. Later, when my mother died, he took me with him to Cairo.

WORD FOCUS

VOCABULARY GLOSS

Alif, Ba, Gim, Dal: *the first four letters of the Arabic alphabet (70)*
Allah: *the supreme being in Islam (62)*
bite the dust: *be defeated; feel dead (61)*
diarrhoea: *intestinal distress; also spelled diarrhea (83)*
dowry: *a marriage settlement (61)*
dung cakes: *dried animal body waste used as fuel (67)*
galabeya: *a long, loose white garment worn by men and women in the Middle East (62)*
Koran: *the holy book of Islam (70)*
led to the gallows: *taken to be executed (15)*
of no avail: *ineffective (32)*
Public Prosecutor: *a lawyer who brings charges on behalf of the state (5)*
turned to stone: *became motionless and speechless (41)*

VOCABULARY QUESTIONS

1. This story contains a number of words that describe different emotions or ways of thinking. Look at the following words:

amazed (43) _____

bemused (55) _____

contempt (43) _____

elated (50) _____

fury (23) _____

pondering (77) _____

wrath (19) _____

worked up (22) _____

Define each word. Find the sentence in the text in which it appears. Then categorize each word according to whether the feeling it conveys is negative or positive by putting it in the appropriate box below. Indicate on the scale under each box whether the feeling is weak or strong.

Negative	*Neutral*	*Positive*

STRONG	WEAK	WEAK	STRONG
NEGATIVE	NEGATIVE	POSITIVE	POSITIVE

2. Religious groups use different words to identify their places of worship and religious leaders. Look at the following table, and fill in the place of worship associated with each group.

Religious Group	*Religious Leader*	*Place of Worship*
Christianity	priest/pastor	_____
Hinduism	pujari	_____
Islam	imam	_____
Judaism	rabbi	_____

3. Firdaus talks about "class" when she discusses her past life:

Only my make-up, my hair and my expensive shoes were 'upper class'. With my secondary school certificate and suppressed desires I belonged to the 'middle class'. By birth I was lower class. (60)

"Class" has several different denotations (which refer to the central, or dictionary, meaning of the word) and connotations (which refer to the ideas and feelings that become associated with the word). Using a dictionary, define "class" as El Saadawi uses it here. Then explore why the connotations of "class" are often negative in contemporary American society.

ENGLISH CRAFT

1. Imperative sentences, commands, are used to give commands and make requests. For example, Firdaus says, "Close the window" (54); "Sit down on the ground" (56); "Let me speak. Do not interrupt me" (59). When imperatives are referred to in academic writing, they are often framed in indirect speech, such as *Firdaus asked the doctor to let her speak.* Change the rest of Firdaus's commands into indirect statements, and discuss the effect this change has on how readers may see Firdaus.

2. *Style* refers to the way in which people express themselves in speech and writing. Depending on the situation, style can range from casual to formal. For example, a letter that begins with *Dear Bob, What's happening?* would be considered casual. Similarly, an essay that begins with *A funny thing happened the other day* is more casual than one that begins with *Psychologists define fun as an activity that reduces stress.*

   In writing, an author's style involves such features as choice of words, type and length of sentences and paragraphs, and organization of the text itself. Look carefully at these features in El Saadawi's text to compare and contrast the first part of the story, which focuses on the psychiatrist, and the second part of the story, which focuses on Firdaus.

3. *Pronouns* are words that take the place of nouns or noun phrases. The noun that the pronoun replaces is called its *antecedent*. Look at the following sentence, particularly the pronoun *she* and its antecedent *Firdaus*.

   The psychiatrist wanted to interview Firdaus, but she refused.

   There are two nouns identifying women *(psychiatrist, Firdaus),* but only one noun refers to the woman who refused to be interviewed—*Firdaus.* The pronoun *she* refers back to the noun closest to it, which is *Firdaus.* Note that *she* agrees with the noun *Firdaus* in gender (female), number (singular), and person (third person).

   Look at the underlined pronouns in the following passages, and identify their antecedent. You may have to refer back to the text.

   The prison doctor told <u>me</u> that this woman had been sentenced to death for killing a man. Yet <u>she</u> was not like the other female murderers held in the prison. (2)

   'You will never meet anyone like <u>her</u> in or out of prison. She refuses all visitors, and won't speak to <u>anyone</u>. She usually leaves her food untouched, and remains wide awake until dawn. Sometimes the prison warder observes her as she sits staring vacantly into space for hours. One day she asked for pen and paper, then spent hours hunched over <u>them</u>

without moving. The warder could not tell whether she was writing a letter or something else. Perhaps she was not writing anything at all.' (3)

INTERPRETIVE JOURNAL

1. Describe Firdaus's family and the relationship among the father, mother, and children.

2. Discuss what you think Firdaus means when she says that her mother was no longer there:

   . . . instead there was another woman who hit me on my hand and took the mug away from me. My father told me she was my mother. In fact, she looked exactly like my mother; the same long garments, the same face, and the same way of moving. But when I used to look into her eyes I could feel she was not my mother. They were not the eyes that held me up each time I was on the point of falling. (82)

3. Identify and analyze any significant statements that help us understand Firdaus's state of mind while she was growing up.

4. The psychiatrist reminds herself and her readers that she is a scientist, doing scientific research. Does her interaction with Firdaus meet the criteria of scientific objectivity?

ESSAY QUESTION

This excerpt tells us about Firdaus's growing-up years and her position in her family and society. Discuss how her role as a female in these early years shaped her life.

Nancy Mairs

Challenge: An Exploration

Preview

Challenges and choices confront people every day of their lives.
Identify some of the challenges and choices you have faced, and discuss how one of them has shaped your life.

Word Preview

You can familiarize yourself with the following words by looking
them up in the dictionary. You can broaden your knowledge of these
words by pronouncing them and understanding how they are used
in context.

venerable (1)	euphemism (11)	Down's syndrome (12)
stamina (1)	designation (11)	obsessively (13)
sojourners (2)	cripple (11)	squandered (14)
multiple sclerosis (2)	limbs (11)	doddering (14)
accumulated (3)	squeamishness (11)	maneuvering (14)
trundling (3)	transformations (11)	intrinsically (14)
colleague (5)	remonstrated (12)	escarpment (14)
hovered (7)	dose (12)	adversity (15)
pummeled (9)	analogy (12)	degenerative (15)
prognostication (9)	Alzheimer's (12)	self-recrimination (15)

1   In recent months I've had to give a good bit of thought to the concept of challenge because I have, in the venerable tradition of explorers,
stepped off the edge of my known world and have encountered, in the
wilderness beyond, numerous tests of my stamina and pluck. "Go west,
middle-aged woman" came the call, and I responded by accepting the
offer of a lectureship in the UCLA Writing Programs. Since my husband and son had responsibilities in Tucson, and my daughter was finishing her senior year at Smith College, in quite the opposite direction,
I had to set off on my venture alone.

2   I'm not accustomed to venturing out alone. In our twenty-odd years of marriage, George and I have almost always been together, most of that time accompanied by children and assorted sojourners and a series of cats remarkable for its length and diversity: the Mino, Ho Tei, Ho's Anna, Kitten Little, the Princess Saralinda, Katy, Balthasar, Mimi, Freya, Gwydion, Burton Rustle, Bête Noire, Vanessa Bell, Lionel Tigress, Eclipse, and most recently a wicked little black scrap called Sophia and her brother Sebastian. And for well over half that time, I've been increasingly crippled by multiple sclerosis. Thus, not only was I uncertain that I could be content without human and feline companionship; I wasn't even sure that I could take care of myself and my household of one on my own. But there didn't seem to be any safe way of finding out. I'd simply have to do it and watch what happened.

3   Our plan was to give me as well-supported a start as possible. During the summer I accumulated the goods it seemed I'd need: some just for fun, like a little television, and others purely practical, like a hand-held electric can opener and a collapsible shopping cart for trundling groceries and laundry. These we would load into my aging Volvo station wagon, and on the eighteenth of September George would drive me across the desert and settle me in the small apartment I'd rented.

4   Then life did what life so often does to mice and men. Three days before our scheduled departure came the telephone call one always dreads: George's father had died, quickly and without suffering, that afternoon at his home in Vermont. Suddenly all our plans seemed meaningless. All that mattered was to get George onto a plane immediately for an indefinite trip East.

5   But I was committed to the westward journey. My duties would begin in a week. And so I unpacked my boxes and repacked what I could squeeze into a couple of suitcases and a couple of carry-on bags and flew to Los Angeles on the day we had planned to arrive, prepared to camp out in my apartment until George could bring me my car and household goods. At the airport I rented a zippy little red Nova and set out through the streets of Los Angeles (the freeways, I knew, were beyond any bravery I had ever summoned, and in fact I have yet to set wheel upon them) to locate my new home. And I did! Foolish with elation, I pulled up in front of a block-long white apartment building in one corner of which, as though among the Anasazi at Mesa Verde, I would crouch in my own small space. A colleague from the Writing Programs and his wife lived there too, and with their help I unloaded the car, bought some groceries, and began to settle in.

6   I was exhausted but pretty pleased with myself. I was taking on tasks I'd never dreamed I could handle, not just moving to Los Angeles but even arranging the whole procedure myself. In a Greek tragedy, my self-

congratulation would be known as *hubris,* and the chorus would make plain to you that my downfall was inevitable. According to the cautionary puritanical wisdom of my Yankee youth, "Pride goeth before a fall." Note that both visions of the human lot share the image of collapse.

7   I fell flat on my face. Literally. About thirty hours after my arrival, as I stepped off the elevator into my garage, I tripped and pitched forward, striking my head on the concrete floor. When I came to, the face of a paramedic hovered near my eyes, a circle of dimmer, curious faces floating beyond.

8   "I'm so frightened," I said.

9   "Don't worry," said the paramedic as he settled me onto a stretcher. "You're going to be just fine." Perhaps he says that to everyone, the laboring woman and the black boy with the bullet in his butt and the security guard pummeled by a thief, all of whom I saw in the emergency room at Brotman Medical Center that night. No doubt paramedics specialize in the power of positive thinking rather than actual prognostication. At any rate, in my case he was right. I got x-rayed and stitched up and spent a couple of days under observation in an extra bed in the Michael Jackson Burn Center and was sent home, looking just as though someone had rammed a California plum into my left eye socket, in time to make the second day of orientation at UCLA, where I worked for the following six months, on a campus just about as ill-suited to the needs and limitations of the physically disabled as you can imagine: steps everywhere, parking spaces nowhere, slippery brick sidewalks, women's rooms on every other floor, elevator doors that snap quicker than Godzilla's jaws.

10   In the context of all these upheavals and adjustments, during which I spent all but a few hours each week alone, I meditated at length on challenge: What it is. What it's good for. Whether I want anything at all to do with it.

11   Recently I've become aware of a new euphemism for the disabled (which is itself, if not a euphemism, at least a designation so abstract as to be nearly meaningless): the "physically challenged." I don't like euphemisms, which constitute a verbal trick for pretending that what is real and sometimes ugly about our lives isn't happening, or is happening but "really" isn't so bad, or that what is happening in our lives is for the best, maybe even for our own good. I don't think any of those thoughts about my multiple sclerosis or my sixteen-year-old niece's blindness or any other radical loss or limitation. For this reason, as I've pointed out elsewhere, I call myself a cripple. I do so because the word is the most accurate and precise I've found, meaning that I no longer have full use of my limbs. That's all it means, by the way (look it up in your dictionary), and I'm not really clear where all the emotional baggage people toss onto it comes from. But in contemporary society the

baggage is there for "cripple," as it is for "death" (people aren't permitted simply to die: they "pass on" or "away," "go to their just reward," or "enter into heaven," though maybe they no longer sleep, like the Victorians, "in the arms of Morpheus"). And I think the squeamishness about the two words is related. We really don't want to confront the radical transformations of our bodies.

12   Hence a phrase like "physically challenged," which struck me as pure bellywash from the moment I heard it over the telephone last spring from a pleasant MS person in California who'd just read an excerpt from my book *Plaintext*. "You shouldn't call yourself a cripple," she remonstrated. "In our group we refer to ourselves as the physically challenged. It suggests a much healthier attitude." I believe people have the right to call themselves whatever they please. And I'm all for healthy attitudes. Lord knows mine gets pretty peaked much of the time. But I don't think a cure for its anemia is a dose of language like "physically challenged" for the simple reason that I have no idea what that phrase means. (I didn't ask my caller, but I supposed one might by analogy call someone with Alzheimer's or Down's syndrome "mentally challenged," with the same fuzzy results; and sure enough, a few weeks ago I came across just that phrase.) The purpose of a word is to identify a phenomenon precisely and distinguish it from all other phenomena. And though, when I'm faced with one of the pigeon-toed shopping carts at the Safeway which, with all my strength, I can barely wrestle up one aisle and down the next, I *know* that I'm physically challenged, I don't see how that phrase distinguishes me from anyone else who works hard or plays hard—from, say, the latest climber struggling up the face of Mount Everest. And, lurching along from ice cream to paper towels, *I am different* from that woman in her parka and goggles, face cracked and blackened, setting out on the last day's exhausted plod to the summit. Not better, or worse, but different. And I have to recognize that difference, not disguise it, in order to live authentically, that is, according to my true self.

13   So I toss aside "physically challenged" on the grounds that it enables me to pretend that difference doesn't matter. But I have another and more urgent reason as well. We are living, rock star Madonna reminds us, in a material world, and we're all material boys and girls. As a society we are obsessively attached, thanks largely to slick advertising campaigns with budgets big enough to feed entire countries for years, to the emblems of sheer physicality: to BMWs and powerful stereo systems and Big Macs with fries and movies every Saturday night and above all to our bodies, which we starve and roast and stretch and pummel and sanitize (deodorant, toothpaste, mouthwash, shampoo, cologne . . .) in a frenetic attempt to "make statements" about ourselves, we say, to let

the world know who we are, as though identity really rode in a BMW or flaunted bronzed skin.

14   I hear in "physically challenged" the same sort of emphasis, the concern with the body's tasks, its difficulties, its accomplishments. These are real, God knows. But I'm not sure they're particularly important. I admit that I have squandered a vast deal of energy and attention doddering from my apartment door to the chute at the end of the hall and maneuvering a bulging plastic sack of Coke cans and old newspapers into the stinking hole, but I don't believe that what I do with my trash is an intrinsically interesting question. What I do with my inward being—with the woman raging at her own wastefulness and weakness, terrified of losing her balance, lonely for her husband who has always made her trash disappear before—that's a different matter, a matter of some urgency, I think. How we respond to physical demands, all of us— Nancy at the Safeway and the woman crouched on the escarpment in the shadow of Mount Everest's summit, everyone reading this essay, whether "disabled" or not, our loved ones, our enemies—and what choices we make in the face of danger, and difficulty, and loss determine the true shape and depth of our being. I think of us all as "spiritually challenged." I think of spiritual challenge as the human condition.

15   Perhaps those of us who are disabled enjoy some advantages in this area—some special knowledge about coping with adversity, for instance. I can't really say. To do so might lead to some form of silly one-upmanship of the spirit ("my condition is more spiritually challenging than your condition"). But I can say that disability provides ample opportunity for spiritual work and growth. Those of us with degenerative diseases must learn to accommodate uncertainty equably, for instance, and to make our plans for the future as leaps of faith rather than sure bets. We must practice patience with the general populace of "temporarily abled persons," who often seem to us as heedless as children. We must learn—a task particularly difficult for women, I find—to articulate our needs clearly and insist on our rights to treatment that enables us to function most fully; but we must also learn not to ask for more than we need out of the typical human weakness for ease at any price. We must accept responsibility for ourselves and our own well-being, and we mustn't give up too readily the difficult tasks we set ourselves. But—a truth I am only beginning to confront as my right side, always my "good" side, quickly weakens—we must also be willing to let go gracefully of tasks that have become impossible, with as little anger and self-recrimination as possible.

16   Anyone who can accomplish such feats—and the many more that disability demands—will be a saint indeed. Myself, I don't know anyone who's come even close. But sainthood isn't really my concern. Just

challenge, and our responses to it. And I say, let's not hide behind meaningless phrases in an attempt to fool ourselves that our lives are somehow easier than they are; let's look at our lives as squarely, and as lovingly, as we can. And let's not be deflected by concerns about our bodies, their images and their illnesses, from what is most significant about our selves: that we can grow in courage, in grit, in spirit, not in spite of who we are but because of who we are.

WORD FOCUS

VOCABULARY GLOSS

Anasazi: *Native American group from the American Southwest whose culture suddenly disappeared in the fourteenth century (5)*

cautionary puritanical wisdom of my Yankee youth: *advice given during upbringing that reflects particular American values (6)*

the chorus: *in a play, a group of actors who explain various aspects of the plot to the audience (6)*

emotional baggage: *memories of painful past experiences that a person has for the rest of his or her life (11)*

Go west: *move westward for opportunity and self-improvement (1)*

Godzilla's jaws: *the snapping mouth of a mythical movie dinosaur (9)*

hubris: *extreme self-confidence (6)*

human lot: *a reference to one's fortune in life—fate or destiny (6)*

in grit: *with bravery and determination despite problems (16)*

look at . . . squarely: *confront something directly and honestly (16)*

Morpheus: *the Greek god of sleep (11)*

one-upmanship: *always trying to do better than someone else (15)*

pigeon-toed: *with toes pointing inward, toward each other (12)*

Pride goeth before a fall: *an idiom meaning that excessive pride can lead to one's downfall (6)*

pure bellywash: *absolutely not true (12)*

set wheel: *began to drive; a variant of the idiom "set foot on" or "venture out" (5)*

slick advertising campaigns: *sophisticated yet deceptive marketing practices (13)*

what life . . . does to mice and men: *a reference to the fact that plans made by living creatures can go wrong (4)*

VOCABULARY QUESTIONS

1. *Euphemisms* are words or phrases with positive connotations that substitute for words that may hurt or offend. Mairs says that after her accident she became aware of new euphemisms such as "physically challenged" in place of "disabled" (11). Euphemisms like these, she says, deny the reality of a person's limitations. She prefers to be called a "cripple" (11). Do you agree that specific words have an effect on how a person, place, or thing is perceived?

2. Mairs states that she needs to live "authentically" (12). Define "authentically" and discuss what it means in terms of the statement she makes.

3. When Mairs first arrived at her new home with her groceries, she reports, "I fell flat on my face. Literally" (7). What specific information about this incident does the word "literally" convey? How would the meaning change if the word *figuratively* were substituted for "literally"?

ENGLISH CRAFT

1. In writing, punctuation can help us organize information. Although punctuation allows us to group certain ideas together, it also lets us insert information. Four punctuation marks operate in this way: the colon; pairs of commas; the dash or pairs of dashes; and parentheses. Look at the following examples from Mairs's text.

The Colon

The colon [:] introduces explanatory information such as a definition or a list. As you can see from the examples below, the list can also act as a definition.

The information following the colon defines the telephone call that people dread.

"Three days before our scheduled departure came the telephone call one always dreads: **George's father had died, quickly and without suffering, that afternoon at his home in Vermont.**" (4)

The information following the colon is a list that identifies the goods Mairs seemed to need.

"During the summer I accumulated the goods it seemed I'd need: **some just for fun, like a little television, and others purely practical, like a hand-held electric can opener and a collapsible shopping cart for trundling groceries and laundry.**" (3)

Pairs of Commas

Pairs of commas [,xxx,] frame inserted information that the author wants to add without changing the meaning of the sentence. Note that you can remove the commas and the information within the commas, and keep the grammatical structure and meaning of the sentence.

"In recent months I've had to give a good bit of thought to the concept of challenge because I have, **in the venerable tradition of explorers,** stepped off the edge of my known world and have encountered, **in the wilderness beyond,** numerous tests of my stamina and pluck." (1)

The Dash and Pairs of Dashes

The single dash or pairs of dashes [—xxx—] frame inserted information that the author wants to emphasize or make clearer.

Note: to make a dash on your word processor, use two hyphens without spaces on either side.

The single dash [xxx—] introduces clarifying information. It is set off from the main clause by the single dash.

"Perhaps those of us who are disabled enjoy some advantages in this area—**some special knowledge about coping with adversity, for instance.**" (15)

The pair of dashes [—xxx—] inserts information into the body of the sentence. A pair of dashes in this case is similar to a pair of commas; however, the dash signals more emphasis.

"Anyone who can accomplish such feats—**and the many more that disability demands**—will be a saint indeed." (16)

Parentheses

Parentheses [(xxx)] frame inserted information that the author wants to convey without changing the structure of the sentence. In writing, the parentheses signal that the information contained is less important, connected, or significant to the sentence than that conveyed by the dash or comma.

"That's all it means, by the way **(look it up in your dictionary),** and I'm not really clear where all the emotional baggage people toss onto it comes from." (11)

In order to practice using these different ways of adding information to your writing, write four sentences about Mairs's text using the colon, a pair of commas, the single dash or pairs of dashes, and parentheses.

2. In academic writing, the conclusion of an essay should emerge from the content of the essay. Rather than ending an essay by summarizing with phrases such as *in summary* or *in conclusion,* the writer should focus on the central ideas of the essay.

One way the writer can achieve this is by repeating a key word or phrase that points the reader to a new way of thinking about the concept. The writer can use the conclusion to convince or drive home the point of the thesis. In the conclusion of "Challenge: An Exploration" Mairs observes, "But sainthood isn't really my concern. Just challenge, and our responses to it" (16). Compare and contrast this final paragraph with the opening paragraph. Discuss their different functions and, if applicable, how they are connected.

3. Key words of a thesis claim often reappear throughout an essay, either repeated exactly or in a different form. For example, Mairs's exploration of the concept "challenge" in this essay might be expressed in the various forms of the word "challenge": a noun, verb, gerund, or as a synonym such as *test* or *difficulty.*

   First identify Mairs's thesis claim, the focus of her essay. Then look at the parts of Mairs's essay listed below, and identify how key words support, expand, or connect concepts in each of these sections:

Essay title _____

Paragraph 1 _____

Paragraph 8 _____

Paragraph 9 _____

Paragraph 14 _____

INTERPRETIVE JOURNAL

1. Public buildings reflect the attitudes of a society toward its people and their needs. Describe a public building—a restaurant, a university, a shopping center—and discuss how it reflects society's awareness of and attitude toward the needs of all people in the community.

2. Mairs says that the United States as a society is obsessively attached to "emblems of sheer physicality" (13). Choose two advertisements from a popular magazine that illustrate "emblems of sheer physicality." Do you think these advertisements include or exclude different groups in society?

3. Write a paragraph discussing in detail why you think Mairs calls her essay "Challenge: An Exploration."

ESSAY QUESTION

Although Mairs does her best to fit into mainstream society, she still feels "different" (12). Discuss the ways in which you see her as different—not just in terms of her physical disabilities, but in terms of her stance on language and how language defines difference. In this essay you might want to consider whether or not difference means exclusion from mainstream society.

Individuality and Acceptance
Sequence of Essay Assignments

READINGS

Bharati Mukherjee, excerpt from *The Tiger's Daughter*

Nawal El Saadawi, excerpt from *Woman at Point Zero*

Nancy Mairs, "Challenge: An Exploration," excerpt from *Carnal Acts*

The following assignments form a sequence of interrelated topics. They become progressively more challenging as they ask you to interact with more texts. Assignment 1 asks you to write about a topic in Mukherjee's story ; Assignment 2 asks you to reconsider your first essay in light of Saadawi's text; and Assignment 3 asks you to consider all three texts as you establish your point of view on the assigned topic.

These assignments can be written as a sequence or they can be written individually. However you approach these essays, each one you write should be supported with citations from the text and examples. Whenever possible, include your own experience and knowledge of the subject.

ASSIGNMENT 1

MUKHERJEE

When Reena accuses Tara of becoming "too self-centered and European" (9), Tara feels separated from her friend even though they grew up in the same country sharing the same values. Discuss how Tara's actions and her arguments with her friends reflect the confusion she feels about belonging to both the country where she was born and the country where she now lives.

ASSIGNMENT 2

EL SAADAWI AND MUKHERJEE

Although Firdaus, one of the narrators in *Woman at Point Zero,* has always remained within her own culture, she feels like an outsider. Looking closely at the people around her, the environment, and the cultural norms that she grew up within, analyze the cause of Firdaus's feeling of not belonging. Compare her situation and fate to that of Tara in the excerpt from *The Tiger's Daughter.*

ASSIGNMENT 3

MAIRS, EL SAADAWI, AND MUKHERJEE

Discuss the ways in which Tara, Firdaus, and Mairs stand out as individuals in their society, and how that individuality separates them to some extent from the group. Analyze carefully the avenues of protest that are available to each woman in her society.

Chapter 4

Dignity and Perspective

Dignity involves both personal and public respect. Although it is common to identify dignity as a mark of honor in the powerful, it is less common to do so in the defeated or the dominated. And yet, political and spiritual leaders frequently refer to the essential dignity of humankind. It is useful to explore whether dignity is inherent or a matter of perspective.

ABOUT THE AUTHORS

Black Elk (1863–1950)

Black Elk, a holy man of the Oglala Sioux tribe of the northwestern plains of the United States, shared with John Neihardt his native people's experiences at the close of the nineteenth century. The excerpts "The Butchering at Wounded Knee" and "The End of the Dream" are taken from the collection of stories published by Neihardt entitled *Black Elk Speaks: Being the Life Story of a Holy Man of the Oglala Sioux* (1932). The excerpts give Black Elk's perspective on the American Cavalry attack on a group of Native Americans at the battle of Wounded Knee in 1890 and his realization that an important era in the history of his people had ended.

Rigoberta Menchú (b. 1959)

Rigoberta Menchú's autobiography *I, Rigoberta Menchú* (1984) presents Guatemalan Indian perspectives with quiet dignity and pride. Menchú's story of this indigenous people is recorded and translated by anthropologist Elisabeth Burgos-Debray. The first two chapters of the autobiography, "The Family" and "Birth Ceremonies," reveal both the vulnerability and the strength of the Guatemalan Indians. Menchú received the Nobel Prize for Peace in 1992.

Ronald Takaki (b. 1939)

Historian Ronald Takaki, professor of ethnic studies at the University of California at Berkeley, raises issues of historical bias in the public record of the American experience. As a third-generation Japanese American, Takaki brings both personal and academic credentials to this analysis. The reading excerpted here from his book *A Different Mirror* (1993) details the experiences and contributions of various ethnic groups that constitute the United States today.

Black Elk
The Butchering at Wounded Knee *and* The End of the Dream

Preview

Write about a significant moment or event in the history of your culture. How did you learn about this piece of history? Why is this event important?

Word Preview

You can familiarize yourself with the following words by looking them up in the dictionary. You can broaden your knowledge of these words by pronouncing them and understanding how they are used in context.

cannon (2)
whipped (8)
cavalrymen (9)
ravine (38)
buckskin (41)

The Butchering at Wounded Knee

1   That evening before it happened, I went in to Pine Ridge and heard these things, and while I was there, soldiers started for where the Big Foots were. These made about five hundred soldiers that were there next morning. When I saw them starting I felt that something terrible was going to happen. That night I could hardly sleep at all. I walked around most of the night.

2   In the morning I went out after my horses, and while I was out I heard shooting off toward the east, and I knew from the sound that it must be wagon-guns (cannon) going off. The sounds went right through my body, and I felt that something terrible would happen.

3   When I reached camp with the horses, a man rode up to me and said: "Hey-hey-hey! The people that are coming are fired on! I know it!"

4   I saddled up my buckskin and put on my sacred shirt. It was one I had made to be worn by no one but myself. It had a spotted eagle outstretched on the back of it, and the daybreak star was on the left shoulder, because when facing south that shoulder is toward the east. Across the breast, from the left shoulder to the right hip, was the flaming rainbow, and there was another rainbow around the neck, like a necklace, with a star at the bottom. At each shoulder, elbow, and wrist was an eagle feather; and over the whole shirt were red streaks of lightning. You will see that this was from my great vision, and you will know how it protected me that day.

5   I painted my face all red, and in my hair I put one eagle feather for the One Above.

6   It did not take me long to get ready, for I could still hear the shooting over there.

7   I started out alone on the old road that ran across the hills to Wounded Knee. I had no gun. I carried only the sacred bow of the west that I had seen in my great vision. I had gone only a little way when a band of young men came galloping after me. The first two who came up were Loves War and Iron Wasichu. I asked what they were going to do, and they said they were just going to see where the shooting was. Then others were coming up, and some older men.

8   We rode fast, and there were about twenty of us now. The shooting was getting louder. A horseback from over there came galloping very fast toward us, and he said: "Hey-hey-hey! They have murdered them!" Then he whipped his horse and rode away faster toward Pine Ridge.

9   In a little while we had come to the top of the ridge where, looking to the east, you can see for the first time the monument and the burying ground on the little hill where the church is. That is where the terrible thing started. Just south of the burying ground on the

little hill a deep dry gulch runs about east and west, very crooked, and it rises westward to nearly the top of the ridge where we were. It had no name, but the Wasichus sometimes call it Battle Creek now. We stopped on the ridge not far from the head of the dry gulch. Wagon guns were still going off over there on the little hill, and they were going off again where they hit along the gulch. There was much shooting down yonder, and there were many cries, and we could see cavalrymen scattered over the hills ahead of us. Cavalrymen were riding along the gulch and shooting into it, where the women and children were running away and trying to hide in the gullies and the stunted pines.

10   A little way ahead of us, just below the head of the dry gulch, there were some women and children who were huddled under a clay bank, and some cavalrymen were there pointing guns at them.

11   We stopped back behind the ridge, and I said to the others: "Take courage. These are our relatives. We will try to get them back." Then we all sang a song which went like this:

12   "A thunder being nation I am, I have said.
A thunder being nation I am, I have said.
You shall live.
You shall live.
You shall live.
You shall live."

13   Then I rode over the ridge and the others after me, and we were crying: "Take courage! It is time to fight!" The soldiers who were guarding our relatives shot at us and then ran away fast, and some more cavalrymen on the other side of the gulch did too. We got our relatives and sent them across the ridge to the northwest where they would be safe.

14   I had no gun, and when we were charging, I just held the sacred bow out in front of me with my right hand. The bullets did not hit us at all.

15   We found a little baby lying all alone near the head of the gulch. I could not pick her up just then, but I got her later and some of my people adopted her. I just wrapped her up tighter in a shawl that was around her and left her there. It was a safe place, and I had other work to do.

16   The soldiers had run eastward over the hills where there were some more soldiers, and they were off their horses and lying down. I told the others to stay back, and I charged upon them holding the sacred bow out toward them with my right hand. They all shot at me, and I could hear bullets all around me, but I ran my horse right close to them, and then swung around. Some soldiers across the gulch began shooting at me too, but I got back to the others and was not hurt at all.

17   By now many other Lakotas, who had heard the shooting, were coming up from Pine Ridge, and we all charged on the soldiers. They ran eastward toward where the trouble began. We followed down along the dry gulch, and what we saw was terrible. Dead and wounded women and children and little babies were scattered all along there where they had been trying to run away. The soldiers had followed along the gulch, as they ran, and murdered them in there. Sometimes they were in heaps because they had huddled together, and some were scattered all along. Sometimes bunches of them had been killed and torn to pieces where the wagon-guns hit them. I saw a little baby trying to suck its mother, but she was bloody and dead.

18   There were two little boys at one place in this gulch. They had guns and they had been killing soldiers all by themselves. We could see the soldiers they had killed. The boys were all alone there, and they were not hurt. These were very brave little boys.

19   When we drove the soldiers back, they dug themselves in, and we were not enough people to drive them out from there. In the evening they marched off up Wounded Knee Creek, and then we saw all that they had done there.

20   Men and women and children were heaped and scattered all over the flat at the bottom of the little hill where the soldiers had their wagon-guns, and westward up the dry gulch all the way to the high ridge, the dead women and children and babies were scattered.

21   When I saw this I wished that I had died too, but I was not sorry for the women and children. It was better for them to be happy in the other world, and I wanted to be there too. But before I went there I wanted to have revenge. I thought there might be a day, and we should have revenge.

22   After the soldiers marched away, I heard from my friend, Dog Chief, how the trouble started, and he was right there by Yellow Bird when it happened. This is the way it was:

23   In the morning the soldiers began to take all the guns away from the Big Foots, who were camped in the flat below the little hill where the monument and burying ground are now. The people had stacked most of their guns, and even their knives, by the tepee where Big Foot was lying sick. Soldiers were on the little hill and all around, and there were soldiers across the dry gulch to the south and over east along Wounded Knee Creek too. The people were nearly surrounded, and the wagon-guns were pointing at them.

24   Some had not yet given up their guns, and so the soldiers were searching all the tepees, throwing things around and poking into everything. There was a man called Yellow Bird, and he and another man were standing in front of the tepee where Big Foot was lying sick. They

had white sheets around and over them, with eyeholes to look through, and they had guns under these. An officer came to search them. He took the other man's gun, and then started to take Yellow Bird's. But Yellow Bird would not let go. He wrestled with the officer, and while they were wrestling, the gun went off and killed the officer. Wasichus and some others have said he meant to do this, but Dog Chief was standing right there, and he told me it was not so. As soon as the gun went off, Dog Chief told me, an officer shot and killed Big Foot who was lying sick inside the tepee.

25   Then suddenly nobody knew what was happening, except that the soldiers were all shooting and the wagon-guns began going off right in among the people.

26   Many were shot down right there. The women and children ran into the gulch and up west, dropping all the time, for the soldiers shot them as they ran. There were only about a hundred warriors and there were nearly five hundred soldiers. The warriors rushed to where they had piled their guns and knives. They fought soldiers with only their hands until they got their guns.

27   Dog Chief saw Yellow Bird run into a tepee with his gun, and from there he killed soldiers until the tepee caught fire. Then he died full of bullets.

28   It was a good winter day when all this happened. The sun was shining. But after the soldiers marched away from their dirty work, a heavy snow began to fall. The wind came up in the night. There was a big blizzard, and it grew very cold. The snow drifted deep in the crooked gulch, and it was one long grave of butchered women and children and babies, who had never done any harm and were only trying to run away.

The End of the Dream

29   After the soldiers marched away, Red Crow and I started back toward Pine Ridge together, and I took the little baby that I told you about. Red Crow had one too.

30   We were going back to Pine Ridge, because we thought there was peace back home; but it was not so. While we were gone, there was a fight around the Agency, and our people had all gone away. They had gone away so fast that they left all the tepees standing.

31   It was nearly dark when we passed north of Pine Ridge where the hospital is now, and some soldiers shot at us, but did not hit us. We rode into the camp, and it was all empty. We were very hungry because we had not eaten anything since early morning, so we peeped into the tepees until we saw where there was a pot with papa (dried meat) cooked

in it. We sat down in there and began to eat. While we were doing this, the soldiers shot at the tepee, and a bullet struck right between Red Crow and me. It threw dust in the soup, but we kept right on eating until we had our fill. Then we took the babies and got on our horses and rode away. If that bullet had only killed me, then I could have died with papa in my mouth.

32   The people had fled down Clay Creek, and we followed their trail. It was dark now, and late in the night we came to where they were camped without any tepees. They were just sitting by little fires, and the snow was beginning to blow. We rode in among them and I heard my mother's voice. She was singing a death song for me, because she felt sure I had died over there. She was so glad to see me that she cried and cried.

33   Women who had milk fed the little babies that Red Crow and I brought with us.

34   I think nobody but the little children slept any that night. The snow blew and we had no tepees.

35   When it was getting light, a war party went out and I went along; but this time I took a gun with me. When I started out the day before to Wounded Knee, I took only my sacred bow, which was not made to shoot with; because I was a little in doubt about the Wanekia religion at that time, and I did not really want to kill anybody because of it.

36   But I did not feel like that any more. After what I had seen over there, I wanted revenge; I wanted to kill.

37   We crossed White Clay Creek and followed it up, keeping on the west side. Soon we could hear many guns going off. So we struck west, following a ridge to where the fight was. It was close to the Mission, and there are many bullets in the Mission yet.

38   From this ridge we could see that the Lakotas were on both sides of the creek and were shooting at soldiers who were coming down the creek. As we looked down, we saw a little ravine, and across this was a big hill. We crossed and rode up the hillside.

39   They were fighting right there, and a Lakota cried to me: "Black Elk, this is the kind of a day in which to do something great!" I answered: "How!"[1]

40   Then I got off my horse and rubbed earth on myself, to show the Powers that I was nothing without their help. Then I took my rifle, got on my horse and galloped up to the top of the hill. Right below me the soldiers were shooting, and my people called out to me not to go down there; that there were some good shots among the soldiers and I should get killed for nothing.

41   But I remembered my great vision, the part where the geese of the

1. Signifying assent.

north appeared. I depended upon their power. Stretching out my arms with my gun in the right hand, like a goose soaring when it flies low to turn in a change of weather, I made the sound the geese make—br-r-r-p, br-r-r-p, br-r-r-p; and, doing this, I charged. The soldiers saw, and began shooting fast at me. I kept right on with my buckskin running, shot in their faces when I was near, then swung wide and rode back up the hill.

42   All this time the bullets were buzzing around me and I was not touched. I was not even afraid. It was like being in a dream about shooting. But just as I had reached the very top of the hill, suddenly it was like waking up, and I was afraid. I dropped my arms and quit making the goose cry. Just as I did this, I felt something strike my belt as though some one had hit me there with the back of an ax. I nearly fell out of my saddle, but I managed to hold on, and rode over the hill.

43   An old man by the name of Protector was there, and he ran up and held me, for now I was falling off my horse. I will show you where the bullet struck me sidewise across the belly here (showing a long deep scar on the abdomen). My insides were coming out. Protector tore up a blanket in strips and bound it around me so that my insides would stay in. By now I was crazy to kill, and I said to Protector: "Help me on my horse! Let me go over there. It is a good day to die, so I will go over there!" But Protector said: "No, young nephew! You must not die to-day. That would be foolish. Your people need you. There may be a better day to die." He lifted me into my saddle and led my horse away down hill. Then I began to feel very sick.

44   By now it looked as though the soldiers would be wiped out, and the Lakotas were fighting harder; but I heard that, after I left, the black Wasichu soldiers came, and the Lakotas had to retreat.

45   There were many of our children in the Mission, and the sisters and priests were taking care of them. I heard there were sisters and priests right in the battle helping wounded people and praying.

46   There was a man by the name of Little Soldier who took charge of me and brought me to where our people were camped. While we were over at the Mission Fight, they had fled to the O-ona-gazhee[2] and were camped on top of it where the women and children would be safe from soldiers. Old Hollow Horn was there. He was a very powerful bear medicine man, and he came over to heal my wound. In three days I could walk, but I kept a piece of blanket tied around my belly.

47   It was now nearly the middle of the Moon of Frost in the Tepee (January). We heard that soldiers were on Smoky Earth River and were coming to attack us in the O-ona-gazhee. They were near Black Feather's

2. Sheltering place, an elevated plateau in the Badlands, with precipitous sides, and inaccessible save by one narrow neck of land easily defended.

place. So a party of about sixty of us started on the war-path to find them. My mother tried to keep me at home, because, although I could walk and ride a horse, my wound was not all healed yet. But I would not stay; for, after what I had seen at Wounded Knee, I wanted a chance to kill soldiers.

48   We rode down Grass Creek to Smoky Earth, and crossed, riding down stream. Soon from the top of a little hill we saw wagons and cavalry guarding them. The soldiers were making a corral of their wagons and getting ready to fight. We got off our horses and went behind some hills to a little knoll, where we crept up to look at the camp. Some soldiers were bringing harnessed horses down to a little creek to water, and I said to the others: "If you will stay here and shoot at the soldiers, I will charge over there and get some good horses." They knew of my power, so they did this, and I charged on my buckskin while the others kept shooting. I got seven of the horses; but when I started back with these, all the soldiers saw me and began shooting. They killed two of my horses, but I brought five back safe and was not hit. When I was out of range, I caught up a fine bald-faced bay and turned my buckskin loose. Then I drove the others back to our party.

49   By now more cavalry were coming up the river, a big bunch of them, and there was some hard fighting for a while, because there were not enough of us. We were fighting and retreating, and all at once I saw Red Willow on foot running. He called to me: "Cousin, my horse is killed!" So I caught up a soldier's horse that was dragging a rope and brought it to Red Willow while the soldiers were shooting fast at me. Just then, for a little while, I was a wanekia[3] myself. In this fight Long Bear and another man, whose name I have forgotten, were badly wounded; but we saved them and carried them along with us. The soldiers did not follow us far into the Badlands, and when it was night we rode back with our wounded to the O-ona-gazhee.

50   We wanted a much bigger war-party so that we could meet the soldiers and get revenge. But this was hard, because the people were not all of the same mind, and they were hungry and cold. We had a meeting there, and were all ready to go out with more warriors, when Afraid-of-His-Horses came over from Pine Ridge to make peace with Red Cloud, who was with us there.

51   Our party wanted to go out and fight anyway, but Red Cloud made a speech to us something like this: "Brothers, this is a very hard winter. The women and children are starving and freezing. If this were summer, I would say to keep on fighting to the end. But we cannot do this. We must think of the women and children and that it is very bad for them.

---

3. A "make-live," savior.

So we must make peace, and I will see that nobody is hurt by the soldiers."

52   The people agreed to this, for it was true. So we broke camp next day and went down from the O-ona-gazhee to Pine Ridge, and many, many Lakotas were already there. Also, there were many, many soldiers. They stood in two lines with their guns held in front of them as we went through to where we camped.

53   And so it was all over.

54   I did not know then how much was ended. When I look back now from this high hill of my old age, I can still see the butchered women and children lying heaped and scattered all along the crooked gulch as plain as when I saw them with eyes still young. And I can see that something else died there in the bloody mud, and was buried in the blizzard. A people's dream died there. It was a beautiful dream.

55   And I, to whom so great a vision was given in my youth—you see me now a pitiful old man who has done nothing, for the nation's hoop is broken and scattered. There is no center any longer, and the sacred tree is dead.

WORD FOCUS

VOCABULARY GLOSS

the Agency: *U.S. government office on the reservation (30)*

Big Foots: *a subdivision of the Lakota tribe led by Chief Big Foot (1)*

corral: *a fenced area in which to hold horses and livestock (48)*

dirty work: *murderous acts (28)*

down yonder: *down below (9)*

dry gulch: *a dried-up ravine or shallow canyon (9)*

dug themselves in: *dug trenches for protection (19)*

fired on: *attacked with guns (3)*

the flat: *the plain (20)*

good shots: *individuals who fire guns accurately (40)*

horseback: *a rider on a horse (8)*

Lakotas: *an American Indian tribe, part of the Sioux people (17)*

medicine man: *a tribal doctor, a holy man (46)*

Mission: *religious outpost (37)*

One Above: *a supreme being (5)*

other world: *the world of the dead (21)*
the Powers: *divine forces or native gods (40)*
tepee: *a Native American cone-shaped tent (23)*
Wasichus: *a Native American name for white people (9)*

VOCABULARY QUESTIONS

1. The word "butchering" is the focus word in the title of Black Elk's narrative. Discuss the effect of using "butchering" instead of possible synonyms such as *killing, fighting,* or *slaying.*

2. The second section of this passage is entitled "The End of the Dream." The following are three different but related meanings of the word "dream":

   - A series of images occurring during sleep

   - A condition or a hope that is longed for

   - Something that works exceptionally well

   Write a paragraph discussing which meanings apply to the word "dream" as it is used in the title. Consult your dictionary for other definitions of "dream," and in your discussion consider that more than one meaning may apply.

ENGLISH CRAFT

1. Black Elk's narrative sounds like a story a local hero might tell his friends or family. In fact, Black Elk's narrative is an example of oral history—something spoken first and then written down. Narrations typically show the following structure:

Beginning:	Sets the events in time and/or space
Middle:	Provides a related series of events, usually ordered chronologically
End:	Presents the closing event, often with resolution

   Use this pattern to analyze the structure of Black Elk's story. In your analysis, point to specific parts of the text that meet these criteria.

2. In writing, expressing relationships between events and concepts can be accomplished through coordinating and subordinating conjunctions.
   The **coordinating conjunctions** *and, but, or, nor, for,* and *yet* join independent clauses of equal weight and signal different logical relationships. In speech and stories, for example, the coordinating conjunction

and is often used to express general logical relationships such as *result, purpose, contrast, condition,* and *similarity.*

The **subordinating conjunctions** *although, even though, because, since, when,* and *while* introduce dependent clauses and express these relationships more specifically. Academic writing requires the identification and inferring of specific relationships such as *comparison, reason, purpose, result, cause and effect,* and *conditions.*

Look at the sentences in the boxes that follow:

The Coordinating Conjunction **and**		
First Unit		*Second Unit*
There were only about a hundred warriors	and	there were nearly five hundred soldiers (26)
Logical Relationship	comparison/contrast	

The use of coordination here emphasizes a point of similarity and/or difference between the two units.

By using subordination, we can analyze this comparison further. We can draw inferences beyond the scope of the exact words of the text.

Subordinating Conjunctions **although** *and* **because**		
	First Unit	*Second Unit*
Although	the Indians had about a hundred warriors	they fought equally to the 500 soldiers.
Logical Relationship	continues comparison/contrast while revealing an unexpected result	

First Unit		*Second Unit*
The 100 Indians fought fiercely and desperately	because	they faced extinction against the power of the 500 soldiers.
Logical Relationship	continues comparison/contrast while introducing a specific reason	

Look at the following paragraph from Black Elk. In a brief paragraph of your own, interpret this excerpt using at least two subordinating conjunctions to make clear the logical relationships you are developing.

There were two little boys at one place in this gulch. They had guns and they had been killing soldiers all by themselves. We could see the soldiers they had killed. The boys were all alone there, and they were not hurt. These were very brave little boys. (18)

3. *Determiners* in English precede a noun and, in fact, signal to the reader that a noun will follow. Determiners include articles, demonstratives, possessives, and quantifiers.

Determiners			
Articles	*Demonstratives*	*Possessives*	*Quantifiers*
a/an	this these	my our	one . . . five
the	that those	your your	first . . . fifth
		his their	
		her	
		its	any some

Although all these determiners occur frequently in English, the articles *a/an* and *the* are usually considered the most difficult to understand and use. The indefinite article *a/an* indicates that knowledge is general or not specific. The definite article *the* indicates that knowledge about a subject is shared. Look at the following box for general guidelines for article usage.

Indefinite and Definite Articles		
	a/an	*the*
Knowledge	• indicates one of a class or group of things (e.g., *a school, a breed of dog*)	• refers to the existence of one thing in the world or in the immediate environment (e.g., *the sun, the neighborhood school*) • refers to recognized institutions (e.g., *the government*)

Textual	• mentions something in the text for the first time	• precedes a noun that is followed by a definition or a specific explanation (e.g., *the school that I attended*)
		• refers to something that has already been mentioned
		• establishes an association with something already mentioned

Examine the following excerpts from Black Elk's text. Provide possible reasons for the choice of the articles in bold type:

In the morning I went out after my horses, and while I was out I heard shooting off toward **the** east, and I knew from the sound that it must be wagon-guns (cannon) going off. **The** sounds went right through my body, and I felt that something terrible would happen. (2)

. . . you can see for **the** first time **the** monument and **the** burying ground on **the** little hill where **the** church is. That is where **the** terrible thing started. Just south of **the** burying ground on **the** little hill **a** deep dry gulch runs about east and west . . . (9)

When it was getting light, **a** war party went out and I went along; but this time I took **a** gun with me. When I started out the day before to Wounded Knee, I took only my sacred bow . . . (35)

INTERPRETIVE JOURNAL

1. The American West has been portrayed differently from the way Black Elk talks about it. Television and movies, for example, have often stereotyped white settlers and soldiers as the heroes and Native Americans as the villains. Choose some scenes in this narrative that either support or counter these stereotypes.

2. The battle that took place at Wounded Knee is a well-recorded piece of American history, and you will find references to it in many history textbooks. Black Elk's account may differ somewhat from these accounts. Go to the library and find a historical account of Wounded Knee, and compare and contrast these accounts.

3. At the end of the section entitled "The End of the Dream," Black Elk says that "the nation's hoop is broken and scattered" (55). Discuss what he means by this statement. What nation is he referring to?

ESSAY QUESTION

Black Elk reveals his passion for justice and revenge after seeing the corpses of the men, women, and children killed by the soldiers. Compare Black Elk's urge to strike back with the feelings that later generations of Native Americans (or other cultural groups) might have about the incident. Consider what might happen when feelings for justice and revenge are carried over from one generation to another.

Rigoberta Menchú
The Family *and* Birth Ceremonies

Preview

Ceremonies mark important events in the lives of individuals and communities. Describe a ceremony you are familiar with, the symbols and actions associated with the ceremony, and what they convey to the people who are a part of it.

Word Preview

You can familiarize yourself with the following words by looking them up in the dictionary. You can broaden your knowledge of these words by pronouncing them and understanding how they are used in context.

testimony (1)	vast (12)	colonization (25)
indigenous (3)	midwife (15)	inter-related (27)
cultivating (4)	scandal (16)	bourgeois (28)
evicted (5)	sorcerers (17)	symbolizes (28)
incurred (5)	placenta (18)	vital (30)
estates (6)	endure (18)	impose (31)
founded (9)	integration (19)	embody (31)
malnutrition (9)	baptism (21)	exemplary (31)
dense (10)		

The Family

'We have always lived here: we have the right to go on living where we are happy and where we want to die. Only here can we feel whole; nowhere else would we ever feel complete and our pain would be eternal.'
—POPOL VUH

1   My name is Rigoberta Menchú. I am twenty-three years old. This is my testimony. I didn't learn it from a book and I didn't learn it alone. I'd like to stress that it's not only *my* life, it's also the testimony of my people. It's hard for me to remember everything that's happened to me in my life since there have been many very bad times but, yes, moments of joy as well. The important thing is that what has happened to me has happened to many other people too: My story is the story of all poor Guatemalans. My personal experience is the reality of a whole people.

• • • • • • • •

2   I must say before I start that I never went to school, and so I find speaking Spanish very difficult. I didn't have the chance to move outside my own world and only learned Spanish three years ago. It's difficult when you learn just by listening, without any books. And, well, yes, I find it a bit difficult. I'd like to start from when I was a little girl, or go back even further to when I was in my mother's womb, because my mother told me how I was born and our customs say that a child begins life on the first day of his mother's pregnancy.

• • • • • • • •

3   There are twenty-two indigenous ethnic groups in Guatemala, twenty-three including the *mestizos,* or *ladinos,* as we call them. Twenty-three groups and twenty-three languages. I belong to one of them—the Quiché people—and I practise Quiché customs, but I also know most of the other groups very well through my work organising the people. I come from San Miguel Uspantán, in the northwest province of El Quiché. I live near Chajul in the north of El Quiché. The towns there all have long histories of struggle. I have to walk six leagues, or 24 kilometres, from my house to the town of Uspantán. The village is called Chimel, I was born there. Where I live is practically a paradise, the country is so beautiful. There are no big roads, and no cars. Only people can reach it. Everything is taken down the mountainside on horseback or else we carry it ourselves. So, you can see, I live right up in the mountains.

Editor's Note: This translation uses British conventions in spelling and punctuation.

4   My parents moved there in 1960 and began cultivating the land. No-one had lived up there before because it's so mountainous. But they settled there and were determined not to leave no matter how hard the life was. They'd first been up there collecting the *mimbre* that's found in those parts, and had liked it. They'd started clearing the land for a house, and had wanted to settle there a year later but they didn't have the means. Then they were thrown out of the small house they had in the town and had no alternative but to go up into the mountains. And they stayed there. Now it's a village with five or six *caballerias* of cultivated land.

5   They'd been forced to leave the town because some *ladino* families came to settle there. They weren't exactly evicted but the *ladinos* just gradually took over. My parents spent everything they earned and they incurred so many debts with these people that they had to leave the house to pay them. The rich are always like that. When people owe them money they take a bit of land or some of their belongings and slowly end up with everything. That's what happened to my parents.

6   My father was an orphan, and had a very hard life as a child. He was born in Santa Rosa Chucuyub, a village in El Quiché. His father died when he was a small boy, leaving the family with a small patch of maize. But when that was finished, my grandmother took her three sons to Uspantán. She got work as a servant to the town's only rich people. Her boys did jobs around the house like carrying wood and water and tending animals. But as they got bigger, her employer said she didn't work enough for him to go on feeding such big boys. She had to give away her eldest son, my father, to another man so he wouldn't go hungry. By then he could do heavy work like chopping wood or working in the fields but he wasn't paid anything because he'd been given away. He lived with these *ladinos* for nine years but learned no Spanish because he wasn't allowed in the house. He was just there to run errands and work, and was kept totally apart from the family. They found him repulsive because he had no clothes and was very dirty. When my father was fourteen he started looking around for some way out. His brothers were also growing up but they weren't earning anything either. My grandmother earned barely enough to feed them. So my father went off to find work on the *fincas* near the coast. He was already a man and started earning enough money to send to my grandmother and he got her away from that family as soon as he could. She'd sort of become her employer's mistress although he had a wife. She had to agree because she'd nowhere else to go. She did it out of necessity and anyway there were plenty more waiting to take her place. She left to join her eldest son in the coastal estates and the other boys started working there as well.

7   We grew up on those *fincas* too. They are on the south coast, part
of Escuintla, Suchitepequez, Retalhuleu, Santa Rose, Jutiapa, where
coffee, cotton, cardamom and sugar are grown. Cutting cane was usually men's work and the pay was a little higher. But at certain times of
the year, both men and women were needed to cut cane. At the beginning things were very hard. They had only wild plants to eat, there
wasn't even any maize. But gradually, by working very hard, they managed to get themselves a place up in the *Altiplano*. Nobody had worked
the land there before. My father was eighteen by this time and was my
grandmother's right arm. He had to work day and night to provide for
my grandmother and his brothers. Unfortunately that was just when
they were rounding young men up for military service and they took my
father off, leaving my grandmother on her own again with her two sons.
My father learnt a lot of bad things in the army, but he also learnt to be
a man. He said they treated you like an object and taught you everything
by brute force. But he did learn how to fight. He was in the army for a
long hard year and when he got back home he found my grandmother
was dying. She had a fever. This is very common among people who
come from the coast where it's very hot straight to the *Altiplano* where
it's very cold. The change is too abrupt for them. There was no money
to buy medicine or to care for my grandmother and she died. My father
and his brothers were left without parents or any other relatives to help
them. My father told me that they had a little house made of straw, very
humble, but with their mother dead, there was no point in staying there.
So they split up and got work in different parts of the coast. My father
found work in a monastery but he hardly earned anything there either.
In those days a worker earned thirty to forty *centavos* a day, both in the
fincas and elsewhere.

8   That's when my father met my mother and they got married. They
went through very difficult times together. They met in the *Altiplano*
since my mother was from a very poor family too. Her parents were
very poor and used to travel around looking for work. They were hardly
ever at home in the *Altiplano*.

9   That's how they came to settle up in the mountains. There was no
town there. There was no-one. They founded a village up there. My village has a long history—a long and painful history. The land up there
belonged to the government and you had to get permission to settle
there. When you'd got permission, you had to pay a fee so that you
could clear the land and then build your house. Through all my parents'
efforts in the *fincas,* they managed to get enough money together to pay
the fee, and they cleared the land. Of course, it's not very easy to make
things grow on land that's just been cleared. You don't get a good yield
for at least eight or nine years. So my parents cultivated the land and

eight years later, it started to produce. We were growing up during this period. I had five older brothers and sisters. I saw my two eldest brothers die from lack of food when we were down in the *fincas*. Most Indian families suffer from malnutrition. Most of them don't even reach fifteen years old. When children are growing and don't get enough to eat, they're often ill, and this . . . well . . . it complicates the situation.

10   So my parents stayed there. My mother found the trees and our amazing mountains so beautiful. She said that they'd get lost sometimes because the mountains were so high and not a single ray of light fell through the plants. It's very dense. Well, that's where we grew up. We loved our land very, very much, even if we did have to walk for a long time to get to our nearest neighbour. But, little by little, my parents got more and more people to come up and cultivate the land so there would be more of us to ward off the animals that came down from the mountains to eat our maize when it was ripe, or, when the ears were still green. These animals would come and eat everything. My father said that one of them was what they call a racoon. Soon my mother started keeping hens and a few sheep because there was plenty of room but she didn't have the time to look after them properly so they'd wander off to find other food and not come back. The mountain animals ate some of them, or they just got lost. So they lived there, but unfortunately, it was many years before our land really produced anything and my parents still had to go down and work in the *fincas*. They told us what it was like when they first settled there, but when we children were growing up and could spend four or five months of the year there, we were very happy. There were big rivers rushing down the mountainside below our house. We didn't actually have much time for playing, but even working was fun—clearing the undergrowth while my father cut down trees. Well, you could hear so many different types of birds singing and there were lots of snakes to frighten us as well. We were happy even though it was very cold because of the mountains. And it's a damp sort of cold.

11   I was born there. My mother already had five children, I think. Yes, I had five brothers and sisters and I'm the sixth. My mother said that she was working down on a *finca* until a month before I was born. She had just twenty days to go when she went up to the mountains, and she gave birth to me all on her own. My father wasn't there because he had to work the month out on the *finca*.

12   Most of what I remember is after I was five. We spent four months in our little house in the *Altiplano* and the rest of the year we had to go down to the coast, either in the *Boca Costa* where there's coffee picking and also weeding out the coffee plants, or further down the South coast where there's cotton. That was the work we did mostly, and I went from when I was very little. A very few families owned the vast areas of land

which produce these crops for sale abroad. These landowners are the lords of vast extensions of land, then. So we'd work in the *fincas* for eight months and in January we'd go back up to the *Altiplano* to sow our crops. Where we live in the mountains, that is, where the land isn't fertile, you can barely grow maize and beans. The land isn't fertile enough for anything else. But on the coast the land is rich and you can grow anything. After we'd sown our crops, we'd go down to the coast again until it was time to harvest them, and then we'd make the journey back again. But the maize would soon run out, and we'd be back down again to earn some money. From what my parents said, they lived this harsh life for many years and they were always poor.

Birth Ceremonies

'Whoever may ask where we are, tell them what you know of us and nothing more.' —POPOL VUH

'Learn to protect yourselves, by keeping our secret.' —POPOL VUH

13   In our community there is an elected representative, someone who is highly respected. He's not a king but someone whom the community looks up to like a father. In our village, my father and mother were the representatives. Well, then the whole community becomes the children of the woman who's elected. So, a mother, on her first day of pregnancy goes with her husband to tell these elected leaders that she's going to have a child, because the child will not only belong to them but to the whole community, and must follow as far as he can our ancestors' traditions. The leaders then pledge the support of the community and say: 'We will help you, we will be the child's second parents.' They are known as *abuelos,* 'grandparents' or 'forefathers.' The parents then ask the 'grandparents' to help them find the child some godparents, so that if he's orphaned, he shouldn't be tempted by any of the bad habits our people sometimes fall into. So the 'grandparents' and the parents choose the godparents together. It's also the custom for the pregnant mother's neighbours to visit her every day and take her little things, no matter how simple. They stay and talk to her, and she'll tell them all her problems.

14   Later, when she's in her seventh month, the mother introduces her baby to the natural world, as our customs tell her to. She goes out in the fields or walks over the hills. She also has to show her baby the kind of life she leads, so that if she gets up at three in the morning, does her

chores and tends the animals, she does it all the more so when she's pregnant, conscious that the child is taking all this in. She talks to the child continuously from the first moment he's in her stomach, telling him how hard his life will be. It's as if the mother were a guide explaining things to a tourist. She'll say, for instance: 'You must never abuse nature and you must live your life as honestly as I do.' As she works in the fields, she tells her child all the little things about her work. It's a duty to her child that a mother must fulfil. And then, she also has to think of a way of hiding the baby's birth from her other children.

15   When her baby is born, the mother mustn't have her other children round her. The people present should be the husband, the village leaders, and the couple's parents. Three couples. The parents are often away in other places, so if they can't be there, the husband's father and the wife's mother can perhaps make up one pair. If one of the village leaders can't come, one of them should be there to make up a couple with one of the parents. If none of the parents can come, some aunts and uncles should come to represent the family on both sides, because the child is to be part of the community. The birth of a new member is very significant for the community, as it belongs to the community not just to the parents, and that's why three couples (but not just anybody) must be there to receive it. They explain that this child is the fruit of communal love. If the village leader is not a midwife as well, another midwife is called (it might be a grandmother) to receive the child. Our customs don't allow single women to see a birth. But it does happen in times of need. For instance, I was with my sister when she went into labour. Nobody else was at home. This was when we were being heavily persecuted. Well, I didn't exactly see, but I was there when the baby was born.

16   My mother was a midwife from when she was sixteen right up to her death at forty-three. She used to say that a woman hadn't the strength to push the baby out when she's lying down. So what she did with my sister was to hang a rope from the roof and pull her up, because my brother wasn't there to lift her up. My mother helped the baby out with my sister in that position. It's a scandal if an Indian woman goes to hospital and gives birth there. None of our women would agree to that. Our ancestors would be shocked at many of the things which go on today. Family planning, for example. It's an insult to our culture and a way of swindling the people, to get money out of them.

17   This is part of the reserve that we've maintained to defend our customs and our culture. Indians have been very careful not to disclose any details of their communities, and the community does not allow them to talk about Indian things. I too must abide by this. This is because many religious people have come among us and drawn a false

impression of the Indian world. We also find a *ladino* using Indian clothes very offensive. All this has meant that we keep a lot of things to ourselves and the community doesn't like us telling its secrets. This applies to all our customs. When the Catholic Action[1] arrived, for instance, everyone started going to mass, and praying, but it's not their only religion, not the only way they have of expressing themselves. Anyway, when a baby is born, he's always baptized within the community before he's taken to church. Our people have taken Catholicism as just another channel of expression, not our one and only belief. Our people do the same with other religions. The priests, monks and nuns haven't gained the people's confidence because so many of their things contradict our own customs. For instance, they say; 'You have too much trust in your elected leaders.' But the village elects them *because* they trust them, don't they? The priests say; 'The trouble is you follow those sorcerers,' and speak badly of them. But for our people this is like speaking ill of their own fathers, and they lose faith in the priests. They say; 'Well, they're not from here, they can't understand our world.' So there's not much hope of winning our people's hearts.

18   To come back to the children, they aren't to know how the baby is born. He's born somewhere hidden away and only the parents know about it. They are told that a baby has arrived and that they can't see their mother for eight days. Later on, the baby's companion, the placenta that is, has to be burned at a special time. If the baby is born at night, the placenta is burned at eight in the morning, and if he's born in the afternoon, it'll be burned at five o'clock. This is out of respect for both the baby and his companion. The placenta is not buried, because the earth is the mother and the father of the child and mustn't be abused by having the placenta buried in it. All these reasons are very important for us. Either the placenta is burned on a log and the ashes left there, or else it is put in the *temascal*. This is a stove which our people use to make vapour baths. It's a small hut made of adobe and inside this hut is another one made of stone, and when we want to have a bath, we light a fire to heat the stones, close the door, and throw water on the stones to produce steam. Well, when the woman is about four months pregnant, she starts taking these baths infused with evergreens, pure natural aromas. There are many plants the community uses for pregnant women, colds, headaches, and things like that. So the pregnant mother takes baths with plants prescribed for her by the midwife or the village leader. The fields are full of plants whose names I don't know in Spanish. Pregnant women use orange and peach leaves a lot for bathing and

1. Association created in 1945 by Monsignor Rafael Gonzalez, to try and control the Indian fraternities of the *Altiplano*.

there's another one we call Saint Mary's leaf which they use. The mother
needs these leaves and herbs to relax because she won't be able to rest
while she's pregnant since our women go on working just as hard in the
fields. So, after work, she takes this calming bath so that she can sleep
well, and the baby won't be harmed by her working hard. She's given
medicines to take as well. And leaves to feed the child. I believe that in
practice (even if this isn't a scientific recommendation) these leaves
work very well, because many of them contain vitamins. How else would
women who endure hunger and hard work, give birth to healthy babies?
I think that these plants have helped our people survive.

19   The purity with which the child comes into the world is protected
for eight days. Our customs say that the new-born baby should be alone
with his mother in a special place for eight days, without any of her
other children. Her only visitors are the people who bring her food.
This is the baby's period of integration into the family; he very slowly becomes a member of it. When the child is born, they kill a sheep and
there's a little fiesta just for the family. Then the neighbours start coming to visit, and bring presents. They either bring food for the mother,
or something for the baby. The mother has to taste all the food her
neighbours bring to show her appreciation for their kindness. After the
eight days are over, the family counts up how many visitors the mother
had, and how many presents were received; things like eggs or food
apart from what was brought for the mother, or clothing, small animals,
and wood for the fire, or services like carrying water and chopping wood.
If, during the eight days, most of the community has called, this is very
important, because it means that this child will have a lot of responsibility towards his community when he grows up. The community takes
over all the household expenses for these eight days and the family
spends nothing.

20   After eight days everything has been received, and another animal
is killed as recognition that the child's right to be alone with his mother
is over. All the mother's clothes, bedclothes, and everything she used
during the birth, are taken away by our elected leader and washed. She
can't wash them in the well, so no matter how far away the river is, they
must be carried and washed there. The baby's purity is washed away
and he's ready to learn the ways of humanity. The mother's bed is moved
to a part of the house which has first been washed with water and lime.
Lime is sacred. It strengthens the child's bones. I believe this really is
true. It gives a child strength to face the world. The mother has a bath
in the *temascal* and puts on clean clothes. Then, the whole house is
cleaned. The child is also washed and dressed and put into the new bed.
Four candles are placed on the corners of the bed to represent the four
corners of the house and show him that this will be his home. They

symbolize the respect the child must have for his community, and the responsibility he must feel towards it as a member of a household. The candles are lit and give off an incense which incorporates the child into the world he must live in. When the baby is born, his hands and feet are bound to show him that they are sacred and must only be used to work or do whatever nature meant them to do. They must never steal or abuse the natural world, or show disrespect for any living thing.

21   After the eight days, his hands and feet are untied and he's now with his mother in the new bed. This means he opens the doors to the other members of the community, because neither the family or the community know him yet. Or rather, they weren't shown the baby when he was born. Now they can all come and kiss him. The neighbours bring another animal, and there's a big lunch in the new baby's house for all the community. This is to celebrate his integration 'in the universe,' as our parents used to say. Candles will be lit for him and his candle becomes part of the candle of the whole community, which now has one more person, one more member. The whole community is at the ceremony, or at least, if not all of it, then some of it. Candles are lit to represent all the things which belong to the universe—earth, water, sun, and man—and the child's candle is put with them, together with incense (what we call *pom*) and lime—our sacred lime. Then, the parents tell the baby of the suffering of the family he will be joining. With great feeling, they express their sorrow at bringing a child into the world to suffer. To us, suffering is our fate, and the child must be introduced to the sorrows and hardship, but he must learn that despite his suffering, he will be respectful and live through his pain. The child is then entrusted with the responsibility for his community and told to abide by its rules. After the ceremony comes the lunch, and then the neighbours go home. Now, there is only the baptism to come.

22   When the baby is born, he's given a little bag with a garlic, a bit of lime, salt, and tobacco in it, to hang round his neck. Tobacco is important because it is a sacred plant for Indians. This all means that the child can ward off all the evil things in life. For us, bad things are like spirits, which exist only in our imagination. Something bad, for instance, would be if the child were to turn out to be a gossip—not sincere, truthful, and respectful, as a child should be. It also helps him collect together and preserve all our ancestors' things. That's more or less the idea of the bag—to keep him pure. The bag is put inside the four candles as well, and this represents the promise of the child when he grows up.

23   When the child is forty days old, there are more speeches, more promises on his behalf, and he becomes a full member of the community. This is his baptism. All the important people of the village are

invited and they speak. The parents make a commitment. They promise to teach the child to keep the secrets of our people, so that our culture and customs will be preserved. The village leaders come and offer their experience, their example, and their knowledge of our ancestors. They explain how to preserve our traditions. Then, they promise to be responsible for the child, teach him as he grows up, and see that he follows in their ways. It's also something of a criticism of humanity, and of the many people who have forsaken their traditions. They say almost a prayer, asking that our traditions again enter the spirits of those who have forsaken them. Then, they evoke the names of our ancestors, like Tecun Umán and others who form part of the ceremony, as a kind of chant. They must be remembered as heroes of the Indian peoples. And then they say (I analyse all this later): 'Let no landowner extinguish all this, nor any rich man wipe out our customs. Let our children, be they workers or servants, respect and keep their secrets.' The child is present for all of this, although he's all wrapped up and can scarcely be seen. He is told that he will eat maize and that, naturally, he is already made of maize because his mother ate it while he was forming in her stomach. He must respect the maize; even the grain of maize which has been thrown away, he must pick up. The child will multiply our race, he will replace all those who have died. From this moment, he takes on this responsibility, and is told to live as his 'grandparents' have lived. The parents then reply that their child promises to accomplish all this. So, the village leaders and the parents both make promises on behalf of the child. It's his initiation into the community.

24   The ceremony is very important. It is also when the child is considered a child of God, our one father. We don't actually have the word God but that is what it is, because the one father is the only one we have. To reach this one father, the child must love beans, maize, the earth. The one father is the heart of the sky, that is, the sun. The sun is the father and our mother is the moon. She is a gentle mother. And she lights our way. Our people have many notions about the moon, and about the sun. They are the pillars of the universe.

25   When children reach ten years old, that's the moment when their parents and the village leaders talk to them again. They tell them that they will be young men and women and that one day they will be fathers and mothers. This is actually when they tell the child that he must never abuse his dignity, in the same way his ancestors never abused their dignity. It's also when they remind them that our ancestors were dishonoured by the White Man, by colonization. But they don't tell them the way that it's written down in books, because the majority of Indians can't read or write, and don't even know that they have their own texts. No, they learn it through oral recommendations, the way it has

been handed down through the generations. They are told that the Spaniards dishonoured our ancestors' finest sons, and the most humble of them. And it is to honour these humble people that we must keep our secrets. And no-one except we Indians must know. They talk a lot about our ancestors. And the ten-years ceremony is also when our children are reminded that they must respect their elders, even though this is something their parents have been telling them ever since they were little. For example, if an old person is walking along the street, children should cross over to allow him to pass by. If any of us sees an elderly person, we are obliged to bow and greet them. Everyone does this, even the very youngest. We also show respect to pregnant women. Whenever we make food, we always keep some for any of our neighbours who are pregnant.

26   When little girls are born, the midwives pierce their ears at the same time as they tie their umbilical cords. The little bags round their necks and the thread used to tie their umbilical cord are both red. Red is very significant for us. It means heat, strength, all living things. It's linked to the sun, which for us is the channel to the one god, the heart of everything, of the universe. So red gives off heat and fire and red things are supposed to give life to the child. At the same time, it asks him to respect living things too. There are no special clothes for the baby. We don't buy anything special beforehand but just use pieces of *corte* to wrap him in.

27   When a male child is born, there are special celebrations, not because he's male but because of all the hard work and responsibility he'll have as a man. It's not that *machismo* doesn't exist among our people, but it doesn't present a problem for the community because it's so much part of our way of life. The male child is given an extra day alone with his mother. The usual custom is to celebrate a male child by killing a sheep or some chickens. Boys are given more, they get more food because their work is harder and they have more responsibility. At the same time, he is head of the household, not in the bad sense of the word, but because he is responsible for so many things. This doesn't mean girls aren't valued. Their work is hard too and there are other things that are due to them as mothers. Girls are valued because they are part of the earth, which gives us maize, beans, plants and everything we live on. The earth is like a mother which multiplies life. So the girl child will multiply the life of our generation and of our ancestors whom we must respect. The girl and the boy are both integrated into the community in equally important ways, the two are inter-related and compatible. Nevertheless, the community is always happier when a male child is born and the men feel much prouder. The customs, like the tying of the hands and feet, apply to both boys and girls.

28   Babies are breast-fed. It's much better than any other sort of food. But the important thing is the sense of community. It's something we all share. From the very first day, the baby belongs to the community, not only to the parents and the baby must learn from all of us . . . in fact, we behave just like bourgeois families in that, as soon as the baby is born, we're thinking of his education, of his well-being. But our people feel that the baby's school must be the community itself, that he must learn to live like all the rest of us. The tying of the hands at birth also symbolizes this; that no-one should accumulate things the rest of the community does not have and he must know how to share, to have open hands. The mother must teach the baby to be generous. This way of thinking comes from poverty and suffering. Each child is taught to live like the fellow members of his community.

29   We never eat in front of pregnant women. You can only eat in front of a pregnant woman if you can offer something as well. The fear is that, otherwise, she might abort the baby or that the baby could suffer if she didn't have enough to eat. It doesn't matter whether you know her or not. The important thing is sharing. You have to treat a pregnant woman differently from other women because she is two people. You must treat her with respect so that she recognizes it and conveys this to the baby inside her. You instinctively think she's the image of the baby about to be born. So you love her. Another reason why you must stop and talk to a pregnant woman is because she doesn't have much chance to rest or enjoy herself. She's always worried and depressed. So when she stops and chats a bit, she can relax and feel some relief.

30   When the baby joins the community, with him in the circle of candles—together with his little red bag—he will have his hoe, his machete, his axe and all the tools he will need in life. These will be his playthings. A little girl will have her washing board and all the things she will need when she grows up. She must learn the things of the house, to clean, to wash, and sew her brothers' trousers, for example. The little boy must begin to live like a man, to be responsible and learn to love the work in the fields. The learning is done as a kind of game. When the parents do anything they always explain what it means. This includes learning prayers. This is very important to our people. The mother may say a prayer at any time. Before getting up in the morning, for instance, she thanks the day which is dawning because it might be a very important one for the family. Before lighting the fire, she blesses the wood because that fire is going to cook food for the whole family. Since it's the little girl who is closest to her mother, she learns all of this. Before washing the *nixtamal,* the woman blows on her hands and puts them in the *nixtamal.* She takes everything out and washes it well. She blows on her hands so that her work will bear fruit. She does it before she does

the wash as well. She explains all these little details to her daughter, who learns by copying her. With the men it's the same. Before they start work every day, whatever hour of the morning it is, they greet the sun. They remove their hats and talk to the sun before starting work. Their sons learn to do it too, taking off their little hats to talk to the sun. Naturally, each ethnic group has its own forms of expression. Other groups have different customs from ours. The meaning of their weaving patterns, for example. We realize the others are different in some things, but the one thing we have in common is our culture. Our people are mainly peasants, but there are some people who buy and sell as well. They go into this after they've worked on the land. Sometimes when they come back from working in the *finca,* instead of tending a little plot of land, they'll start a shop and look for a different sort of life. But if they're used to greeting the sun every morning, they still go on doing it. And they keep all their old customs. Every part of our culture comes from the earth. Our religion comes from the maize and bean harvests which are so vital to our community. So even if a man goes to try and make some money, he never forgets his culture springs from the earth.

31   As we grow up we have a series of obligations. Our parents teach us to be responsible; just as they have been responsible. The eldest son is responsible for the house. Whatever the father cannot correct is up to the eldest son to correct. He is like a second father to us all and is responsible for our upbringing. The mother is the one who is responsible for keeping an account of what the family eats, and what she has to buy. When a child is ill, she has to get medicine. But the father has to solve a lot of problems too. And each one of us, as we grow up, has our own small area of responsibility. This comes from the promises made for the child when he is born, and from the continuity of our customs. The child can make the promise for himself when his parents have taught him to do it. The mother, who is closest to the children, does this, or sometimes the father. They talk to their children explaining what they have to do and what our ancestors used to do. They don't impose it as a law, but just give the example of what our ancestors have always done. This is how we all learn our own small responsibilities. For example, the little girl begins by carrying water, and the little boy begins by tying up the dogs when the animals are brought into the yard at night, or by fetching a horse which has wandered off. Both girls and boys have their tasks and are told the reasons for doing them. They learn responsibility because if they don't do their little jobs well, their father has the right to scold them, or even beat them. So, they are very careful about learning to do their jobs well, but the parents are also very careful to explain exactly why the jobs have to be done. The little girl understands the reasons for everything her

mother does. For example, when she puts a new earthenware pot on the fire for the first time, she hits it five times with a branch, so that it knows its job is to cook and so that it lasts. When the little girl asks, 'Why did you do that?' her mother says, 'So that it knows what its job is and does it well.' When it's her turn to cook, the little girl does as her mother does. Again this is all bound up with our commitment to maintain our customs and pass on the secrets of our ancestors. The elected fathers of the community explain to us that all these things come down to us from our grandfathers and we must conserve them. Nearly everything we do today is based on what our ancestors did. This is the main purpose of our elected leader—to embody all the values handed down from our ancestors. He is the leader of the community, a father to all our children, and he must lead an exemplary life. Above all, he has a commitment to the whole community. Everything that is done today, is done in memory of those who have passed on.

WORD FOCUS

VOCABULARY GLOSS

abuelos: *grandparents; elders (13)*

adobe: *bricks made of mud and straw; a dwelling (18)*

Altiplano: *land high up in the mountains (7)*

bourgeois: *educated, middle-class (28)*

caballerias: *a measurement of land equal to about two and a half acres (4)*

centavos: *money; coins (7)*

corte: *local handwoven cloth (26)*

fiesta: *a holiday or celebration (19)*

fincas: *farms; plantations; estates (7)*

grandmother's right arm: *her main support (7)*

machete: *a large, sharp knife used for cutting vegetation (30)*

machismo: *an attribute that indicates extreme manliness and power (27)*

mestizos/ladinos: *people who are Spanish-speaking and of mixed South American Indian and Spanish ancestry (3)*

mimbre: *a tree used for making baskets and furniture (4)*

nixtamal: *both the pot in which maize is cooked, and the dough used to make tortillas (30)*

pom: *a special kind of incense (21)*

Tecun Umán: *a commander of the Quiché forces who died in 1524 (23)*

temascal: *a steam bath made with hot stones; vapor baths (18)*

weaving patterns: *designs in cloth (30)*

VOCABULARY QUESTIONS

1. Menchú says that "Indians have been very careful not to disclose any details of their communities, and the community does not allow them to talk about Indian things" (17). What does "disclose" mean in this sentence? Why do you think Menchú chooses the word "disclose" instead of synonyms such as *show* and *share?*

2. Discuss the meaning of the word "testimony" in the following sentence: "I'd like to stress that it's not only *my* life, it's also the testimony of my people" (1).

3. After a close reading of the following paragraphs, consider the reasons Menchú gives for the different treatment of female and male children. Look up the following words in your dictionary and define them: *explanation, justification,* and *rationalization.* Use these words to analyze the two paragraphs:

When little girls are born, the midwives pierce their ears at the same time as they tie their umbilical cords. The little bags round their necks and the thread used to tie their umbilical cord are both red. Red is very significant for us. It means heat, strength, all living things. It's linked to the sun, which for us is the channel to the one god, the heart of everything, of the universe. So red gives off heat and fire and red things are supposed to give life to the child. At the same time, it asks him to respect living things too. There are no special clothes for the baby. We don't buy anything special beforehand but just use pieces of *corte* to wrap him in.

When a male child is born, there are special celebrations, not because he's male but because of all the hard work and responsibility he'll have as a man. It's not that *machismo* doesn't exist among our people, but it doesn't present a problem for the community because it's so much part of our way of life. The male child is given an extra day alone with his mother. The usual custom is to celebrate a male child by killing a sheep or some chickens. Boys are given more, they get more food because their work is harder and they have more responsibility. At the same time, he is head of the household, not in the bad sense of the word, but because he is responsible for so many things. This doesn't mean girls aren't valued. Their work is hard too and there are other things that are due to them as mothers. Girls are valued because they are part of the earth, which gives us maize, beans, plants and everything we live on. The earth is like a mother which multiplies life. So the girl child will multiply the life of our generation and of our ancestors whom we must respect. The girl and the boy are both integrated into the community in equally important ways, the two are inter-related and compatible. Nevertheless, the community is always happier when a male child is born and the men feel much prouder. The customs, like the tying of the hands and feet, apply to both boys and girls. (26, 27)

ENGLISH CRAFT

1. In academic writing, authors cite *evidence* from other texts as a means to support and broaden their own statements. Evidence can come from many sources:

   - quotations from texts
   - mention of related ideas through reference and allusion
   - examples from texts
   - personal experience or knowledge
   - generally known facts

   Look at the end of Menchú's story beginning with "When the baby joins the community, with him in the circle of candles . . ." (30). Write a paragraph about the initiation of the child into the community. Support the topic sentence claims of your paragraph by using different sources of evidence.

2. Specific kinds of words link concepts from sentence to sentence and from paragraph to paragraph. These include articles, personal pronouns, and **demonstrative adjectives and pronouns.** The demonstratives *this, that, these,* and *those* can tie sentences together by pointing both backward and forward in a text, and by doing so tie the essay together both conceptually and structurally.

   The demonstratives *this, that, these,* and *those* can act as both adjectives and pronouns. Note that they also allow us to make distinctions between things that are singular and plural *(this/these)* or near and far *(that/those).*

Demonstrative Adjectives		*Demonstrative Pronouns*	
this person	*these* people	this	these
that person	*those* people	that	those

Look at the following examples, and discuss how the demonstratives tie the text together. Do they point forward, backward, or in both directions? Are they singular or plural? Do they take the place of a noun, and if so, what noun? Do they point to things that are near or far? Do they tie concepts together?

Demonstrative Adjectives

The mother must teach the baby to be generous. **This** way of thinking comes from poverty and suffering. (28)

[My parents had] been forced to leave the town because some *ladino* families came to settle there. . . . My parents spent everything they earned and they incurred so many debts with **these** people that they had to leave the house to pay them. (5)

My grandmother earned barely enough to feed them. So my father went off to find work on the *fincas* near the coast. . . . We grew up on **those** *fincas* too. They are on the south coast . . . (6, 7)

Demonstrative Pronouns

My name is Rigoberta Menchú. I am twenty-three years old. **This** is my testimony. I didn't learn it from a book and I didn't learn it alone. (1)

When little girls are born, the midwives pierce their ears at the same time as they tie their umbilical cords. . . . When a male child is born, there are special celebrations, not because he's male but because of all the hard work and responsibility he'll have as a man. . . . **This** doesn't mean girls aren't valued. (26, 27)

INTERPRETIVE JOURNAL

1. Menchú observes, "My father learnt a lot of bad things in the army, but he also learnt to be a man. He said they treated you like an object and taught you everything by brute force" (7). What does it mean to be treated like an object? What is the connection between learning "to be a man" and being taught "everything by brute force"? What may be difficult about learning "to be a man or a woman" in today's society?

2. People in technological societies may stereotype native cultures in negative ways. Make a list of some of these negative stereotypes. Does Menchú's description of the ceremonies surrounding the birth of a child support or argue against such stereotypes?

3. Compare and contrast (1) the playthings that the boys and girls of Menchú's society receive, and (2) those typical for children today. What

do these playthings reveal about the expectations parents have for their children?

4. Although Menchú talks with pride about individual achievement in her narrative, she also emphasizes the strong sense of community. How does personal achievement fit in with Menchú's sense of community?

ESSAY QUESTION

Menchú reports that village leaders talk to the children at age ten about becoming "men and women," "fathers and mothers" (25). She observes, "This is actually when they tell the child that he must never abuse his dignity, in the same way his ancestors never abused their dignity" (25). Discuss what the rule "never abuse [one's] dignity" means in Menchú's community. Be sure to define what "dignity" means to both you and Menchú.

Ronald Takaki
Excerpt from *A Different Mirror*

Preview

Mirrors both reflect and distort images. In many societies, mirrors are associated with superstitions and have symbolic functions. Discuss some of the beliefs and practices you can associate with mirrors.

Word Preview

You can familiarize yourself with the following words by looking them up in the dictionary. You can broaden your knowledge of these words by pronouncing them and understanding how they are used in context.

appropriation (2)	mused (2)	jarring (3)
indigenous (2)	terrain (2)	ubiquitous (4)

predominate (4)
minority (5)
ethnic (5)
perplexed (6)
preeminence (6)
backlash (6)
permissiveness (6)
befouled (6)
homogeneous (7)
fragmentization (7)
acculturate (7)
rend (7)
supplant (7)
boycott (9)
hysteria (9)
nadir (10)
rampage (10)
mesmerized (10)
melee (10)
binary (11)
prologue (12)
malevolence (12)
primordial (12)
pluralism (12)
antagonisms (12)

malaise (12)
revisionism (16)
proliferation (16)
seminal (16)
mosaic (17)
scrutinizing (17)
inordinate (18)
freighted (19)
heathen (20)
unassimilable (20)
tyrannical (20)
integral (21)
colonized (21)
proximity (21)
mestizo (21)
foreshadowed (22)
pioneers (22)
mainstream (22)
solidarity (22)
persecution (23)
surrogate (23)
bigotry (23)
virulence (23)
crucible (24)
moccasins (24)

oppressors (26)
scabs (26)
impassioned (27)
elite (27)
clannishness (27)
nerds (27)
liminality (28)
overblown (29)
inaugural (32)
mystic (32)
hearthstone (32)
consecrated (32)
bayonet (32)
consummation (32)
authenticity (35)
deity (36)
phenomenal (36)
calamitous (36)
distraught (36)
disarray (36)
crisscross (38)
proposition (38)
concreteness (38)
riddled (38)
riveted (39)

1   I had flown from San Francisco to Norfolk and was riding in a taxi to my hotel to attend a conference on multiculturalism. Hundreds of educators from across the country were meeting to discuss the need for greater cultural diversity in the curriculum. My driver and I chatted about the weather and the tourists. The sky was cloudy, and Virginia Beach was twenty minutes away. The rearview mirror reflected a white man in his forties. "How long have you been in this country?" he asked. "All my life," I replied, wincing. "I was born in the United States." With a strong southern drawl, he remarked: "I was wondering because your English is excellent!" Then, as I had many times before, I explained: "My grandfather came here from Japan in the 1880s. My family has been here, in America, for over a hundred years." He glanced at me in the mirror. Somehow I did not look "American" to him; my eyes and complexion looked foreign.

2   Suddenly, we both became uncomfortably conscious of a racial divide separating us. An awkward silence turned my gaze from the mirror

to the passing landscape, the shore where the English and the Powhatan Indians first encountered each other. Our highway was on land that Sir Walter Raleigh had renamed "Virginia" in honor of Elizabeth I, the Virgin Queen. In the English cultural appropriation of America, the indigenous peoples themselves would become outsiders in their native land. Here, at the eastern edge of the continent, I mused, was the site of the beginning of multicultural America. Jamestown, the English settlement founded in 1607, was nearby: the first twenty Africans were brought here a year before the Pilgrims arrived at Plymouth Rock. Several hundred miles offshore was Bermuda, the "Bermoothes" where William Shakespeare's Prospero had landed and met the native Caliban in *The Tempest.* Earlier, another voyager had made an Atlantic crossing and unexpectedly bumped into some islands to the south. Thinking he had reached Asia, Christopher Columbus mistakenly identified one of the islands as "Cipango" (Japan). In the wake of the admiral, many peoples would come to America from different shores, not only from Europe but also Africa and Asia. One of them would be my grandfather. My mental wandering across terrain and time ended abruptly as we arrived at my destination. I said good-bye to my driver and went into the hotel, carrying a vivid reminder of why I was attending this conference.

· · · · · · · · ·

3   Questions like the one my taxi driver asked me are always jarring, but I can understand why he could not see me as American. He had a narrow but widely shared sense of the past—a history that has viewed Americans as European in ancestry. "Race," Toni Morrison explained, has functioned as a "metaphor" necessary to the "construction of Americanness": in the creation of our national identity, "American" has been defined as "white."[1]

4   But America has been racially diverse since our very beginning on the Virginia shore, and this reality is increasingly becoming visible and ubiquitous. Currently, one-third of the American people do not trace their origins to Europe; in California, minorities are fast becoming a majority. They already predominate in major cities across the country—New York, Chicago, Atlanta, Detroit, Philadelphia, San Francisco, and Los Angeles.

5   This emerging demographic diversity has raised fundamental questions about America's identity and culture. In 1990, *Time* published a cover story on "America's Changing Colors." "Someday soon," the magazine announced, "white Americans will become a minority group."

1. Toni Morrison, *Playing in the Dark: Whiteness in the Literary Imagination* (Cambridge, Mass., 1992), p. 47.

How soon? By 2056, most Americans will trace their descent to "Africa, Asia, the Hispanic world, the Pacific Islands, Arabia—almost anywhere but white Europe." This dramatic change in our nation's ethnic composition is altering the way we think about ourselves. "The deeper significance of America's becoming a majority nonwhite society is what it means to the national psyche, to individuals' sense of themselves and their nation—their idea of what it is to be American."[2]

6   Indeed, more than ever before, as we approach the time when whites become a minority, many of us are perplexed about our national identity and our future as one people. This uncertainty has provoked Allan Bloom to reaffirm the preeminence of Western civilization. Author of *The Closing of the American Mind,* he has emerged as a leader of an intellectual backlash against cultural diversity. In his view, students entering the university are "uncivilized," and the university has the responsibility to "civilize" them. Bloom claims he knows what their "hungers" are and "what they can digest." Eating is one of his favorite metaphors. Noting the "large black presence" in major universities, he laments the "one failure" in race relations—black students have proven to be "indigestible." They do not "melt as have *all* other groups." The problem, he contends, is that "blacks have become blacks": they have become "ethnic." This separatism has been reinforced by an academic permissiveness that has befouled the curriculum with "Black Studies" along with "Learn Another Culture." The only solution, Bloom insists, is "the good old Great Books approach."[3]

7   Similarly, E. D. Hirsch worries that America is becoming a "tower of Babel," and that this multiplicity of cultures is threatening to rend our social fabric. He, too, longs for a more cohesive culture and a more homogeneous America: "If we *had* to make a choice between the *one* and the *many,* most Americans would choose the principle of unity, since we cannot function as a nation without it." The way to correct this fragmentation, Hirsch argues, is to acculturate "disadvantaged children." What do they need to know? "Only by accumulating shared symbols, and the shared information that symbols represent," Hirsch answers, "can we learn to communicate effectively with one another in our national community." Though he concedes the value of multicultural education, he quickly dismisses it by insisting that it "should not be allowed to supplant or interfere with our schools' responsibility to ensure

2. William A. Henry III, "Beyond the Melting Pot," in "America's Changing Colors," *Time,* vol. 135, no. 15 (April 9, 1990), pp. 28–31.

3. Allan Bloom, *The Closing of the American Mind: How Higher Education Has Failed Democracy and Impoverished the Souls of Today's Students* (New York, 1987), pp. 19, 91–93, 340–341, 344.

our children's mastery of American literate culture." In *Cultural Literacy: What Every American Needs to Know,* Hirsch offers a long list of terms that excludes much of the history of minority groups.[4]

8   While Bloom and Hirsch are reacting defensively to what they regard as a vexatious balkanization of America, many other educators are responding to our diversity as an opportunity to open American minds. In 1990, the Task Force on Minorities for New York emphasized the importance of a culturally diverse education. "Essentially," the *New York Times* commented, "the issue is how to deal with both dimensions of the nation's motto: 'E pluribus unum'—'Out of many, one.' " Universities from New Hampshire to Berkeley have established American cultural diversity graduation requirements. "Every student needs to know," explained University of Wisconsin's chancellor Donna Shalala, "much more about the origins and history of the particular cultures which, as Americans, we will encounter during our lives." Even the University of Minnesota, located in a state that is 98 percent white, requires its students to take ethnic studies courses. Asked why multiculturalism is so important, Dean Fred Lukermann answered: As a national university, Minnesota has to offer a national curriculum—one that includes all of the peoples of America. He added that after graduation many students move to cities like Chicago and Los Angeles and thus need to know about racial diversity. Moreover, many educators stress, multiculturalism has an intellectual purpose. By allowing us to see events from the viewpoints of different groups, a multicultural curriculum enables us to reach toward a more comprehensive understanding of American history.[5]

9   What is fueling this debate over our national identity and the content of our curriculum is America's intensifying racial crisis. The alarming signs and symptoms seem to be everywhere—the killing of Vincent Chin in Detroit, the black boycott of a Korean grocery store in Flatbush, the hysteria in Boston over the Carol Stuart murder, the battle between white sportsmen and Indians over tribal fishing rights in Wisconsin, the Jewish-black clashes in Brooklyn's Crown Heights, the black-Hispanic competition for jobs and educational resources in Dallas, which *Newsweek* described as "a conflict of the have-nots," and the Willie Horton campaign commercials, which widened the divide between the suburbs and the inner cities.[6]

4. E. D. Hirsch, Jr., *Cultural Literacy: What Every American Needs to Know* (Boston, 1987), pp. xiii, xvii, 2, 18, 96. See also "The List," pp. 152–215.

5. Edward Fiske, "Lessons," *New York Times,* February 7, 1990; "University of Wisconsin-Madison: The Madison Plan," February 9, 1988; interview with Dean Fred Lukermann, University of Minnesota, 1987.

6. "A Conflict of the Have-Nots," *Newsweek,* December 12, 1988, pp. 28–29.

10   This reality of racial tension rudely woke America like a fire bell in
the night on April 29, 1992. Immediately after four Los Angeles police
officers were found not guilty of brutality against Rodney King, rage ex-
ploded in Los Angeles. Race relations reached a new nadir. During the
nightmarish rampage, scores of people were killed, over two thousand
injured, twelve thousand arrested, and almost a billion dollars' worth of
property destroyed. The live televised images mesmerized America. The
rioting and the murderous melee on the streets resembled the fighting
in Beirut and the West Bank. The thousands of fires burning out of control and the dark smoke filling the skies brought back images of the
burning oil fields of Kuwait during Desert Storm. Entire sections of
Los Angeles looked like a bombed city. "Is this America?" many shocked
viewers asked. "Please, can we get along here," pleaded Rodney King,
calling for calm. "We all can get along. I mean, we're all stuck here for
a while. Let's try to work it out."[7]

11   But how should "we" be defined? Who are the people "stuck here"
in America? One of the lessons of the Los Angeles explosion is the recognition of the fact that we are a multiracial society and that race can no
longer be defined in the binary terms of white and black. "We" will have
to include Hispanics and Asians. While blacks currently constitute 13
percent of the Los Angeles population, Hispanics represent 40 percent.
The 1990 census revealed that South Central Los Angeles, which was
predominantly black in 1965 when the Watts rebellion occurred, is now
45 percent Hispanic. A majority of the first 5,438 people arrested were
Hispanic, while 37 percent were black. Of the fifty-eight people who
died in the riot, more than a third were Hispanic, and about 40 percent
of the businesses destroyed were Hispanic-owned. Most of the other
shops and stores were Korean-owned. The dreams of many Korean immigrants went up in smoke during the riot: two thousand Korean-
owned businesses were damaged or demolished, totaling about $400
million in losses. There is evidence indicating they were targeted. "After
all," explained a black gang member, "we didn't burn our community,
just *their* stores."[8]

12   "I don't feel like I'm in America anymore," said Denisse Bustamente
as she watched the police protecting the firefighters. "I feel like I am far
away." Indeed, Americans have been witnessing ethnic strife erupting

7. Rodney King's statement to the press, *New York Times,* May 2, 1992, p. 6.
8. Tim Rutten, "A New Kind of Riot," *New York Review of Books,* June 11, 1992, pp. 52–53;
Maria Newman, "Riots Bring Attention to Growing Hispanic Presence in South-Central
Area," *New York Times,* May 11, 1992, p. A10; Mike Davis, "In L.A. Burning All Illusions,"
The Nation, June 1, 1992, pp. 744–745; Jack Viets and Peter Fimrite, "S.F. Mayor Visits
Riot-Torn Area to Buoy Businesses," *San Francisco Chronicle,* May 6, 1992, p. A6.

around the world—the rise of neo-Nazism and the murder of Turks in Germany, the ugly "ethnic cleansing" in Bosnia, the terrible and bloody clashes between Muslims and Hindus in India. Is the situation here different, we have been nervously wondering, or do ethnic conflicts elsewhere represent a prologue for America? What is the nature of malevolence? Is there a deep, perhaps primordial, need for group identity rooted in hatred for the other? Is ethnic pluralism possible for America? But answers have been limited. Television reports have been little more than thirty-second sound bites. Newspaper articles have been mostly superficial descriptions of racial antagonisms and the current urban malaise. What is lacking is historical context; consequently, we are left feeling bewildered.[9]

13   How did we get to this point, Americans everywhere are anxiously asking. What does our diversity mean, and where is it leading us? *How* do we work it out in the post–Rodney King era?

14   Certainly one crucial way is for our society's various ethnic groups to develop a greater understanding of each other. For example, how can African Americans and Korean Americans work it out unless they learn about each other's cultures, histories, and also economic situations? This need to share knowledge about our ethnic diversity has acquired new importance and has given new urgency to the pursuit for a more accurate history.

15   More than ever before, there is a growing realization that the established scholarship has tended to define America too narrowly. For example, in his prize-winning study *The Uprooted,* Harvard historian Oscar Handlin presented—to use the book's subtitle—"The Epic Story of the Great Migrations That Made the American People." But Handlin's "epic story" excluded the "uprooted" from Africa, Asia, and Latin America—the other "Great Migrations" that also helped to make "the American People." Similarly, in *The Age of Jackson,* Arthur M. Schlesinger, Jr., left out blacks and Indians. There is not even a mention of two marker events—the Nat Turner insurrection and Indian removal, which Andrew Jackson himself would have been surprised to find omitted from a history of his era.[10]

16   Still, Schlesinger and Handlin offered us a refreshing revisionism, paving the way for the study of common people rather than princes and presidents. They inspired the next generation of historians to examine

9. Rick DelVecchio, Suzanne Espinosa, and Carl Nolte, "Bradley Ready to Lift Curfew," *San Francisco Chronicle,* May 4, 1992, p. A1.

10. Oscar Handlin, *The Uprooted: The Epic Story of the Great Migrations That Made the American People* (New York, 1951); Arthur M. Schlesinger, Jr., *The Age of Jackson* (Boston, 1945).

groups such as the artisan laborers of Philadelphia and the Irish immigrants of Boston. "Once I thought to write a history of the immigrants in America," Handlin confided in his introduction to *The Uprooted*. "I discovered that the immigrants *were* American history." This door, once opened, led to the flowering of a more inclusive scholarship as we began to recognize that ethnic history was American history. Suddenly, there was a proliferation of seminal works such as Irving Howe's *World of Our Fathers: The Journey of the East European Jews to America,* Dee Brown's *Bury My Heart at Wounded Knee: An Indian History of the American West,* Albert Camarillo's *Chicanos in a Changing Society,* Lawrence Levine's *Black Culture and Black Consciousness,* Yuji Ichioka's *The Issei: The World of the First Generation Japanese Immigrants,* and Kerby Miller's *Emigrants and Exiles: Ireland and the Irish Exodus to North America.*[11]

17   But even this new scholarship, while it has given us a more expanded understanding of the mosaic called America, does not address our needs in the post–Rodney King era. These books and others like them fragment American society, studying each group separately, in isolation from the other groups and the whole. While scrutinizing our specific pieces, we have to step back in order to see the rich and complex portrait they compose. What is needed is a fresh angle, a study of the American past from a comparative perspective.

18   While all of America's many groups cannot be covered in one book, the English immigrants and their descendants require attention, for they possessed inordinate power to define American culture and make public policy. What men like John Winthrop, Thomas Jefferson, and Andrew Jackson thought as well as did mattered greatly to all of us and was consequential for everyone. A broad range of groups has been selected: African Americans, Asian Americans, Chicanos, Irish, Jews, and Indians. While together they help to explain general patterns in our society, each has contributed to the making of the United States.

19   African Americans have been the central minority throughout our country's history. They were initially brought here on a slave ship in 1619. Actually, these first twenty Africans might not have been slaves;

11. Handlin, *The Uprooted,* p. 3; Irving Howe, *World of Our Fathers: The Journey of the East European Jews to America and the Life They Found and Made* (New York, 1983); Dee Brown, *Bury My Heart at Wounded Knee: An Indian History of the American West* (New York, 1970); Albert Camarillo, *Chicanos in a Changing Society: From Mexican Pueblos to American Barrios in Santa Barbara and Southern California, 1848–1930* (Cambridge, Mass., 1979); Lawrence W. Levine, *Black Culture and Black Consciousness: Afro-American Folk Thought from Slavery to Freedom* (New York, 1977); Yuji Ichioka, *The Issei: The World of the First Generation Japanese Immigrants* (New York, 1988); Kerby A. Miller, *Emigrants and Exiles: Ireland and the Irish Exodus to North America* (New York, 1985).

rather, like most of the white laborers, they were probably indentured servants. The transformation of Africans into slaves is the story of the "hidden" origins of slavery. How and when was it decided to institute a system of bonded black labor? What happened, while freighted with racial significance, was actually conditioned by class conflicts within white society. Once established, the "peculiar institution" would have consequences for centuries to come. During the nineteenth century, the political storm over slavery almost destroyed the nation. Since the Civil War and emancipation, race has continued to be largely defined in relation to African Americans—segregation, civil rights, the underclass, and affirmative action. Constituting the largest minority group in our society, they have been at the cutting edge of the Civil Rights Movement. Indeed, their struggle has been a constant reminder of America's moral vision as a country committed to the principle of liberty. Martin Luther King clearly understood this truth when he wrote from a jail cell: "We will reach the goal of freedom in Birmingham and all over the nation, because the goal of America is freedom. Abused and scorned though we may be, our destiny is tied up with America's destiny."[12]

20   Asian Americans have been here for over one hundred and fifty years, before many European immigrant groups. But as "strangers" coming from a "different shore," they have been stereotyped as "heathen," exotic, and unassimilable. Seeking "Gold Mountain," the Chinese arrived first, and what happened to them influenced the reception of the Japanese, Koreans, Filipinos, and Asian Indians as well as the Southeast Asian refugees like the Vietnamese and the Hmong. The 1882 Chinese Exclusion Act was the first law that prohibited the entry of immigrants on the basis of nationality. The Chinese condemned this restriction as racist and tyrannical. "They call us 'Chink,' " complained a Chinese immigrant, cursing the "white demons." "They think we no good! America cuts us off. No more come now, too bad!" This precedent later provided a basis for the restriction of European immigrant groups such as Italians, Russians, Poles, and Greeks. The Japanese painfully discovered that their accomplishments in America did not lead to acceptance, for during World War II, unlike Italian Americans and German Americans, they were placed in internment camps. Two-thirds of them were citizens by birth. "How could I as a 6-month-old child born in this country," asked Congressman Robert Matsui years later, "be declared by my own Government to be an enemy alien?" Today, Asian Americans

---

12. Abraham Lincoln, "The Gettysburg Address," in *The Annals of America,* vol. 9, *1863–1865: The Crisis of the Union* (Chicago, 1968), pp. 462–463; Martin Luther King, *Why We Can't Wait* (New York, 1964), pp. 92–93.

represent the fastest-growing ethnic group. They have also become the focus of much mass media attention as "the Model Minority" not only for blacks and Chicanos, but also for whites on welfare and even middle-class whites experiencing economic difficulties.[13]

21   Chicanos represent the largest group among the Hispanic population, which is projected to outnumber African Americans. They have been in the United States for a long time, initially incorporated by the war against Mexico. The treaty had moved the border between the two countries, and the people of "occupied" Mexico suddenly found themselves "foreigners" in their "native land." As historian Albert Camarillo pointed out, the Chicano past is an integral part of America's westward expansion, also known as "manifest destiny." But while the early Chicanos were a colonized people, most of them today have immigrant roots. Many began the trek to El Norte in the early twentieth century. "As I had heard a lot about the United States," Jesus Garza recalled, "it was my dream to come here." "We came to know families from Chihuahua, Sonora, Jalisco, and Durango," stated Ernesto Galarza. "Like ourselves, our Mexican neighbors had come this far moving step by step, working and waiting, as if they were feeling their way up a ladder." Nevertheless, the Chicano experience has been unique, for most of them have lived close to their homeland—a proximity that has helped reinforce their language, identity, and culture. This migration to El Norte has continued to the present. Los Angeles has more people of Mexican origin than any other city in the world, except Mexico City. A mostly mestizo people of Indian as well as African and Spanish ancestries, Chicanos currently represent the largest minority group in the Southwest, where they have been visibly transforming culture and society.[14]

22   The Irish came here in greater numbers than most immigrant groups. Their history has been tied to America's past from the very beginning. Ireland represented the earliest English frontier: the conquest of Ireland occurred before the colonization of America, and the Irish were the first group that the English called "savages." In this context,

---

13. Interview with old laundryman, in "Interviews with Two Chinese," circa 1924, Box 326, folder 325, Survey of Race Relations, Stanford University, Hoover Institution Archives; Congressman Robert Matsui, speech in the House of Representatives on the 442 bill for redress and reparations, September 17, 1987, *Congressional Record* (Washington, D.C., 1987), p. 7584.

14. Camarillo, *Chicanos in a Changing Society*, p. 2; Juan Nepomuceno Seguín, in David J. Weber (ed.), *Foreigners in Their Native Land: Historical Roots of the Mexican Americans* (Albuquerque, N. Mex., 1973), p. vi; Jesus Garza, in Manuel Gamio, *The Mexican Immigrant: His Life Story* (Chicago, 1931), p. 15; Ernesto Galarza, *Barrio Boy: The Story of a Boy's Acculturation* (Notre Dame, Ind., 1986), p. 200.

the Irish past foreshadowed the Indian future. During the nineteenth century, the Irish, like the Chinese, were victims of British colonialism. While the Chinese fled from the ravages of the Opium Wars, the Irish were pushed from their homeland by "English tyranny." Here they became construction workers and factory operatives as well as the "maids" of America. Representing a Catholic group seeking to settle in a fiercely Protestant society, the Irish immigrants were targets of American nativist hostility. They were also what historian Lawrence J. McCaffrey called "the pioneers of the American urban ghetto," "previewing" experiences that would later be shared by the Italians, Poles, and other groups from southern and eastern Europe. Furthermore, they offer contrast to the immigrants from Asia. The Irish came about the same time as the Chinese, but they had a distinct advantage: the Naturalization Law of 1790 had reserved citizenship for "whites" only. Their compatible complexion allowed them to assimilate by blending into American society. In making their journey successfully into the mainstream, however, these immigrants from Erin pursued an Irish "ethnic" strategy: they promoted "Irish" solidarity in order to gain political power and also to dominate the skilled blue-collar occupations, often at the expense of the Chinese and blacks.[15]

23   Fleeing pogroms and religious persecution in Russia, the Jews were driven from what John Cuddihy described as the "Middle Ages into the Anglo-American world of the *goyim* 'beyond the pale.' " To them, America represented the Promised Land. This vision led Jews to struggle not only for themselves but also for other oppressed groups, especially blacks. After the 1917 East St. Louis race riot, the Yiddish *Forward* of New York compared this anti-black violence to a 1903 pogrom in Russia: "Kishinev and St. Louis—the same soil, the same people." Jews cheered when Jackie Robinson broke into the Brooklyn Dodgers in 1947. "He was adopted as the surrogate hero by many of us growing up at the time," recalled Jack Greenberg of the NAACP Legal Defense Fund. "He was the way we saw ourselves triumphing against the forces of bigotry and ignorance." Jews stood shoulder to shoulder with blacks in the Civil Rights Movement: two-thirds of the white volunteers who went south during the 1964 Freedom Summer were Jewish. Today Jews are considered a highly successful "ethnic" group. How did they make such great socioeconomic strides? This question is often reframed by neoconservative intellectuals like Irving Kristol and Nathan Glazer to read: if Jewish immigrants were able to lift themselves from poverty into the mainstream through self-help and education without welfare and affirmative action, why can't blacks? But what this thinking overlooks is the

15. Lawrence J. McCaffrey, *The Irish Diaspora in America* (Washington, D.C., 1984), pp. 6, 62.

unique history of Jewish immigrants, especially the initial advantages of many of them as literate and skilled. Moreover, it minimizes the virulence of racial prejudice rooted in American slavery.[16]

24   Indians represent a critical contrast, for theirs was not an immigrant experience. The Wampanoags were on the shore as the first English strangers arrived in what would be called "New England." The encounters between Indians and whites not only shaped the course of race relations, but also influenced the very culture and identity of the general society. The architect of Indian removal, President Andrew Jackson told Congress: "Our conduct toward these people is deeply interesting to the national character." Frederick Jackson Turner understood the meaning of this observation when he identified the frontier as our transforming crucible. At first, the European newcomers had to wear Indian moccasins and shout the war cry. "Little by little," as they subdued the wilderness, the pioneers became "a new product" that was "American." But Indians have had a different view of this entire process. "The white man," Luther Standing Bear of the Sioux explained, "does not understand the Indian for the reason that he does not understand America." Continuing to be "troubled with primitive fears," he has "in his consciousness the perils of this frontier continent. . . . The man from Europe is still a foreigner and an alien. And he still hates the man who questioned his path across the continent." Indians questioned what Jackson and Turner trumpeted as "progress." For them, the frontier had a different "significance": their history was how the West was lost. But their story has also been one of resistance. As Vine Deloria declared, "Custer died for your sins."[17]

25   By looking at these groups from a multicultural perspective, we can comparatively analyze their experiences in order to develop an understanding of their differences and similarities. Race, we will see, has been a social construction that has historically set apart racial minorities from European immigrant groups. Contrary to the notions of scholars like Nathan Glazer and Thomas Sowell, race in America has not been the

16. John Murray Cuddihy, *The Ordeal of Civility: Freud, Marx, Levi Strauss, and the Jewish Struggle with Modernity* (Boston, 1987), p. 165; Jonathan Kaufman, *Broken Alliance: The Turbulent Times between Blacks and Jews in America* (New York, 1989), pp. 28, 82, 83–84, 91, 93, 106.

17. Andrew Jackson, First Annual Message to Congress, December 8, 1829, in James D. Richardson (ed.), *A Compilation of the Messages and Papers of the Presidents, 1789–1897* (Washington, D.C., 1897), vol. 2, p. 457; Frederick Jackson Turner, "The Significance of the Frontier in American History," in *The Early Writings of Frederick Jackson Turner* (Madison, Wis., 1938), pp. 185ff.; Luther Standing Bear, "What the Indian Means to America," in Wayne Moquin (ed.), *Great Documents in American Indian History* (New York, 1973), p. 307; Vine Deloria, Jr., *Custer Died for Your Sins: An Indian Manifesto* (New York, 1969).

same as ethnicity. A broad comparative focus also allows us to see how the varied experiences of different racial and ethnic groups occurred within shared contexts.

26   During the nineteenth century, for example, the Market Revolution employed Irish immigrant laborers in New England factories as it expanded cotton fields worked by enslaved blacks across Indian lands toward Mexico. Like blacks, the Irish newcomers were stereotyped as "savages," ruled by passions rather than "civilized" virtues such as self-control and hard work. The Irish saw themselves as the "slaves" of British oppressors, and during a visit to Ireland in the 1840s, Frederick Douglass found that the "wailing notes" of the Irish ballads reminded him of the "wild notes" of slave songs. The United States annexation of California, while incorporating Mexicans, led to trade with Asia and the migration of "strangers" from Pacific shores. In 1870, Chinese immigrant laborers were transported to Massachusetts as scabs to break an Irish immigrant strike; in response, the Irish recognized the need for interethnic working-class solidarity and tried to organize a Chinese lodge of the Knights of St. Crispin. After the Civil War, Mississippi planters recruited Chinese immigrants to discipline the newly freed blacks. During the debate over an immigration exclusion bill in 1882, a senator asked: If Indians could be located on reservations, why not the Chinese?[18]

27   Other instances of our connectedness abound. In 1903, Mexican and Japanese farm laborers went on strike together in California: their union officers had names like Yamaguchi and Lizarras, and strike meetings were conducted in Japanese and Spanish. The Mexican strikers declared that they were standing in solidarity with their "Japanese brothers" because the two groups had toiled together in the fields and were now fighting together for a fair wage. Speaking in impassioned Yiddish during the 1909 "uprising of twenty thousand" strikers in New York, the charismatic Clara Lemlich compared the abuse of Jewish female garment workers to the experience of blacks: "[The bosses] yell at the girls and 'call them down' even worse than I imagine the Negro slaves were in the South." During the 1920s, elite universities like Harvard worried about the increasing numbers of Jewish students, and new admissions criteria were instituted to curb their enrollment. Jewish students were scorned for their studiousness and criticized for their "clannishness." Recently, Asian-American students have been the

18. Nathan Glazer, *Affirmative Discrimination: Ethnic Inequality and Public Policy* (New York, 1978); Thomas Sowell, *Ethnic America: A History* (New York, 1981); David R. Roediger, *The Wages of Whiteness: Race and the Making of the American Working Class* (London, 1991), pp. 134–136; Dan Caldwell, "The Negroization of the Chinese Stereotype in California," *Southern California Quarterly*, vol. 33 (June 1971), pp. 123–131.

targets of similar complaints: they have been called "nerds" and told there are "too many" of them on campus.[19]

28   Indians were already here, while blacks were forcibly transported to America, and Mexicans were initially enclosed by America's expanding border. The other groups came here as immigrants: for them, America represented liminality—a new world where they could pursue extravagant urges and do things they had thought beyond their capabilities. Like the land itself, they found themselves "betwixt and between all fixed points of classification." No longer fastened as fiercely to their old countries, they felt a stirring to become new people in a society still being defined and formed.[20]

29   These immigrants made bold and dangerous crossings, pushed by political events and economic hardships in their homelands and pulled by America's demand for labor as well as by their own dreams for a better life. "By all means let me go to America," a young man in Japan begged his parents. He had calculated that in one year as a laborer here he could save almost a thousand yen—an amount equal to the income of a governor in Japan. "My dear Father," wrote an immigrant Irish girl living in New York, "Any man or woman without a family are fools that would not venture and come to this plentyful Country where no man or woman ever hungered." In the shtetls of Russia, the cry "To America!" roared like "wild-fire." "America was in everybody's mouth," a Jewish immigrant recalled. "Businessmen talked [about] it over their accounts; the market women made up their quarrels that they might discuss it from stall to stall; people who had relatives in the famous land went around reading their letters." Similarly, for Mexican immigrants crossing the border in the early twentieth century, El Norte became the stuff of overblown hopes. "If only you could see how nice the United States is," they said, "that is why the Mexicans are crazy about it."[21]

30   The signs of America's ethnic diversity can be discerned across the continent—Ellis Island, Angel Island, Chinatown, Harlem, South

19. Tomas Almaguer, "Racial Domination and Class Conflict in Capitalist Agriculture: The Oxnard Sugar Beet Workers' Strike of 1903," *Labor History,* vol. 25, no. 3 (Summer 1984), p. 347; Howard M. Sachar, *A History of the Jews in America* (New York, 1992), p. 183.

20. For the concept of liminality, see Victor Turner, *Dramas, Fields, and Metaphors: Symbolic Action in Human Society* (Ithaca, N.Y., 1974), pp. 232, 237; and Arnold Van Gennep, *The Rites of Passage* (Chicago, 1960). What I try to do is to apply liminality to the land called America.

21. Kazuo Ito, *Issei: A History of Japanese Immigrants in North America* (Seattle, 1973), p. 33; Arnold Schrier, *Ireland and the American Emigration, 1850–1900* (New York, 1970), p. 24; Abraham Cahan, *The Rise of David Levinsky* (New York, 1960; originally published in 1917), pp. 59–61; Mary Antin, quoted in Howe, *World of Our Fathers,* p. 27; Lawrence A. Cardoso, *Mexican Emigration to the United States, 1897–1931* (Tucson, Ariz., 1981), p. 80.

Boston, the Lower East Side, places with Spanish names like Los Angeles and San Antonio or Indian names like Massachusetts and Iowa. Much of what is familiar in America's cultural landscape actually has ethnic origins. The Bing cherry was developed by an early Chinese immigrant named Ah Bing. American Indians were cultivating corn, tomatoes, and tobacco long before the arrival of Columbus. The term *okay* was derived from the Choctaw word *oke,* meaning "it is so." There is evidence indicating that the name *Yankee* came from Indian terms for the English—from *eankke* in Cherokee and *Yankwis* in Delaware. Jazz and blues as well as rock and roll have African-American origins. The "Forty-Niners" of the Gold Rush learned mining techniques from the Mexicans; American cowboys acquired herding skills from Mexican *vaqueros* and adopted their range terms—such as *lariat* from *la reata, lasso* from *lazo,* and *stampede* from *estampida.* Songs like "God Bless America," "Easter Parade," and "White Christmas" were written by a Russian-Jewish immigrant named Israel Baline, more popularly known as Irving Berlin.[22]

31   Furthermore, many diverse ethnic groups have contributed to the building of the American economy, forming what Walt Whitman saluted as "a vast, surging, hopeful army of workers." They worked in the South's cotton fields, New England's textile mills, Hawaii's canefields, New York's garment factories, California's orchards, Washington's salmon canneries, and Arizona's copper mines. They built the railroad, the great symbol of America's industrial triumph. Laying railroad ties, black laborers sang:

> *Down the railroad, um-huh*
> *Well, raise the iron, um-huh*
> *Raise the iron, um-huh.*

Irish railroad workers shouted as they stretched an iron ribbon across the continent:

> *Then drill, my Paddies, drill—*
> *Drill, my heroes, drill,*
> *Drill all day, no sugar in your tay*
> *Workin' on the U.P. railway.*

22. Ronald Takaki, *Strangers from a Different Shore: A History of Asian Americans* (Boston, 1989), pp. 88–89; Jack Weatherford, *Native Roots: How the Indians Enriched America* (New York, 1991), pp. 210, 212; Carey McWilliams, *North from Mexico: The Spanish-Speaking People of the United States* (New York, 1968), p. 154; Stephan Thernstrom (ed.), *Harvard Encyclopedia of American Ethnic Groups* (Cambridge, Mass., 1980), p. 22; Sachar, *A History of the Jews in America,* p. 367.

Japanese laborers in the Northwest chorused as their bodies fought the fickle weather:

> *A railroad worker—*
> *That's me!*
> *I am great.*
> *Yes, I am a railroad worker.*
> *Complaining:*
> *"It is too hot!"*
> *"It is too cold!"*
> *"It rains too often!"*
> *"It snows too much!"*
> *They all ran off.*
> *I alone remained.*
> *I am a railroad worker!*

Chicano workers in the Southwest joined in as they swore at the punishing work:

> *Some unloaded rails*
> *Others unloaded ties,*
> *And others of my companions*
> *Threw out thousands of curses.*[23]

32   Moreover, our diversity was tied to America's most serious crisis: the Civil War was fought over a racial issue—slavery. In his "First Inaugural Address," presented on March 4, 1861, President Abraham Lincoln declared: "One section of our country believes slavery is *right* and ought to be extended, while the other believes it is *wrong* and ought not to be extended." Southern secession, he argued, would be anarchy. Lincoln sternly warned the South that he had a solemn oath to defend and preserve the Union. Americans were one people, he explained, bound together by "the mystic chords of memory, stretching from every battlefield and patriot grave to every living heart and hearthstone all over this broad land." The struggle and sacrifices of the War for Independence had enabled Americans to create a new nation out of thirteen separate colonies. But Lincoln's appeal for unity fell on deaf ears in the South. And the war came. Two and a half years later, at Gettysburg, President Lincoln declared that "brave men" had fought and "consecrated" the

23. Walt Whitman, *Leaves of Grass* (New York, 1958), p. 284; Mathilde Bunton, "Negro Work Songs" (1940), 1 typescript in Box 91 ("Music"), Illinois Writers Project, U.S.W.P.A., in James R. Grossman, *Land of Hope: Chicago, Black Southerners, and the Great Migration* (Chicago, 1989), p. 192; Carl Wittke, *The Irish in America* (Baton Rouge, La., 1956), p. 39; Ito, *Issei*, p. 343; Manuel Gamio, *Mexican Immigration to the United States* (Chicago, 1930), pp. 84–85.

ground of this battlefield in order to preserve the Union. Among the brave were black men. Shortly after this bloody battle, Lincoln acknowledged the military contributions of blacks. "There will be some black men," he wrote in a letter to an old friend, James C. Conkling, "who can remember that with silent tongue, and clenched teeth, and steady eye, and well-poised bayonet, they have helped mankind on to this great consummation. . . ." Indeed, 186,000 blacks served in the Union Army, and one-third of them were listed as missing or dead. Black men in blue, Frederick Douglass pointed out, were "on the battlefield mingling their blood with that of white men in one common effort to save the country." Now the mystic chords of memory stretched across the new battlefields of the Civil War, and black soldiers were buried in "patriot graves." They, too, had given their lives to ensure that the "government of the people, by the people, for the people shall not perish from the earth."[24]

33   Like these black soldiers, the people in our study have been actors in history, not merely victims of discrimination and exploitation. They are entitled to be viewed as subjects—as men and women with minds, wills, and voices.

In the telling and retelling
of their stories,
They create communities
of memory.

They also re-vision history. "It is very natural that the history written by the victim," said a Mexican in 1874, "does not altogether chime with the story of the victor." Sometimes they are hesitant to speak, thinking they are only "little people." "I don't know why anybody wants to hear my history," an Irish maid said apologetically in 1900. "Nothing ever happened to me worth the tellin'."[25]

34   But their stories are worthy. Through their stories, the people who have lived America's history can help all of us, including my taxi driver, understand that Americans originated from many shores, and that all of us are entitled to dignity. "I hope this survey do a lot of good for Chinese people," an immigrant told an interviewer from Stanford University in the 1920s. "Make American people realize that Chinese people are

24. Abraham Lincoln, "First Inaugural Address," in *The Annals of America,* vol. 9, *1863–1865: The Crisis of the Union* (Chicago, 1968), p. 255; Lincoln, "The Gettysburg Address," pp. 462–463; Abraham Lincoln, letter to James C. Conkling, August 26, 1863, in *Annals of America,* p. 439; Frederick Douglass, in Herbert Aptheker (ed.), *A Documentary History of the Negro People in the United States* (New York, 1951), vol. 1, p. 496.

25. Weber (ed.), *Foreigners in Their Native Land,* p. vi; Hamilton Holt (ed.), *The Life Stories of Undistinguished Americans as Told by Themselves* (New York, 1906), p. 143.

humans. I think very few American people really know anything about Chinese." But the remembering is also for the sake of the children. "This story is dedicated to the descendants of Lazar and Goldie Glauberman," Jewish immigrant Minnie Miller wrote in her autobiography. "My history is bound up in their history and the generations that follow should know where they came from to know better who they are." Similarly, Tomo Shoji, an elderly Nisei woman, urged Asian Americans to learn more about their roots: "We got such good, fantastic stories to tell. All our stories are different." Seeking to know how they fit into America, many young people have become listeners; they are eager to learn about the hardships and humiliations experienced by their parents and grandparents. They want to hear their stories, unwilling to remain ignorant or ashamed of their identity and past.[26]

35   The telling of stories liberates. By writing about the people on Mango Street, Sandra Cisneros explained, "the ghost does not ache so much." The place no longer holds her with "both arms. She sets me free." Indeed, stories may not be as innocent or simple as they seem to be. Native-American novelist Leslie Marmon Silko cautioned:

I will tell you something about stories . . .
They aren't just entertainment.
Don't be fooled.

Indeed, the accounts given by the people in this study vibrantly recreate moments, capturing the complexities of human emotions and thoughts. They also provide the authenticity of experience. After she escaped from slavery, Harriet Jacobs wrote in her autobiography: "[My purpose] is not to tell you what I have heard but what I have seen—and what I have suffered." In their sharing of memory, the people in this study offer us an opportunity to see ourselves reflected in a mirror called history.[27]

36   In his recent study of Spain and the New World, *The Buried Mirror,* Carlos Fuentes points out that mirrors have been found in the tombs of ancient Mexico, placed there to guide the dead through the underworld. He also tells us about the legend of Quetzalcoatl, the Plumed Serpent: when this god was given a mirror by the Toltec deity Tezcatlipoca, he saw a man's face in the mirror and realized his own humanity. For us,

26. "Social Document of Pany Lowe, interviewed by C. H. Burnett, Seattle, July 5, 1924," p. 6, Survey of Race Relations, Stanford University, Hoover Institution Archives; Minnie Miller, "Autobiography," private manuscript, copy from Richard Balkin; Tomo Shoji, presentation, Ohana Cultural Center, Oakland, California, March 4, 1988.

27. Sandra Cisneros, *The House on Mango Street* (New York, 1991), pp. 109–110; Leslie Marmon Silko, *Ceremony* (New York, 1978), p. 2; Harriet A. Jacobs, *Incidents in the Life of a Slave Girl, written by herself* (Cambridge, Mass., 1987; originally published in 1857), p. xiii.

the "mirror" of history can guide the living and also help us recognize who we have been and hence are. In *A Distant Mirror,* Barbara W. Tuchman finds "phenomenal parallels" between the "calamitous 14th century" of European society and our own era. We can, she observes, have "greater fellow-feeling for a distraught age" as we painfully recognize the "similar disarray," "collapsing assumptions," and "unusual discomfort."[28]

37   But what is needed in our own perplexing times is not so much a "distant" mirror, as one that is "different." While the study of the past can provide collective self-knowledge, it often reflects the scholar's particular perspective or view of the world. What happens when historians leave out many of America's peoples? What happens, to borrow the words of Adrienne Rich, "when someone with the authority of a teacher" describes our society, and "you are not in it"? Such an experience can be disorienting—"a moment of psychic disequilibrium, as if you looked into a mirror and saw nothing."[29]

38   Through their narratives about their lives and circumstances, the people of America's diverse groups are able to see themselves and each other in our common past. They celebrate what Ishmael Reed has described as a society "unique" in the world because "the world is here"— a place "where the cultures of the world crisscross." Much of America's past, they point out, has been riddled with racism. At the same time, these people offer hope, affirming the struggle for equality as a central theme in our country's history. At its conception, our nation was dedicated to the proposition of equality. What has given concreteness to this powerful national principle has been our coming together in the creation of a new society. "Stuck here" together, workers of different backgrounds have attempted to get along with each other.

> *People harvesting*
> *Work together unaware*
> *Of racial problems,*

wrote a Japanese immigrant describing a lesson learned by Mexican and Asian farm laborers in California.[30]

39   Finally, how do we see our prospects for "working out" America's

28. Carlos Fuentes, *The Buried Mirror: Reflections on Spain and the New World* (Boston, 1992), pp. 10, 11, 109; Barbara W. Tuchman, *A Distant Mirror: The Calamitous 14th Century* (New York, 1978), pp. xiii, xiv.

29. Adrienne Rich, *Blood, Bread, and Poetry: Selected Prose, 1979–1985* (New York, 1986), pp. 199.

30. Ishmael Reed, "America: The Multinational Society," in Rick Simonson and Scott Walker (eds.), *Multi-cultural Literacy* (St. Paul, 1988), p. 160; Ito, *Issei,* p. 497.

racial crisis? Do we see it as through a glass darkly? Do the televised images of racial hatred and violence that riveted us in 1992 during the days of rage in Los Angeles frame a future of divisive race relations—what Arthur Schlesinger, Jr., has fearfully denounced as the "disuniting of America"? Or will Americans of diverse races and ethnicities be able to connect themselves to a larger narrative? Whatever happens, we can be certain that much of our society's future will be influenced by which "mirror" we choose to see ourselves. America does not belong to one race or one group, the people in this study remind us, and Americans have been constantly redefining their national identity from the moment of first contact on the Virginia shore. By sharing their stories, they invite us to see ourselves in a different mirror.[31]

WORD FOCUS

VOCABULARY GLOSS

at the cutting edge: *at the forefront of a movement or of knowledge (19)*

betwixt and between: *in the middle and on the edge of (28)*

beyond the pale: *indicating something that is unacceptable or unreasonable (23)*

blue-collar occupations: *manual labor (22)*

demographic: *relating to the study of human populations by size and composition (5)*

Desert Storm: *military term for the war waged by the United States and its allies against Iraq in 1991 (10)*

E pluribus unum: *(Latin) "out of many, one"—the motto of the United States (8)*

El Norte: *a term for North America (21)*

fell on deaf ears: *was not heard, most often intentionally (32)*

Forty-Niners of the Gold Rush: *people who took part in the search for gold in California in 1849 (30)*

Gold Mountain: *riches believed to exist in the United States (20)*

the good old Great Books approach: *teaching through the classics of the Western world that reflect Western culture (6)*

goyim: *(Yiddish) a non-Jewish person (23)*

---

31. Arthur M. Schlesinger, Jr., *The Disuniting of America: Reflections on a Multicultural Society* (Knoxville, Tenn., 1991); Carlos Bulosan, *America Is in the Heart: A Personal History* (Seattle, 1981), pp. 188–189.

the have-nots: *the poor people (9)*

in the wake of: *as a direct consequence of (2)*

indentured servants: *people bound by contract to work for another (19)*

interethnic working-class solidarity: *unity among workers that goes beyond racial differences (26)*

internment camps: *relocation camps for Americans of Japanese ancestry in the United States during World War II (20)*

manifest destiny: *a belief typical of many Americans in the nineteenth century that the expansion of the United States from coast to coast was a natural consequence of fate (21)*

marker events: *significant events that signal points of change (15)*

NAACP: *an acronym for the National Association for the Advancement of Colored People (23)*

Nisei: *a person born in America whose parents emigrated from Japan (34)*

neo-Nazism: *a new or recent form of racist nationalism (12)*

Opium Wars: *wars fought over the importation of opium into China by Western powers in the mid-nineteenth century (22)*

Paddies: *a derogatory term identifying Irish immigrants in the United States (31)*

Pilgrims: *English religious dissenters who founded the Plymouth Colony (2)*

pogroms: *institutional and societal attacks against Jews (23)*

the Promised Land: *a place that promises happiness; in the Bible, the land promised to Abraham and his children (23)*

psychic disequilibrium: *mental imbalance (37)*

shtetls: *(Yiddish) small Eastern European Jewish communities (29)*

southern drawl: *a term that describes patterns of speech in the southern United States (1)*

stood shoulder to shoulder: *were united with one another to take a stand (23)*

a system of bonded black labor: *American slavery (19)*

thirty-second sound bites: *very brief segments of speech edited from radio or television and typically replayed out of context (12)*

through a glass darkly: *a biblical phrase that means "unclear" or "blurred" (39)*

tower of Babel: *a biblical allusion referring to a confusion of languages (7)*

urban ghetto: *a poor economic area located in a city (22)*

vexatious balkanization: *the breaking up of something into small, hostile units (8)*

went up in smoke: *disappeared; failed (11)*
yen: *a unit of money in Japan (29)*

VOCABULARY QUESTIONS

1. What does Takaki mean by the statement "Indeed, stories may not be as innocent or simple as they seem to be" (35)? What does his choice of the word "indeed" contribute to the total meaning of this sentence?

2. Using words involves not only learning the meanings of words and phrases but also understanding how they can be used most effectively. Dictionaries refer to this as a word's **level of usage.** Three such usage labels are *formal/technical, informal/colloquial,* and *slang.*

   Consider the following list of terms that describe a person whose thoughts, feelings, and behavior are not considered normal in society: *crazy, mad, insane, looney, nuts, hysterical, psychotic, neurotic, mentally ill,* and *dysfunctional.*

Formal/Technical	*Informal/Colloquial*	*Slang*
_____	_____	_____
_____	_____	_____
_____	_____	_____
_____	_____	_____
_____	_____	_____

   a. Using a dictionary, group these terms according to the three categories.

   b. Look at the types of words used in a newspaper such as the *New York Times* or in a magazine such as *Newsweek,* and compare them to those used in tabloid newspapers or in magazines that focus on sensationalism or gossip. Group the words from your comparison according to the three categories, and discuss the audience for which these words are intended.

3. Adjectives add detail to a noun and enable a writer to insert important information into a sentence with a single word. Although adjectives may appear singly throughout a text, a reader understands them in a larger context as concepts that are repeated throughout the text, often as sets of synonyms or antonyms. These related adjectives help a writer expand a concept.

a. Using your text and a dictionary, find synonyms and antonyms for each of the following adjectives from Takaki's text:

Adjectives	Synonyms	Antonyms
indigenous (2)	_____	_____
ubiquitous (4)	_____	_____
homogeneous (7)	_____	_____
integral (21)	_____	_____
phenomenal (36)	_____	_____
calamitous (36)	_____	_____

b. You can also expand your discussion by thinking of nouns that these adjectives might go with. In the following example, the sentences pair the related adjectives *indigenous* and *foreign* with the noun *origins*.

Takaki claims that people's <u>origins</u> are irrelevant when deciding whether or not they are American. Few present residents, he notes, are <u>indigenous</u> to North America, but rather <u>foreign</u> in the sense that they or their ancestors came from some other part of the world.

Following the pattern in the example sentences above, which combine related adjectives with a noun, write a short discussion about Takaki's text. You may pair the sets of related adjectives with the nouns provided below, or you may create your own.

Nouns

result, effect

state, event

extent

relevance

origin

nature or texture

ENGLISH CRAFT

1. Takaki chooses a variety of verbs that indicate his understanding of others' statements or ideas. In place of using *say* or *said,* he chooses verbs that interpret certain aspects of the statements.

   Refer to the phrases below as they appear in the text, and discuss the meanings that each verb conveys. Look through other parts of Takaki's text, and discuss how the verbs he uses interpret the points of others.

- The way to correct this fragmentization, Hirsch **argues** (7)
- Native American novelist Leslie Marmon Silko **cautioned** (35)
- Bloom **claims** (6)
- the charismatic Clara Lemlich **compared** (27)
- Though he **concedes** (7)

2. Commas, important marks in writing, are frequently used to set off and separate elements in sentences. Commas can separate words, phrases, or clauses.

Words, Phrases, and Clauses in a List

Commas are used to separate coordinate words, phrases, and clauses in a list. Consider the following quotation from Takaki, which claims that "alarming signs and symptoms" seem to exist everywhere. Following the dash, he provides a specific list of some signs and symptoms, which are separated with commas.

The alarming signs and symptoms seem to be everywhere—the killing of Vincent Chin in Detroit, the black boycott of a Korean grocery store in Flatbush, the hysteria in Boston over the Carol Stuart murder, the battle between white sportsmen and Indians over tribal fishing rights in Wisconsin, the Jewish-black clashes in Brooklyn's Crown Heights, the black-Hispanic competition for jobs and educational resources in Dallas, which *Newsweek* described as a "conflict of the have-nots," and the Willie Horton campaign commercials, which widened the divide between the suburbs and the inner cities. (9)

Adjectives in a List

Commas are used to separate coordinate adjectives in a list. You can test whether elements are coordinate by asking if their order can be reversed and if the word *and* can be inserted between them. In the following sentence the adjectives democratic, technological, and industrialized describe America equally.

A democratic, technological, and industrialized country like America has to offer itself to all of its citizens and not just a few.

Write several sentences commenting on the text, using commas to separate words, phrases, and clauses.

3. In academic writing, paragraphs typically have a topic sentence claim that organizes the content of that paragraph. Although a topic sentence claim may come at the beginning, middle, or end of a paragraph, it most commonly appears at the beginning of paragraphs in academic writing. Even though there is no rule as to how long a paragraph should be, a paragraph written for an essay should be fully developed and contain

   - a topic sentence claim

   - explanations and analyses of the topic sentence claim

   - supporting details, such as quotations from another text, personal example, or definition

   In an essay, each paragraph may develop its own topic sentence claim that relates directly back to the thesis claim. In many cases, several paragraphs may be required to develop a broad topic sentence claim, which as a series relate back to the thesis claim. Whether each point that is made requires one or a series of paragraphs, all should support the thesis sentence claim.

   a. Read the following paragraph:

   These immigrants made bold and dangerous crossings, pushed by political events and economic hardships in their homelands and pulled by America's demand for labor as well as by their own dreams for a better life. "By all means let me go to America," a young man in Japan begged his parents. He had calculated that in one year as a laborer here he could save almost a thousand yen—an amount equal to the income of a governor in Japan. "My dear Father," wrote an immigrant Irish girl living in New York, "Any man or woman without a family are fools that would not venture and come to this plentyful Country where no man or woman ever hungered." In the shtetls of Russia, the cry "To America!" roared like "wild-fire." "America was in everybody's mouth," a Jewish immigrant recalled. "Businessmen talked [about] it over their accounts; the market women made up their quarrels that they might discuss it from stall to stall; people who had relatives in the famous land went around reading their letters." Similarly, for Mexican immigrants crossing the border in the early twentieth century, El Norte became the stuff of overblown hopes. "If only you could see how nice the United States is," they said, "that is why the Mexicans are crazy about it." (29)

    i. What is the topic sentence claim of the paragraph?

    ii. Where does it occur in the paragraph?

    iii. Identify specific words and phrases that set up the expectation of what will be discussed in the paragraph.

    iv. Discuss whether or not this expectation is fulfilled in the paragraph.

    v. How is the topic sentence claim supported?

  b. Look at paragraphs 17 through 24 of Takaki's text, paying particular attention to the topic sentence claims.

    i. Does each paragraph contain a topic sentence? Where does it appear in the paragraph?

    ii. How is each paragraph developed?

    iii. Is each paragraph separately developed, or do some paragraphs act in a series in order to develop a broad topic sentence claim?

INTERPRETIVE JOURNAL

1. Takaki comments: "Indians were already here, while blacks were forcibly transported to America, and Mexicans were initially enclosed by America's expanding border" (28). How does this statement relate to the commonly held view that America is a nation of immigrants?

2. Takaki makes the following observation: "Like these black soldiers, the people in our study have been actors in history, not merely victims of discrimination and exploitation" (33). What distinction is Takaki making by contrasting "actors in history" and "victims"?

3. Takaki remarks: "Much of what is familiar in America's cultural landscape actually has ethnic origins" (30). How might this statement help people understand the culture, food, and traditions of the United States?

4. Review the four excerpts from the railroad workers' songs (31). What observations about American labor can you make from these four excerpts?

ESSAY QUESTION

The title of Takaki's essay, as well as of the book from which this excerpt is taken, is "A Different Mirror." Write an essay in which you develop a position regarding Takaki's title and his assertion that America should look at itself in a different mirror. In your discussion, you will need to interpret the image of a different mirror and then relate that image to the evidence Takaki presents.

Dignity and Perspective
Sequence of Essay Assignments

READINGS

Black Elk, "The Butchering at Wounded Knee" and "The End of the Dream," excerpts from *Black Elk Speaks: Being the Life Story of a Holy Man of the Oglala Sioux*

Rigoberta Menchú, "The Family" and "Birth Ceremonies," excerpts from *I, Rigoberta Menchú,* trans. Ann Wright

Ronald Takaki, "A Different Mirror," excerpt from *A Different Mirror*

The following assignments form a sequence of interrelated topics. They become progressively more challenging as they ask you to interact with more texts. Assignment 1 asks you to write about a topic in Black Elk's text; Assignment 2 asks you to reconsider your first essay in light of Menchú's text; and Assignment 3 asks you to consider all three texts as you establish your point of view on the assigned topic.

These assignments can be written as a sequence or they can be written individually. However you approach these essays, each one you write should be supported with citations from the text and examples. Whenever possible, include your own experience and knowledge on the subject.

ASSIGNMENT 1

BLACK ELK

In Black Elk's account of the war between his people and the U.S. Cavalry, he reveals how important his community is and the role of each individual in it. Analyze specific incidents in the text that reveal Black Elk's attitude toward his people and his heritage.

ASSIGNMENT 2

MENCHÚ AND BLACK ELK

When Rigoberta Menchú speaks about her origins, she conveys a sense of dignity and pride in her family and ethnic group despite their history of exploitation. Analyze this sense of pride in both Menchú's and Black Elk's accounts.

ASSIGNMENT 3

TAKAKI, MENCHÚ, AND BLACK ELK

When Takaki uses the image of a mirror to build up his sense of American history, he emphasizes the need to reinterpret our understanding of what it means to be connected or alienated. What do the perspectives of Takaki, Menchú, and Black Elk tell you about their cultures? Use the image of the mirror to analyze these histories.

Chapter 5

Bias and Discovery

Bias and discovery are ideas that are not obviously connected in today's society. In current popular thinking, discoveries come from looking "objectively" at the world—in other words, eliminating subjectivity or personal bias from the process. However, some people suggest that in its most basic sense, bias is merely a lens through which all information about the world is filtered. In this view, interpreting the world around us in any way requires some kind of focusing that allows new discoveries to be made within that system.

ABOUT THE AUTHORS

Harry Mark Petrakis (b. 1923)

Novelist and short-story writer Harry Mark Petrakis was born in St. Louis, Missouri, and grew up in and around Chicago. The son of immigrant Greek parents, he has closely observed the conflicts and tensions of first- and second-generation immigrants in the United States. "The Judgment," from *Collected Stories* (1987), portrays the struggle to assimilate in a new country and the impact that previous experience has on the perspectives of individuals.

Elie Wiesel (b. 1928)

Novelist and 1986 Nobel Peace Prize laureate Elie Wiesel has devoted his life to educating others about the plight of Jews around the world and other humanitarian issues. He was born in Transylvania, was subjected to imprisonment at Auschwitz, was educated after the war in France, and eventually was naturalized as an American citizen. In "Fear," excerpted from *The Jews of Silence* (1956), Wiesel relates his attempts to understand the reasons for the fears and suspicions that he encountered in the Russian Jewish community.

Jeremy Campbell (b. 1931)

Jeremy Campbell's essay "Farewell the Open Mind" is a chapter in *The Improbable Machine* (1989), which addresses the subject of artificial intelligence. Campbell proposes that artificial intelligence is essentially doomed because it is patterned after a faulty theory— that the human mind is logical.

Harry Mark Petrakis
The Judgment

Preview

We often evaluate people on the basis of first impressions and later may feel differently about them. Discuss a time when your feelings about a person changed. Did that person do something to make that change occur, or did the change occur because of certain factors within yourself?

Word Preview

You can familiarize yourself with the following words by looking them up in the dictionary. You can broaden your knowledge of these words by pronouncing them and understanding how they are used in context.

stocky (1)	dire (11)	defiled (27)
robust (1)	dowry (11)	jubilant (29)
rudiments (2)	shabby (13)	ardor (41)
incurred (3)	monotonous (13)	epidemic (46)
somber (6)	nostalgia (13)	ministrations (46)
menial (6)	maudlin (18)	console (47)
ridiculed (6)	soddenly (18)	retribution (48)
surly (6)	salvaged (19)	resignation (55)
indignantly (7)	surfeited (20)	anesthetize (56)

facet (64)	futility (73)	conserve (86)
vehemence (67)	reminiscent (73)	irrevocable (91)
vigilant (68)	insensate (74)	stoically (93)
ominous (68)	mocked (79)	vengeful (96)

1   Elias Karnezos entered the United States as an immigrant from Greece in 1919. He was twenty-six years old, the son of a farmer from a village near Tripolis, in the Peloponnese. He was short, stocky, with robust arms and shoulders, strong hands, and thick black hair. His good health and ebullient spirits made him confident he would achieve success and make a fortune in the new land.

2   A friend who had emigrated from the same village a few years earlier, working as a bellboy in a Chicago hotel, obtained a job for Elias as a shine boy in a neighborhood shoe-repair shop. Elias shined shoes zestfully while singing songs of his village. The old shoemaker liked him and began teaching him the rudiments of his craft.

3   When conventions were quartered in the hotel where his friend worked, Elias joined him as a bellboy. From his paycheck and tips, he sent money home to his parents and to repay the debt he had incurred for his passage to America. Whatever remained after deducting for rent and food, he spent in roistering with a group of young sports. They gambled, danced, drank, and visited whores with jocular enthusiasm. Some of the first words Elias learned in English remained his favorite ones: "Sonofabitch!" "Goddam!" "Jesus Christ!" He never used these words in anger but simply as explosive and fervent expressions of his excitement and delight.

4   When the old shoemaker died, the owner of the store gave Elias the job with a substantial raise. Elias bought several new suits and a wide-brimmed Borsalino like those worn by gangsters of that period. He gained a reputation as a dandy and a generous man with friendship and money.

5   Among the cronies with whom he gambled were two brothers named Varvari from a village not far from his own in Greece. Playing poker in their apartment, he saw Katina, a younger sister the brothers had brought a few months earlier from Greece.

6   The girl was sixteen, tiny and slim-boned, with a somber face. She had never attended school and could not read or write. At the pleading of their parents the brothers had reluctantly brought her to America to have her educated and married. But they found it simpler to utilize her as a menial. She scrubbed, cleaned, washed, and cooked for them and their friends without complaint. She was shuttered by shyness and paralyzed by ignorance and terror. Her brothers ridiculed her constantly,

mocking her ignorance by tossing newspapers and magazines at her and demanding she read them aloud. When they grew surly because they were losing in the games, they pinched her and threatened her with beatings.

7   "Why don't you leave the poor girl alone?" Elias cried indignantly.

8   "Sticking up for her is a waste of time," one of her brothers sneered. "She's dumb as a sheep and hasn't as much meat on her skinny frame as a starving chicken."

9   Katina knew Elias was defending her and fled with flushed cheeks back to the sanctuary of the kitchen.

10   In the following weeks, on visits to the apartment, Elias found excuses to enter the kitchen. It took him a while to overcome Katina's shyness and fear. One night he brought her a small box of sweet chocolates and saw her laugh with pleasure for the first time. He noticed then with surprise that she was a pretty girl, her hair black and lustrous, her features delicate, her eyes bright and alert. And she was so tiny that, despite his own short stature, he felt huge and tall beside her.

11   Her brothers thought him crazy and wavered between encouraging his interest to get Katina off their hands and avoiding the dire prospect of losing their indentured servant. The fact that Elias did not seem concerned about the traditional old-country dowry decided the brothers to accept his proposal of marriage to their sister.

12   Elias and Katina were married in a small church ceremony. He wore a rented tuxedo too small for his brawny shoulders and she wore a cheap white gown grudgingly paid for by her brothers. On the first night of their weekend honeymoon in the hotel where he worked as a bellboy, Elias took his bride's virginity with gentleness and patience. Despite her fear and shock at the sight of her blood, he was surprised at the fierce passion in her small, slim body.

· · · · · · · ·

13 They lived in a shabby, two-room apartment overlooking an alley a block from the shoe-repair shop. For the first few months after their marriage he came home after work every night to the dinner Katina prepared. But he found her meekness and silence oppressive, and in the monotonous hours of the evening he ached with nostalgia for the revelries of the nights before his marriage. He began meeting his cronies again, explaining to Katina there were shoes to be repaired after hours in the shop. When she did not question his excuses, he discarded even that flimsy pretense, slipping easily back into his routine of drinking, gambling, and visiting the jovial, bountiful whores who laughed and shrieked in his arms.

14   When he arrived home late at night, stinking of wine and the

colognes and powders of other women, he climbed heavily into bed beside Katina. He heard her fitful breathing.

15   "Katina?"

16   She did not answer.

17   "Katina, I know you're awake."

18   She did not move. He reached under the covers and groped clumsily with his fingers for her naked body under the cotton nightgown, a maudlin gesture of remorse and affection. She twisted violently away from him, and untroubled within his drunken euphoria, he fell soddenly asleep, unaware of the tears of shame and fury Katina cried into her pillow as he snored.

19   Katina's life resumed the pattern of her labor in the service of her brothers. She scrubbed, washed, and cooked for Elias and the friends he brought home. In addition, she received him into her body for the occasional spurtings of passion he salvaged from his whores.

20   Elias could not understand that Katina's inability to read and write locked her into a dark obsession with her own grievances. Although she had feared the cruelty of her brothers, their brutalities seemed trivial to those she now endured. She felt betrayed, her rage at Elias compounded of her own unsatisfied passion and the way he selfishly surfeited his needs. She began resisting his caresses, subduing her desire in a corset of tightly laced hate.

21   "What the hell's the matter with you?" he would say in aggravation. "You're stiff as a carrot! What's wrong with you?"

22   "Leave me alone!"

23   "What the hell is wrong?" he cried.

24   "Ask your whores!" she said hoarsely.

25   Stung by the justice of her condemnation, he would turn away from her in the bed.

26   "Goddam women!" he would mumble under his breath. "None of them understand a man needs a little fun. . . ."

27   At other times, however, when drinking dulled his guilt, he forced himself upon her. They warred with their bodies, his strength pitted against her spirit. Though she was determined to deny herself any pleasure, there were moments Katina's body betrayed her will and she cried out with a wild, unwilling joy. Afterward she bathed and scrubbed her breasts and thighs as if they had been defiled.

· · · · · · · ·

28   In the second year of their marriage Katina became pregnant. She accepted the doctor's diagnosis with resentment and distress. But as the baby grew within her body, she felt herself softening, curling warm and alive, the world less grim and forbidding.

29   Elias was jubilant. He sang loudly as he pounded on the last, cut down his drinking, reduced his gambling, and subdued his whoring except for a few infrequent lapses when desire drove him wild. On those occasions he did not linger after he was relieved but would hurry to dress.

30   "Where you going so fast, honey?" a whore named Anneta, who was fond of him, asked.

31   "I'm going to have a son," Elias said, as if that anticipated event explained everything.

32   In the evenings after work he went home to Katina eagerly. He treated her with an awkward, uncommon gentleness as he watched her tiny belly rise and swell. At night in bed when he felt her stirring restlessly to find a comfortable position, he spoke to her softly.

33   "Are you all right?"

34   "I am all right," she answered quietly.

35   "Do you have any pain?"

36   "I have no pain," she said.

37   "Can I get you anything? A glass of water or some tea?"

38   "I am all right!" she said impatiently. "Go to sleep!"

39   In the silence that followed he slid his body carefully closer to her, gently touching her bare foot with his own toes. He was overwhelmed with gratefulness when she did not pull away.

· · · · · · · ·

40   The baby was born in the spring of that year, a dark-haired, brown-eyed boy they named Peter. When he beheld the infant in Katina's arms for the first time, Elias cried with pride and joy. In that sacred moment he swore he would never touch a whore again.

41   Their lives mended in the delight of their son. After each day's work Elias rushed home to play with the baby. Katina scolded him for his ardor but enjoyed the baby herself, her days filled with the wonder of his beauty and his growth.

42   The following year, Katina gave birth to a baby girl. Almost a year to the day after that birth, in the same month that Elias purchased the shoe-repair shop for his own business, Katina gave birth to a second daughter, their third child. For all three children she was a devoted and capable mother, unhindered by her inability to read and write.

43   Contented in his home and family, Elias worked vigorously, and his business prospered. He bought a second shoe-repair shop and then a large dry-cleaning business. He had more than thirty employees working for him, joined a fraternal lodge and a businessmen's association, bought a new car, the first he had ever owned, and learned, not without some minor mishaps, to drive it.

44   For a while Katina firmly refused to allow the children or herself to

ride with Elias, but when her apprehension lessened, she looked forward to their drives into the country on Sunday afternoons. Another favorite pastime was when they invited a score of friends to the park on summer weekends. Elias would buy a whole lamb and roast it over a charcoal fire and a spit, drinking and dancing and singing until it was time to eat.

45   And every Sunday morning they dressed the children and themselves in their best clothing and went to the Greek church. Standing stiffly beside Katina as they held the children in their arms, Elias felt his family blessed and sanctioned by God.

· · · · · · · ·

46   When Peter was three years old, the girls about one and two, an epidemic of influenza struck the city. All three children became ill, but only their son suffered complications. In the space of two nights, despite the frantic ministrations of a doctor and a nurse, the boy died.

47   In the anguish that followed their son's death Elias sought to comfort Katina, feeling a mother's loss even a greater calamity than his own. Yet he could not console himself. During the day he would suddenly burst into tears. Every small boy he passed on the street cut like a knife into his heart.

48   Katina, tearing at her hair in grief, came to feel the boy's death was a punishment for her acquittal and acceptance of the corruptions and debaucheries of Elias. By forgiving her husband's lechery, she had had delivered upon her a terrible retribution. She swore she would live the remainder of her life seeking to protect her daughters and herself, convinced that, in the end, God would exact damnation on Elias. Katina made her decision to mourn and remember, and to suppress every small pleasure and joy.

49   "What can I do?" Elias cried. "Sit in a dark room, day and night, remembering the boy?"

50   "Say your prayers and go to church!" Katina cried. "Light candles! Ask God's forgiveness!"

51   "Candles won't bring me back my son," Elias said bitterly.

52   "He is with God now."

53   "He doesn't belong to God!" Elias said. "He belongs to me!"

54   "Wait!" Katina cried. "Wait! God will answer your blasphemy!"

55   "I'm not saying nothing against God," Elias said. A resignation and despair swept his spirit. "I'm only saying that goddam candles won't bring me back my son."

56   In a frantic effort to anesthetize his sorrow, he invited friends to dinner several evenings a week. He spent money lavishly on wine, lamb, olives, and cheese. He sat at the head of the table, shouting for his guests to eat and drink. His arduous efforts at gaiety faltered before the somber

presence of Katina. Sometimes she spoke a few words to one of the guests, but mostly she remained silent and unsmiling, casting her mournful shadow over the gathering. The uncomfortable guests would leave soon after dinner.

57   Sometimes at night, their daughters asleep, Elias and Katina in bed in their darkened room, he'd make an effort to embrace his wife. She pulled away as if the touch of his body had burned her.

58   "Let me love you a little," he pleaded. "It will be good for both of us."

59   "Never again," Katina said, her voice cold and relentless. "Never again for as long as we live. That is what God has decreed."

60   "How do you know that?" he cried in a low, hoarse whisper. "Why should he want that from us?" When she did not answer he turned away from her, trying to separate and calm the waves of fear and desire that swept his body. He remembered the oath he had taken, after the birth of his son, never to touch a whore again. He saw the balance of his life, cold and unloved.

61   "Sonofabitch," he murmured softly. "Sonofabitch."

62   Upon his small daughters Elias lavished all the generosity and affection his wife rejected. Despite her disapproval, he bought them frilly expensive dresses and small ermine coats. He spoiled them rampantly, loved to have them come running into his arms when he entered the door in the evening, their fingers eagerly searching his pockets for the gifts he always carried.

63   In contrast to his indulgences, Katina taught the girls the crafts of cooking and sewing, sternly pushing them to their books and studies, although she had no comprehension of the things they were studying.

64   When Elias sought to help the girls with some facet of their schoolwork, she turned on him resentfully.

65   "You think that's the way it really is?" she said scornfully. "You think because you can read, you know what's going on? You know nothing about life and the way people really are! You are a fool!"

66   To reinforce her argument she drew upon all the flotsam that floated unmoored in her head. Ignorant of the barest fundamentals of the knowledge in books, she lived in a teeming cupboard of superstition, myth, village theology, memories, fears, rumors, and the gossip of neighbors.

67   If Elias tried to argue with her, she'd burst into a rage. The girls would flee to their room and Elias would shield himself behind a newspaper, trying vainly to understand the reason for her vehemence and fury.

• • • • • • • •

68   The years passed. The girls grew into dark-haired, dark-eyed young beauties. Katina was a vigilant tyrant, refusing to allow them to attend

dances at school or parties in the homes of friends. The only organization she permitted them to join was the choir of the Greek church. On
the holidays, she allowed them to invite a few friends into their home,
but she subjected every boy who entered to so baleful a scrutiny, he
fled, vowing never to return. When her daughters complained, Katina
silenced them with angry, ominous warnings.

69   "All men are animals!" she cried. "Seeking to destroy girls, turn
them into sluts! That won't happen to you while I'm alive!"

· · · · · · · ·

70 In the year their eldest daughter graduated from high school, Elias
suffered a disastrous fire that totally destroyed his dry-cleaning shop
full of the clothing of his customers. His insurance covered only a frac-
tion of their losses, yet he felt his honor required he pay the full
amounts. When he had fulfilled this obligation, he was almost penni-
less, left with a single small shoe-repair shop, a shoemaker, a shine
boy, and himself.

71   These reversals reinforced Katina's conviction that Elias was a shallow and indulgent man who accidentally managed some success that, in
the end, his stupidity caused him to destroy. He, in turn, began to believe she was right in calling him a blockhead and a fool.

· · · · · · · ·

72 Within a year after their graduations, both daughters left home to be
married. For the first time in twenty-five years, Elias and Katina were
alone.

73   Elias aged quickly. Although he was only in his middle fifties, his
thick black hair was mottled with strands of white. Futility cut deeper
creases into the flesh of his cheeks and darkened the hollow circles
about his eyes. He sought desperately to salvage his shattered business
under a persistent burden of failure and defeat. He let the shoemaker go
and returned to the last himself. But the years had dulled his fingers,
and his poor workmanship was the final blow that caused him to close
his business. They moved to a smaller apartment, grimly reminiscent of
the dark rooms they had lived in during the first years of their marriage.
Elias managed to pay the rent and buy food on a small insurance annu-
ity he had taken out years before.

74   He looked for work but there was nothing for a man of his years
without any special skill. He retreated to spending his hours before the
television set, waiting for the visits of his daughters and the small grandchildren that had been born in the past few years. When they came to
see him, he hugged them playfully, tickling and kissing them with delight. Katina shrieked that he would hurt them, confuse them with his

insensate shouts. He'd make an effort to ignore her but, finally, pained and subdued, he'd let the children alone.

75   When they sat at the table, he slipped into the bountiful role he had always loved, urging food upon the children, wine upon his sons-in-law. Everything he did incurred Katina's displeasure.

76   "Shut up, old man!" she cried. "You think everybody guzzles and eats like you do! Not a dollar in your pocket and you still eat and drink like a pig!"

77   "Goddam, leave me alone," he'd say weakly and shake his head in resignation.

78   When he began to recite a story, some episode out of his past, his eyes would glitter and he'd laugh gaily. At some point in his excited recounting, Katina entered like a chorus.

79   "He was your good friend, that one, wasn't he? As long as you had money in your pocket and wine and food on your table. Where is he now?" She mocked him. "Where are all your other friends? Now that you have nothing but the pants you wear each day and the pants you wear on Sunday, where are all your friends? Answer me that, old fool!"

80   In order to evade Katina's nagging, he began leaving the house each morning, gathering with a few other old men in a coffee shop a couple of blocks away. They passed the hours telling stories of their youth.

81   Through the owner of the coffee shop, Elias heard of an old Italian shoemaker in the neighborhood who wanted to sell his small shop and return to Italy to die. Elias visited the shabby, narrow store, the fixtures decrepit, the machinery ancient. But the old shoemaker was willing to sell out for five hundred dollars, and the rent was only fifty dollars a month.

82   Elias borrowed two hundred and fifty dollars from his elder daughter's husband as a down payment on the purchase price and promised to pay the shoemaker the balance within six months.

83   When Katina learned of what he had done, she shrieked at him in fury and denounced her daughters for aiding him in his folly.

84   "Just wait a few months and I'll show you!" he cried. "I'll be on my feet again in no time! Jesus Christ, watch if I don't show you!"

85   Once more he rose with renewed hope at dawn and walked briskly to his shop, feeling a delight in turning on the lights, putting on his apron, starting the machinery. Yet, despite working from dawn until seven or eight o'clock in the evening, he barely made enough money to pay his rent. Rather than confront Katina's scorn, he borrowed a few dollars from one of his daughters and gave it to his wife at the end of the week as if it were a profit.

86   In the winter of that year, the wind and snow sweeping through the desolate streets, he sat huddled for warmth beside the small coal-burning

stove, wearing his coat to conserve on fuel, staring through the window, vainly waiting for a customer to appear. Sometimes a whole day passed without a single person entering the store. The few pairs of shoes he repaired stood forlorn on the counter. At the end of the day he locked and shuttered his shop and despondently walked the few blocks home to the dinner Katina had prepared for him.

87   A new distress rose to plague him. His vision began to blur and the few customers who brought him work complained about the poor quality of the repair. Apprehensive of complaining to Katina, he kept the knowledge of his failing sight to himself for months. Only when he finally slashed his fingers on the shoe machines did he ask one of his daughters to take him to the doctor. An examination disclosed he had ripened cataracts in both eyes.

88   He entered the hospital for surgery, a dreadful period of darkness, sustained only by the faith that he would be able to see again. When the bandages were finally removed, his vision remained clouded by the failure of his eyes to heal properly. He sat for hours before the television set, watching the screen for that instant when the blurred faces and figures would once more come into focus. Instead of improving, his sight grew slowly worse. Each time one of his daughters took him back to the doctor for re-examination, he pleaded for help.

89   "Goddam, Doctor!" he cried. "Maybe something, some new medicine can make me see better. I can't work or read a paper! A man can't live like this!"

90   He could not accept the doctor's explanation that there had been incurable damage to the retina of his eyes, that although he might not become totally blind, his sight would slowly diminish and he would have to exist in a world of shadows.

91   With that irrevocable diagnosis, Katina ceased to nag him, fed him patiently, tended his needs without complaint. He was so grateful for her kindness, he was often moved to tears.

92   "I'll get better, Ma," he promised her fervently, holding tightly to her hand. "They'll find some medicine, some new treatment. You'll see, I'll find another store, get a new start, look after us both once more."

93   He marveled how calmly and stoically she accepted his plight. He praised her constancy and devotion to his daughters.

94   "Jesus Christ, that woman has become an angel," he said. "The way she takes care of me every minute. That's what she is, an angel."

95   But as the weeks passed and his hope faltered, his anguish grew and the bonds holding him to life weakened. There was a night he woke with a strange heat burning through his body. He started to call to Katina, who slept in the bedroom across the hall, then slipped again into a fitful sleep. In his fevered dreams he saw the faces of his father and

mother, the fields and groves about his village, the ship on which he journeyed to America. He saw the cronies of his early revels, the glittering bodies of whores, the laughing, carefree black men who worked for him, the mountain of shoes he had mended. He saw the countless wine casks he had emptied, the lambs roasting on the spit, the dancing friends who had shared his joy. He saw the cherub's cheeks of his son, the flowered mound of his grave, the eyes of his grandchildren glowing in the light of candles on the holiday tables. Above them all he saw the figure of Katina.

96   He could not be certain whether she was part of his dream or whether he had wakened to find her standing over him, grown to a vast and stunning height, huge and broad as he had once felt when she was small and slim. But he suddenly recognized her as a vengeful, merciless, and satisfied witness to his fate.

97   In the great flood of water rising to engulf his body, a torrent rushing to clear his eyes, he uttered a single perplexed and bewildered cry, the last sound he made before he died.

WORD FOCUS

VOCABULARY GLOSS

accepted his plight: *lived with his unpleasant situation (93)*
baleful: *menacing (68)*
blasphemy: *irreverent words or acts toward a deity (54)*
Borsalino: *a type of hat (4)*
corset: *a stiff undergarment that shapes a woman's body (20)*
cronies: *buddies; close friends (5)*
cupboard: *a cabinet for storing kitchen utensils or food (66)*
dandy: *a man who is overly concerned with being fashionably dressed (4)*
debaucheries: *wild behavior usually associated with sex and alcohol (48)*
ebullient: *bubbling and enthusiastic (1)*
flotsam: *floating wreckage (66)*
a fraternal lodge: *a club for men only (43)*
guzzles: *drinks quickly and greedily, often to excess (76)*
indentured servant: *a person bound by contract to work for another for a given period of time (11)*
jocular: *jovial; joking (3)*
last: *a form shaped like a foot used by shoemakers (29)*

Peloponnese: *the southern peninsula of Greece (1)*
revelries: *loud parties or celebrations (13)*
roistering: *celebrating in a loud, noisy way (3)*
a shine boy: *a boy who polishes shoes (2)*
sticking up for her: *taking her side; defending her (8)*
whores: *prostitutes; sexually promiscuous women (3)*
young sports: *young people who are enjoying life (3)*

VOCABULARY QUESTIONS

1. In describing Katina, Petrakis points out that she lived "in a teeming cupboard of superstition, myth, village theology, memories, fears, rumors, and the gossip of neighbors" (66). Each of these terms contributes to an overall picture of Katina from different perspectives. Using your dictionary, define each of the terms. Then explain the image of these terms as a "teeming cupboard." What picture of Katina do you get from this image?

2. Adjectives that are placed before a noun highlight certain aspects of that noun. That is, they can give additional information about the noun; for example, features such as size, shape, quality, character, and location. Consider the following phrases that Petrakis uses, and discuss what specific information each of these adjectives brings to the noun:

   - dire prospect (11)
   - maudlin gesture (18)
   - monotonous hours (13)
   - robust arms (1)
   - somber face (6)
   - vengeful, merciless, and satisfied witness (96)

   Write a brief paragraph about one of the characters or incidents in the text, using this pattern of an adjective modifying a noun.

ENGLISH CRAFT

1. Most essays written in college are to some degree based on the writings of other authors; this requires that students understand how to incorporate others' works into their own writing. Effective use of quotations involves both presentation and interpretation. When they are three lines

in length or less, quotations must be grammatically incorporated into the sentence structure of an essay. Then the process must be taken a step further through interpretation.

Look at the following example. The writer makes a topic sentence claim about the story "The Judgment," supports that claim with a quotation—which is incorporated into the sentence both grammatically and logically—and then interprets the quotation:

Throughout their married life, Katina became more and more unhappy with her marriage. Although her husband Elias was often unfaithful, used bad language, and spent too much money, these were not the primary reasons that her hatred grew. Her disgust for her husband had little to do with him and his actions. Her hatred was fed daily by the dark cupboard of her mind that was filled with "superstition, myth, village theology, memories, fears, rumors, and the gossip of neighbors" (197).* Katina was an uneducated woman, an unhappy woman who could not understand happiness. Instead, she learned to feel a sense of satisfaction through half truths and lies.

Write a paragraph using the following quotation: " 'He doesn't belong to God!' Elias said. 'He belongs to me!' " (53). Be sure to incorporate it into a sentence both grammatically and logically, and interpret it in relation to the topic sentence claim.

2. One of the ways that writers can organize information within a paragraph is through *parallelism*. Parallel constructions use the same grammatical structures to bring together various pieces of information in one sentence. Many different sentence parts can be joined by parallelism: individual words, phrases, and clauses.

Petrakis uses parallelism extensively throughout this story. Look at the underlined parallel structures in the following sentences:

She <u>scrubbed</u>, <u>cleaned</u>, <u>washed</u>, and <u>cooked</u> for them and their friends without complaint. (6)

She was <u>shuttered by shyness</u> and <u>paralyzed by ignorance and terror</u>. (6)

He sang loudly as he <u>pounded on the last</u>, <u>cut down his drinking</u>, <u>reduced his gambling</u>, and <u>subdued his whoring</u> except for a few infrequent lapses when desire drove him wild. (29)

Find three other parallel structures in the text. Then use parallel constructions of your own to make observations about characters or incidents in the text.

*Editor's note: Writers use page number references in academic writing.

INTERPRETIVE JOURNAL

1. A story can present issues that people confront on a daily basis. What immigration issues does Elias Karnezos face during his early years of living and working in the United States? How relevant are these issues today?

2. Compare and contrast Katina's life before and after her marriage to Elias.

3. After their son's death, "Elias sought to comfort Katina, feeling a mother's loss even a greater calamity than his own" (47). Discuss how Katina reacts to her husband's pain and sympathy.

4. Discuss what Katina and Elias do to hurt each other, and show where each lacks understanding of the other person.

ESSAY QUESTION

Consider the title of this story, "The Judgment." What role does judgment play in the story in terms of the two central characters, Elias and Katina? Identify and analyze all the different types of judgments being made throughout the story. How would you evaluate the characters' actions?

Elie Wiesel
Fear

Preview

Fear is an emotion everyone experiences at some time or other for a variety of reasons. Describe in detail at least two times when you felt afraid. Specify whether your fear was of people, incidents, or something less tangible.

Word Preview

You can familiarize yourself with the following words by looking them up in the dictionary. You can broaden your knowledge of these words by pronouncing them and understanding how they are used in context.

phenomenon (1)	proscribed (8)	analogies (16)
diplomatic (1)	rehabilitation (8)	persecution (16)
enigma (1)	ascertain (9)	malicious (17)
impenetrable (2)	futile (9)	misinformed (19)
interstices (2)	badgered (9)	embellishing (19)
lurked (2)	imminence (9)	paranoia (19)
irrational (4)	entreaties (9)	infamous (21)
justification (4)	intricacies (10)	sanctuary (22)
rationalization (4)	render (11)	edicts (22)
unravel (4)	repellent (12)	comrade (22)
dislodge (4)	immersed (12)	banished (23)
maniacal (5)	slandering (12)	afflicted (23)
fictitious (5)	derision (13)	choir (24)
propaganda (5)	oppressed (15)	pulpit (24)
populace (5)	sanctify (15)	intoned (24)
alleviated (5)	erupt (16)	congregation (24)
infectious (6)	communal (16)	witless (27)
abyss (8)	hysteria (16)	receded (29)
liquidated (8)	succumbed (16)	

1   What are they afraid of? I don't know. Perhaps, afraid to ask, neither do they. I wasn't afraid to ask, but I never got an answer. Official government guides abruptly denied the existence of any such phenomenon, and the Western diplomatic observers whom I consulted simply said that the whole matter was an enigma to them. As for Jews, they smiled at me sadly. "You're an outsider. You wouldn't understand."

2   I cannot say, then, whether their fear is justified, but I know for a fact that it exists, and that its depths are greater than I had imagined possible. In city after city it confronted me like an impenetrable wall; on the other side, peering out of its own interstices, lurked only the final unknown.

3   Time after time, people with whom I had been talking slipped away without saying good-by or left me in the middle of a sentence. A person who had conversed with me one day denied knowing me the next. Once a technician who had arranged to meet me in the synagogue to give me particulars concerning a brother in Philadelphia never came. In Moscow I met a French Jew who told me he had come to Russia to visit a sister he had not seen since the war. When he arrived at her house in Lvov she refused to let him in. Later she appeared at his hotel and, in the five minutes she allowed herself to stay, begged him to leave the city, to go back to Moscow, or better, to France. "What did I do?" he cried. And I, to calm him, said, "Nothing. Try to understand, can't you? She's afraid." He began to shout. "Of whom? Of what?" I had no answer.

4   Perhaps there is none. Perhaps, in the absence of all objective correlatives, their dark and irrational fear exists simply as a thing in itself, without reason or purpose, serving no useful function, incapable of a reasoned justification. It exists because it exists, and it is therefore impossible to fight. No argument, no amount of careful rationalization can hope to unravel the nature of this fear, let alone dislodge its presence.

5   So far as anyone can tell, the years of terror are over. Stalin's maniacal hold on the country is a chapter in past history. During the last ten years something has *happened* in Russia; changes have taken place which cannot be lightly dismissed as the fictitious products of an efficient propaganda machine. The general populace is beginning to enjoy the benefits of society. Tensions have been noticeably alleviated. If you stop a man in the street, he will not hesitate to talk with you. The person in the airplane seat next to yours will join you in conversation, perhaps even tell jokes. From time to time you may meet an English-speaking citizen who will admit that the worker's homeland has yet to become a paradise on earth. Young people twisting in Russian night clubs would put San Franciscans to shame.

6   It is only the Jews then who live in permanent fear, in this infectious mystery. "Yes," one occasionally acknowledges, "times have changed, and for the better." But no explanation follows that remark.

7   "You wouldn't understand anyway."

8   It is true; I do not understand. Why are they so suspicious? Why do they behave like a community of terrorized captives, on the brink of some awful abyss? No one denies that the Jews have benefited from the recent easing of tension. Writers who had been liquidated or proscribed are now undergoing rehabilitation. Tens of thousands of Jews convicted of "Jewish nationalism" and sentenced to prison have been released. It is no longer dangerous to be known as a Yiddish writer; now and again one hears of whole evenings devoted to Yiddish songs and public readings of Yiddish works. A Yiddish magazine—never mind the quality of the writing—appears regularly each month. The legendary figure of Solomon Mikhoels[1] has been revived, and today even Ilya Ehrenburg[2] takes public pride in the fact that certain Jewish writers were among his closest friends.

9   Why are they afraid? I tried during my stay to ascertain precisely the consequence of boldness, but it was a futile effort. I badgered my hosts with questions. Is someone who speaks with a Jew from abroad thrown into prison? If you are seen strolling with a guest from America or Israel, will you be persecuted? One shred of evidence was all I required, a single example to convince me of the clear and present danger, of the imminence of some fatal blow. All my entreaties failed. "Do me a favor," one Jew told me, "don't ask simple questions." Another said, "If I told you, you wouldn't believe me. And even if you did you wouldn't understand."

10   I realized suddenly that there was no common language between us, that they persist in thinking in terms of "we" and "you." No wonder they refuse to speak to strangers; what's the use of talking? No matter what one says, the meaning is lost. Fear has created a language of its own, and only one who lives with it day after day can ever hope to master the intricacies of its syntax.

11   I did, however, succeed in discovering the answer to one riddle . . . not *what* they fear, but whom: Informers, Jewish agents of the secret police who attend synagogue to observe the behavior of their fellow Jews. They have eyes to see, ears to hear, hands to write. You must always know who stands behind you, as you know beyond doubt before whom you will be called to render your accounts.

1. Leading Yiddish actor and producer, murdered during the Stalin purges of 1949. T.N.

2. b. 1891, Soviet Jewish author; one of a handful who survived the Stalin era. T.N.

12   At first I refused to believe this. The idea of Jews informing on Jews was too repellent, especially in the House of God. But they believe it. Any number of times—in Moscow, in Leningrad, and particularly in Kiev—I was cautioned by a wink or a low whisper, "Watch out for that one; he works for *them*." Their suspicion can reach the pitch of terror. No one trusts anyone. A Jew profoundly immersed in prayer is pointed out as a fake, a government agent, worshiping not the God of Israel but his enemies. "But how do you know that?" I found myself protesting. "Mightn't you be slandering an honest man for no good reason?"

13   "Are you telling *us* what is right and what is not?" Their gaze moves between grief and derision. "Do you mean to instruct *us* in matters of guilt and innocence?" Wounded and ashamed, one can only keep silent before such outbursts. Whether their suspicions are founded on fact or not is clearly unimportant. *They* regard them as factual, and their conviction only serves to compound the fear in which they live.

14   Occasionally I was a witness to incidents that would have seemed funny or absurd had they not been so tragic. "Do you see that redhead," someone would whisper in my ear, "sitting in the third row, pretending to pray with all his might? Keep away from him; he's one of theirs." Not an hour later the redhead himself would approach with lowered voice. "The Jew you were talking with before . . . we know him. He works for them."

15   You cannot understand these Jews and that, more than anything else, is what shocks you so. Holidays and Sabbaths, when you see them standing outside or gathered in the synagogue, they look oppressed and poor; they seem to be walking, bent over, through a world of the dead, their eyes reflecting sad and distant mysteries. You pity them. Somehow you understand their sadness. Their sadness, but not their fear. I found myself trembling as I asked what had happened to create this wall between us, what it was that prevented me from comprehending in the slightest degree the reason for their fear. Am I not a Jew like them? Are we not brothers in the same ancient tradition, sharing a common belief in the eternity of Israel? Do we not observe together the commandment bidding us to sanctify our lives? That such a gap should stretch between us seems impossible. Yet, apparently, everything is possible. Fear remains the one point of contact that binds us to one another, but we stand on opposing sides of the line, facing each other. All I can do is pray that my pain reaches out to them, as their fear reaches out to touch me.

16   If, driven by fear, they were to erupt in communal hysteria, I would feel less pain. If they screamed, wept, succumbed to a mass nervous breakdown, I would know how to react, what to do . . . especially what

to think. Analogies would come to mind from recent Jewish history or from the period of the Russian pogroms. But there is nothing in the history of the Jewish people to compare with this enclosed and silent fear. Perhaps it follows its own rules, perhaps not. Perhaps it follows no rules whatsoever but instead denies all logic and escapes all human understanding. Such fear, in its absolute power, can descend only upon those suffering from an overwhelming sense of persecution. Shut off from help, its victims are swiftly brought to the edge of despair, where devoid of hope they await the end.

17   The situation does on rare occasion reach the level of a larger delusion. On "Kol Nidrei"[3] night two young Russians hurled a rock through a window of the Moscow synagogue. They may have been drunk, or simply malicious. In any event the incident was quickly over. No one got excited. But the next morning, in a second synagogue, it was rumored that a serious clash had broken out between the Jews and their attackers.

18   A similar story came to my attention in Tbilisi, where I was approached one night on a side street by two Jews who asked me to tell everyone I saw about the "terrible things" that had occurred a few days before in Kotaisi, a town about four hundred kilometers away. What had happened? Riots, bloodshed. A number of Jews had been injured, a few imprisoned. I looked into the matter; it was all a lie. No one had been injured, no one imprisoned.

19   Why was I misinformed? One person I asked suggested that the two were informers who meant to mislead me into spreading false reports. Another said they were good men who had simply spoken out of fear, embellishing what they had heard with details of their own imagining. They had acted under the influence of that mass paranoia which from time to time attacks the Russian Jewish community.

· · · · · · · ·

20   My first encounter with that community and with the fear that pervades it took place on the night I arrived in Russia. It was Yom Kippur[4] eve, and as I stood in the Great Synagogue of Moscow, I thought I had come to pray in the company of Marannos,[5] Jews who once each year

3. Prayer for remission of vows and oaths, chanted on the eve of Yom Kippur. T.N.

4. Day of Atonement, the most solemn day of the Jewish year, culmination of the Ten Days of Repentance begun on New Year's Day, Rosh HaShanah. Jews traditionally observe a twenty-four hour fast on Yom Kippur. T.N.

5. Specifically, Spanish and Portuguese Jews who openly professed Christianity during and after the medieval Inquisition but continued to practice Judaism in private; hence, "secret Jews." T.N.

decided to leave their places of hiding and worship their Creator in public. I felt like a stranger, a gentile, among them.

21   Yet, on the surface at least, I might have been in any prewar synagogue in Europe or America, not in the very heart of the Russian capital, ten minutes away from the golden domes of the Kremlin and from the infamous "Lublianka," headquarters of the secret service, its darkened cellars once the final home of many who were tortured and condemned to die simply because they were Jews.

22   The sanctuary was brightly lit and crowded. Many were wearing white holiday robes and prayer shawls. As usual the number of older people was large, but there were also many of middle age and quite a few between the ages of twenty and thirty. Three generations had come together—grandfather, who still remembered the edicts of the Czar; his son, who had spent years in a labor camp in Siberia; and his grandson . . . but what was he doing here? Someone, a comrade at school or at work, must have reminded him that after all he, too, was a Jew, only a Jew—by force if not by choice.

23   The old people prayed with all their hearts, the younger generation sat listening in silence. They seemed thoughtful, worried, distracted. But this was only natural; it was Yom Kippur, the Day of Judgment. Who shall live and who shall die, who shall be banished and who set free, who shall be afflicted and who shall be at rest. Thoughts like these occupy the mind of every Jew on this night, wherever he may be. But here they are of immediate moment.

24   The prayers went on in an orderly fashion, with traditional melodies sung by a cantor and choir. The scrolls of the Torah[6] were removed from the ark, and as the procession wound around the pulpit the elderly rabbi, Yehuda-Leib Levin, declared in a trembling voice, *"Or zarua latzaddik . . .* Light is sown for the righteous, and gladness for the pure of heart." What light? What gladness? The cantor sang "Kol Nidrei." Here and there one heard a quiet sigh. A woman sobbed. And as the final blessing was intoned, "Blessed art Thou who hast kept us alive, and hast sustained us, and enabled us to reach this day," a shudder passed through the congregation. Another year.

25   Suddenly I sensed my neighbors eying me peculiarly. Their look was unfriendly, insulting. They were examining me, trying to tear an imaginary mask from my face and thus reveal the true purpose of my presence among them. I heard whispers. "Does anyone know him?" No one. "Does anyone know where he's from or why he's here?" No one knew. No one could possibly know. I had spoken to no one, had in fact

---

6. The Pentateuch, or Five Books of Moses. T.N.

just arrived, almost directly from the airport. Barely seven hours before I had been in Paris.

26   Their suspicion did not surprise me, although it did trouble me somewhat. I tried to start a conversation; they pretended not to hear. The fact that I had deliberately chosen to sit in the main part of the synagogue instead of in the visitors' section only increased their mistrust. When I spoke, they pretended not to understand Yiddish. Despite the crowding and the close quarters, a kind of distance opened between us.

27   It was only when I began to pray aloud, in witless desperation, that the barriers fell. The Prince of Prayer had come to my aid. They listened closely, then drew nearer; their hearts opened. They crowded around me. The crush was unbearable, but I loved it. And the questions poured out. Are there Jews in America? In Western Europe? Are they well off? Any news from Israel? Can it resist its enemies? All they wanted was to hear me talk. They refused to answer my questions. "Better not ask," said one. Another said the same. "We can't say, we can't talk," said a third. Why not? "Because. It's dangerous." They turned to me with hunted looks. I could never be one of them, because I would never be in their place. The wall of fear had risen to cut us off.

28   "Don't talk," one said to me. "Just pray. That is enough. How good it is to know there are young Jews in the world who still know how to pray." I felt like an outsider, a sinner. . . .

29   I forgot the rabbi and the cantor and the choir. Even God receded from my mind. I closed my eyes and raised my voice in prayer. Never in my life have I prayed with such a sense of devotion.

WORD FOCUS

VOCABULARY GLOSS

ark: *a chest containing the Ten Commandments written on stone tablets, which was carried by the Hebrews during their wandering in the desert; today, a similar chest is used in Jewish congregations to house the Torah (24).*

cantor: *someone who sings in prayer services (24)*

commandment: *a reference to any of the Ten Commandments (15)*

czar: *a Russian monarch before the Revolution of 1917 (22)*

gentile: *a person who is not Jewish (20)*

Kol Nidrei: *the first prayer recited on Yom Kippur (17)*

Kremlin: *the center of government in the former Soviet Union (21)*

labor camp in Siberia: *a place of imprisonment and forced labor in desolate areas of central and eastern Russia (22)*

pogroms: *institutional and societal attacks on Jews (16)*

prayer shawls: *fringed shawls worn by Jews during prayer (22)*

rabbi: *a teacher or religious leader of a Jewish congregation (24)*

Sabbaths: *days of rest and worship (15)*

Stalin: *Russian premier (1941–1953) (5)*

synagogue: *a place of Jewish worship (3)*

syntax: *the rules that describe the ordering and connecting of words in phrases, clauses, and sentences (10)*

Yiddish: *a language spoken by Central and Eastern European Jews (8)*

Yom Kippur: *Jewish Day of Atonement (20)*

VOCABULARY QUESTIONS

1. The title of this story is "Fear." Make a list of the words in the story that are associated with fear, and find other synonyms for "fear" in your dictionary. Write down the definition for each word. Then, according to their intensity, rank them on a scale of one to ten, one being the least frightened and ten being the most frightened.

2. "Strolling" (9) is a manner of walking. What is the attitude of people when they are strolling rather than walking? Using your dictionary and a thesaurus, make a list of the words associated with walking. Then group these words according to the attitude and manner of walking they reflect.

3. Discuss the difference between being "misinformed" (19) and being uninformed. Use these words in a paragraph to make statements about the text.

ENGLISH CRAFT

1. Focusing on basic aspects of a text—such as how it begins, how it ends, and how the beginning and end relate to other parts of the text—helps a reader to understand the text better. The box that follows lists some important characteristics of the different parts of expository texts that are useful in this process.

Beginning—sets up expectations	Middle—makes connections that support and extend the expectations set up in the beginning	End—ties together the expectations set up in the beginning and the connections explored in the middle
• Poses a problem or interesting situation to attract reader's attention	• Explores specific features of the problem or situation	• Ties together key ideas with expectations
• Places the problem or situation in a larger context of human concern	• Deepens reader's understanding of the problem or situation	• May point the reader in new directions
• Narrows reader's attention to limited aspects of the problem or situation that can be handled in the rest of the text.		

Using the box as a guide, identify the beginning, middle, and end parts of Wiesel's text. Analyze these sections in detail according to the criteria in the box.

2. The need for an *s/es* ending on third person singular, present tense verbs is often confusing because that same ending has other meanings when it is attached to nouns. The distinction is important because subject-verb agreement is critical in academic writing.

s/es word ending on →	verbs means singular	nouns means plural
	• read<u>s</u>	• book<u>s</u>
	• watch<u>es</u>	• watch<u>es</u>

Write a paragraph about Wiesel's essay in which you summarize his beliefs, observations, or experiences. Use third person singular, present tense verb forms wherever possible.

3. *Paraphrasing* is a valuable tool in referring to the writings of other authors while maintaining your own style. It involves rewriting someone else's idea in your own words. Paraphrasing helps you avoid overloading an essay with quotations that contain important information but are not critical to your thesis or topic sentence claims. Paraphrase paragraph 2 of this text, and discuss its key idea.

INTERPRETIVE JOURNAL

1. In trying to analyze reasons for the fear that he senses around him, the narrator observes that "in the absence of all objective correlatives, their dark and irrational fear exists simply as a thing in itself . . ." (4). Explain the term "objective correlatives" as it is used in this claim, and discuss the relationship between fear and an objective correlative. What speculations does Wiesel make about the existence of fear?

2. Texts often create a mood or feeling. Discuss the mood that the author creates and the parts of the text that develop this mood. You should look at particular words and sentences, as well as incidents referred to in the text.

3. What information does the author give about himself in this essay? Write a short biographical sketch based on the information you gather.

4. When someone warns the author about a red-headed person being "one of theirs," the author observes that the incident would be "funny or absurd" if it had not been so "tragic" (14). Consider the incident, and discuss how it could be both "absurd" and "tragic."

ESSAY QUESTION

In this essay, Wiesel is making an intellectual and emotional journey in order to understand the fear that seems to dominate the lives of the people he meets. Discuss this journey—his frame of mind when he begins, the experiences that he learns from, and his ultimate understanding of himself and the Jewish community.

Jeremy Campbell
Farewell the Open Mind

Preview

What does the term *open mind* suggest to you? Think of a situation in which having an open mind would be valuable. Can being open-minded also create problems?

Word Preview

You can familiarize yourself with the following words by looking them up in the dictionary. You can broaden your knowledge of these words by pronouncing them and understanding how they are used in context.

presuppositions (3)	disconfirmed (11)	proletariat (24)
phantoms (4)	fluke (13)	venturesome (25)
automaton (7)	axioms (13)	nightmarish (26)
aesthetic (8)	big bang theory (16)	conjecture (26)
paradoxical (10)	schemas (17)	opaque (26)
nonlogical (11)	morass (18)	headquarters (27)
preconceptions (11)	paradigm (19)	

1 Can an intelligence that is perfectly open make sense of the world? In a limited organ such as the brain, working under the constraints of space and time in a real world, reason cannot explore all possibilities, but needs to be guided by organized structures of knowledge stored in memory. And the essence of organized knowledge is that it tilts the mind toward a particular interpretation of reality and tilts it away from other interpretations. Our mental categories, with their best examples and basic levels, enable us to anticipate that things and people will behave in certain ways, and that is good, because it amplifies the restricted data of experience. At the same time, it suggests that common sense and a certain bias go hand in hand. We may not have one without the other. Unless the mind is partly blinkered, it cannot know the world at all.

2   Psychologists have noticed lately that the mind's natural tendency to approach everyday problems from a certain point of view, from a definite perspective, can result in the sort of thinking that is irrational according to the norms of logic. People may give different answers to the same question, depending on its form, because the way in which the question is worded determines the point of view they take. In a celebrated puzzle devised by Daniel Kahneman and Amos Tversky, some students were asked which of two programs they would choose to prepare for the outbreak of a rare Asian disease which is expected to kill six hundred people. The programs were identical, but they were described in two different ways to two different groups of students: "If program A is adopted, two hundred people will be saved," or "If program A is adopted, four hundred people will die." Three out of four students chose this program when it was worded in terms of lives saved, and four out of five rejected it when it was worded in terms of lives lost. Evidently, how people reason about a problem can be influenced by manipulating their point of view. The "dirty little secret" of opinion polling is that error is more likely to arise from the way a question is worded than from faulty methods of sampling.

3   No mind could be more open, more free from points of view, presuppositions, and biases, it might be thought, than the mind of a scientist. Francis Bacon, who is regarded as the prophet of modern science and the shaper of the modern skeptical intellect, insisted that a scientist must first clear his head of all inherent biases. It was foolish of the logicians, Bacon declared, to hold the operations of the mind in such high respect, because the mind looks at the world through the lens of its own knowledge, beliefs, opinions, and prejudices. In fact, Bacon said, the intellect is more prone to error than the senses are. "For let men please themselves as they will in admiring and almost adoring the human mind, this is certain: that as an uneven mirror distorts the rays of objects according to its own figure and section, so the mind, when it receives impressions of objects through the senses, cannot be trusted to report them truly, but in forming its notions mixes up its own nature with the nature of things."

4   The understanding, in Bacon's view, imposes on the external world an order and pattern that are in the mind but not in reality. Each person is inclined to interpret what he learns in the light of his own peculiar and singular disposition. Philosophy itself is one of the chief obstacles to the truly open mind, because philosophies are really fictions, phantoms, theatrical shows, stage plays, that have a false relationship to experience and lead us to see the universe as if it were an invention, not as it really is.

5   Much of Bacon's scorn for the amateurish methods prevalent in his day was aimed at their faulty logical underpinnings. The Baconian tradition, which modern science has inherited, took logic as the foundation of its thought and practice.

6   Lately, however, the idea that science is an exclusively logical, perfectly open-minded process has been seriously undermined. Scholars who have taken a closer look at what actually happens when the Baconian program of stripping away nature's secrets bears important fruit in the form of new theories, have discovered that the methods used, the cast of mind of the investigator, is not as Baconian as we might imagine.

7   In economics, for example, the concept of "rational man," who always chooses in such a way that the expected benefits of his choice will exceed the expected costs, is not a logical deduction, or a fact derived from observation. It is an assumption, a point of view, which can be neither proved nor disproved, and yet it is a cornerstone of economic theorizing. Rational man is a sort of automaton, acting in a perfectly consistent fashion. He is a stereotype. No such creature ever drew breath in the real world; he represents a highly restricted and even warped view of human life. All the same, economists find the concept useful for the very reason that it rules out other, less rational kinds of behavior, and thus directs their thinking. They do not claim that the concept can explain all of human experience, and in fact it places sweeping limits on economics as a science. Yet economists need rational man, because without a point of view, without partly closing the mind, it would be impossible to organize the information they collect, and thus impossible to understand any of it.

8   Even in the hard sciences, such as physics and chemistry, the minds of the great investigators have not been wholly free from the phantoms Bacon deplored. In a splendid study of the roads by which scientists such as Kepler, Newton, and Einstein journeyed to their discoveries, Gerald Holton, a Harvard historian of science, maintains that presuppositions, themes, and points of view may actually play a central role in penetrating nature's mysteries. These mental biases do so, Holton argues, because in the process of closing a scientist's mind to certain possibilities, they also open it up to other more daring and original avenues of inquiry. Einstein, for example, was influenced in his thinking by a whole collection of concepts that were more aesthetic than logical. He began with certain built-in nonlogical assumptions about the physical world; that nature is not unreasonably complex, that the universe is essentially harmonious and intelligible to human beings. Ideas about symmetry and simplicity were powerful considerations in his work, and

they created a set of expectations about nature, not unlike the expectations that are generated by knowledge structures in commonsense thinking about the everyday world, though very different in some ways.

9   Einstein did not bring an "open" mind to the riddles of space and time. He was able to resist the allure of prevailing notions by adhering unswervingly to the preconceptions implicit in the equations of Clerk Maxwell, and these led to ideas that were startlingly different from those of nearly all his contemporaries. It was a bias, of a highly rarefied and very special kind, that brought Einstein to new knowledge about the universe which, like Galileo's, seemed absurd in the light of ordinary observation and flew in the face of common sense. They were at odds with the established beliefs of the naked mind. As he became increasingly persuaded of the importance of preexisting concepts in making his discoveries, Einstein joked about his transformation from a physicist into a "metaphysicist." At the same time, he freely acknowledged his debt to Kant, whose "Copernican revolution" in the theory of the mind was founded on the insight that we cannot observe the world as it really is, but can only interpret it by means of implicit mental structures that are not in themselves logical.

10   In scientific investigation, Gerald Holton finds, men and women of genius are especially apt to bring themes and other forms of subtle bias to their work. "Themes force upon people notions that are usually regarded as paradoxical, ridiculous or outrageous," he writes. They enable bold adventurers in the scientific enterprise to disregard fashion and the firmly entrenched beliefs that seem so rational, so self-evident, and so right at the time when they are widely held. In physics, unlike logic, "paradox" can be a road to hidden truths.

11   Thus a form of prejudice, a certain point of view, creates a blindness that blocks a scientist's mental vision in certain directions, while extending it in other, perhaps more interesting, directions. The implicit themes that influenced Einstein were not so much descriptions of the universe itself, of its objective properties, as they were constraints on the ways in which he thought about the universe. In Holton's view, such themes have little to do with logic or with direct observation of the facts. A scientist engages in logical reasoning while developing an explicit, formal theory, but in the early stages of discovery, nonlogical or even illogical elements may be present in his thinking, and behind these are preconceptions that can neither be proved true nor disconfirmed.

12   An especially dramatic example of a bias of this sort was Newton's premise, which he tried to avoid stating openly, that God is the cause of all natural forces, including gravity. This theme, which could not possibly be demonstrated, logically or in any other way, was a means of

filling in the gaps in the impoverished data at Newton's disposal. It enabled him to think and reason in an efficient way in the presence of information that was incomplete and of poor quality. In a similar way, the success of Kepler's astronomy depended on the introduction of unashamedly metaphysical presuppositions when his physical suppositions had carried him as far as they could. Kepler's theme of the universe as a machine led him to new knowledge only when it was bolstered by two added preconceptions, that of the universe as a mathematical harmony, and as a theological order.

13   Einstein maintained that new scientific theories are "free creations of thought," but, as Holton points out, if that were really the case, there would be an infinite number of different axioms from which to choose, most of them useless, and success would come only by a lucky accident or fluke, as the scientist in his boundless freedom happened to make a leap to exactly the right axioms. In fact, this freedom is narrowly restricted by the set of themes that tilt the imagination in one direction or another, often without the scientist being aware of the power they exert. This is a highly personal process. A scientist's themes, Holton says, identify him as surely as his fingerprints.

14   A theory acts as a guide to the discovery of new knowledge, because it tells researchers what to look for, what information may be relevant and interesting, and what is not worth pursuing. A theory is a very sophisticated way of making the mind less open than it might otherwise have been, leading a researcher through a maze of possible interpretations to the unique, correct one. A case in point is the curious story of the detection, in 1965, by two astronomers, Arno Penzias and Robert Wilson, of the diffuse background radio static left over from the big bang with which the universe supposedly started fifteen billion years ago. Penzias and Wilson were studying the intensity of radio waves coming from our own galaxy. They were surprised to notice a large amount of microwave noise which scarcely varied in strength no matter where they pointed their antenna, and regardless of the time of day or season of the year. This odd observation suggested that the static did not emanate from the Milky Way, but from the universe in general.

15   Penzias and Wilson were baffled. They assumed at first that something was wrong with their equipment. A couple of pigeons had been nesting in the long horn of the antenna and became major suspects in the mystery, but when the pigeons were shooed away and the horn cleaned out, the noise remained. The two astronomers cast about for all kinds of other explanations, and only after a chance telephone conversation with another radio astronomer, Bernard Burke of MIT, did they surmise that the puzzling activity was a remnant of the birth pangs of

the cosmos. Steven Weinberg, a Harvard astronomer who tells this story, points out that the momentous discovery of background radiation could have been made at least ten years earlier. Theories predicting it had been around for nearly twenty years, but they were unknown to astrophysicists in general. Nobody set out to look for the telltale cosmic static, and when Penzias and Wilson stumbled upon it by accident, they had no idea what they had found. Even the few astronomers who knew about the predictions dating back to the 1940s had not taken them very seriously.

16   Weinberg thinks the reason for this strange neglect was partly a breakdown in communication between people who make theories and people who make observations. The theorists did not think radiation with such a low temperature could be detected with the instruments available at the time. Partly, too, the big bang theory did not lead to a search for radiation because physicists found it hard to take seriously any theory of the early universe, seeing that the circumstances of the cosmic birth are so remote and unfamiliar. The result was that new knowledge about the universe was lying around for years but could not be picked up for want of a theory to produce expectancies, to provide a point of view, and rule out other possibilities. "This is often the way it is in physics—our mistake is not that we take our theories too seriously, but that we do not take them seriously enough," Weinberg says. "I do not think it is possible really to understand the successes of science without understanding how *hard* it is—how easy it is to be led astray, how difficult it is to know at any time what is the next thing to be done."

17   Scientific theories, like schemas and even stereotypes, make sense of the world by excluding certain ways of interpreting ambiguous or incomplete information. This is a form of cognitive economy. A theory is a summary, a device that stores and organizes knowledge, putting together the bits and pieces of data that have been observed into a coherent whole, and also providing a pattern of connections into which future observations can be fitted. It reduces the amount of new information about the world that is needed for understanding, and amplifies that small amount by means of the knowledge it stores.

18   In his landmark book, *The Structure of Scientific Revolutions,* Thomas Kuhn describes the almost random gathering of facts that goes on in the absence of a theory. Pliny's encyclopedic writings, for instance, or works on natural history in the seventeenth century, consist of a morass of unconnected observations, some of which later proved to be highly illuminating when connected by a new theory, and some of which were too complex to fit into any theory for years to come. No natural history can be interpreted without an implicit body of organized knowledge or belief that makes it possible to select, evaluate, and criticize the facts.

If such a pattern is not implicit in the collection of facts, Kuhn argues, it must be supplied from outside, perhaps from metaphysics, or by accident. That being the case, it is not surprising that in the early stages of any science, different investigators who look at the same facts describe and interpret them in different ways.

19   Kuhn's book, which was highly controversial, and remains so, strongly challenged the traditional view that science is a perfectly rational enterprise, governed by logical rules of procedure that never change as time goes on. Scientific knowledge comes rather from seeing the world from a particular point of view. Kuhn makes a distinction between "normal" science, which goes on within a context of accepted ideas he calls a paradigm, and periods of revolution, when scientists break through to a new and different paradigm. Normal science simply extends our knowledge of those facts that a given context of ideas shows to be particularly revealing. During such periods, researchers not only refrain from seeking new theories, but actually resist them when they appear. This is both good and bad for the advancement of understanding. It is good because scientists are able to investigate an aspect of nature more deeply than would be possible if the context of ideas did not exist, and bad because of an intolerance that arises toward novel ways of thinking. During regimes of normal science, the prevailing context of ideas does more than determine what problems are to be solved; it also selects the sort of puzzles that are assumed to have solutions, which is one reason why a hallmark of normal science is that it proceeds at a rapid pace. Preconceptions, points of view, implicit in a particular regime, are the "rules of the game" for these puzzles, constraining the kind of answers that are acceptable and the steps by which they are reached. Only by changing the rules of the game are new sorts of answers possible, and it is a side-effect of the intolerance often bred during periods of normal science that a regime is eventually shattered.

20   The network of prior commitments to concepts, theories, and methods may have long-lasting influences on a science. After about 1630, for example, due mainly to the writings of Descartes, most scientists assumed the universe was made of tiny particles, and everything that happened in the universe could be explained in terms of the shape, size, motion, and interaction of the particles. Such a prejudice drastically limited both the problems and the theories that scientists worked on, in domains as diverse as chemistry, mechanics, optics, and heat.

21   Paradoxically, it is during normal regimes, when science is least open-minded, that it advances with greatest assurance and verve, penetrating nature's mysteries deeply within the limits set by the rules. Only a crisis, Kuhn thinks, enables new theories to emerge, and these are usually produced by workers who are very young or very new to

their field. In all the history of science, Kuhn found no instance in which a theory has been falsified by direct comparison with nature. Usually it is overthrown by a new theory, but even the creation of such a theory is not the rational, open-minded process it might seem. When the rules are in force, scientific choices are rational, within narrowly defined constraints, but when the rules are put aside, during a period of revolution, the choice of a new worldview is in part arbitrary and nonrational, an accident.

22   Kuhn uses the word *stereotypes* to describe the commitment to certain theories, beliefs and methods that enable science to move so fast and confidently in normal periods, suggesting a link between the knowledge structures of everyday common sense and the mental operations of the scientist; both leave the mind unfree, so that it can thread its way through the complexity of the world without drowning in irrelevant detail.

23   So a kind of bias underlies all our efforts to make sense of the world, from the Olympian level of theory-making in physics to the down-to-earth task of reading the ambiguous clues that other people send us in the most routine social encounters. Karl Popper, a modern philosopher who has written with great insight about the open mind, believes that we do not learn by observation, but by creating anticipations, sending up mental trial balloons. Such anticipations, guiding discovery, tilting the mind in a certain direction, amount to a kind of prejudice. What we expect to see influences what we actually do see, and what we find relevant or irrelevant. The process of discovery, as opposed to the testing and criticism of a particular discovery, is never pure, never unbiased.

24   Popper insists that the criticism of a theory must be all the more severe because its creation is the product of a mind that cannot be fully open. As a young man living in Vienna, Popper became a Marxist, only to suffer a sharp disillusionment at the age of seventeen, when he watched several unarmed young socialists being shot to death by police while demonstrating to obtain the release of some agitators. The protest had been instigated by the communists. Popper was shocked by the brutality of the police, but the experience also jolted him into realizing that he had accepted a complex doctrine like Marxism uncritically. He had assumed it was on the side of the proletariat, the majority, and yet even among workers in the factories of Vienna the communists were a minority. Popper came to the conclusion that Marxism, like Freudian psychoanalysis, is full of presuppositions that are nonrational in the sense that any new fact can always be made to confirm the theory, but no fact can ever disprove it.

25   Most philosophers, at least until Frege, had taken it for granted that there is only one kind of knowledge, the interior kind that is either innate or a result of experience. Popper, in a more venturesome spirit, proposes not one, but three varieties of knowledge. They are so different from one another that he assigns them to three distinct "worlds." World 1 is the domain of physical objects, things. World 2 is the realm of our subjective thoughts, ideas, expectations, presuppositions, which limit the openness of the mind. World 3 is knowledge that is out in the public arena for all to see, where trial balloons float but can also be pricked and deflated, where theories are exposed to the bracing and perhaps destructive winds of criticism, doubt, and debate. In World 3, knowledge is stated in an explicit, and usually a written or printed form. It is the world of books, art, science, computers, and logic.

26   Only in World 3 can the mind be described as truly open. Here the products of thought can be examined under the magnifying glass of logic, ideas checked against reality. One of the surprising features of World 3 is that although the systems of knowledge it contains are human inventions, they often take on a life of their own. They turn out to have unexpected properties and regularities never intended or foreseen by their authors. We make discoveries about them in much the same way that explorers make discoveries about such objects of World 1 as continents and oceans. The natural number system, for example, may be a pure creation of the mind, but that does not mean it is fully under the control of its creators. Seemingly simple questions about the nature of numbers may present nightmarish difficulties. The innocent-looking conjecture that every even number can be written as the sum of two prime numbers is in fact so opaque that it has yet to be proved. Logic, too, which was regarded by eighteenth-century minds as a tamed and settled continent, suddenly revealed itself to be inhabited by monsters, in the form of strange and deadly paradoxes.

27   World 2, by contrast, can be talked about in psychological terms only, and is not inherently rational. It is the headquarters of common sense, but common sense is a type of knowledge we cannot fully trust. World 2 knowledge is conjectural only, never certain, and it can lead us astray. It tends to harbor bias and prejudice, and may embrace contradictory beliefs and expectations. In World 2, the mind tends to look for evidence that will confirm its conjectures, rather than for facts that will disprove them.

28   Our conjectures and opinions, expectations and beliefs, are, in Popper's words, "nets in which we try to catch the real world." They are not mirrors of reality, but patterns of connections that help us to construct a fabric of interpretation out of the scattered clues we pick up from the

environment. What the mind catches in these knowledge nets is an imperfect and sometimes seriously biased version of reality, but the alternative, the fully open mind of World 3, would not be able to catch reality at all; it would not even know where to start.

29   What better evidence can there be of the inadequacy of the open mind, than the fact that after nearly four decades of trying to model human intelligence in its World 3 manifestation, artificial-intelligence researchers are at last beginning to talk about new computer architectures that have some of the hallmarks, the shortcomings and strengths, the enabling biases and efficient prejudices, of the World 2 mind?

WORD FOCUS

VOCABULARY GLOSS

avenues of inquiry: *new or different ways of thinking about or approaching concepts (8)*

bears important fruit: *produces significant results (6)*

beliefs of the naked mind: *beliefs that the scientific mind could make unbiased observations (9)*

birth pangs: *labor pains; stress associated with creativity (15)*

blinkered: *partially covered, as a horse's eyes are by blinders (1)*

cast of mind: *frame of reference or perspective (6)*

Copernican revolution: *the change in thinking caused by Copernicus, who claimed that the sun is at the center of the universe (9)*

cornerstone: *a fundamental or essential point (7)*

down-to-earth task: *an everyday, often routine, task (23)*

fabric of interpretation: *a network of ideas (28)*

flew in the face of common sense: *went against accepted belief (9)*

Francis Bacon: *an English Renaissance scholar who proposed the inductive theory of scientific inquiry (3)*

Freudian psychoanalysis: *a twentieth-century theory connecting behavior to the unconscious mind, developed by Sigmund Freud (24)*

hallmark: *a significant and identifying characteristic (19)*

Marxism: *a twentieth-century political theory about economic materialism provided by philosopher Karl Marx (24)*

Milky Way: *galaxy within which our solar system is located (14)*

norms of logic: *criteria for logical thinking (2)*

Olympian level: *elevated or majestic in scope, from Greek mythology (23)*

rules of the game: *accepted practices (19)*

a side-effect: *another aspect of an experience, usually negative (19)*

taken a closer look: *looked at something critically (6)*

trial balloons: *tentative thoughts, ideas, or proposals subjected to public reaction; hypotheses that are tested (23)*

VOCABULARY QUESTIONS

1. Campbell talks about "open-mindedness" and "bias" in ways different from what we are accustomed to. Define open-mindedness and bias in your own terms. Compare your understanding of these words and their dictionary definitions with the way Campbell uses them.

2. The word "stereotype" usually has a negative connotation in today's society. According to Campbell, Thomas Kuhn uses the word in a positive sense. Compare the dictionary definition of "stereotype" with Kuhn's.

3. Campbell claims that "Unless the mind is partly blinkered, it cannot know the world at all" (1). The word "blinkered" is usually associated with the blinders that limit a horse's vision. How is Campbell using this word, and what understanding of the mind does Campbell convey by using this image?

ENGLISH CRAFT

1. Studying the patterns Campbell uses in this essay can help you understand his main points and model your own academic essays. Campbell's introductory paragraph begins with a *hook* to engage the reader's attention and ends with a *thesis claim,* the major point of the essay. The paragraph begins with the question (hook), "Can an intelligence that is perfectly open make sense of the world?" and ends with the answer (thesis claim), "Unless the mind is partly blinkered, it cannot know the world at all" (1).

   Study the sentences between the hook and the thesis claim carefully. What information do they give the reader that leads from the hook to the thesis claim?

2. The following series of boxes is one way to arrange the thesis claim and the topic sentence claims of the first five paragraphs of Campbell's essay. Notice that topic sentence claims related to broader topic sentence claims are indented.

THESIS CLAIM
Unless the mind is partly blinkered, it cannot know the world at all. (1)

BROAD TOPIC SENTENCE CLAIM
Psychologists have noticed lately that the mind's natural tendency to approach everyday problems from a certain point of view, from a definite perspective, can result in the sort of thinking that is irrational according to the norms of logic. (2)

TOPIC SENTENCE CLAIM (directly supports broad topic sentence claim)
No mind could be more open, more free from points of view, presuppositions, and biases, it might be thought, than the mind of a scientist. (3)

TOPIC SENTENCE CLAIM (supports topic sentence claim)
The understanding, in Bacon's view, imposes on the external world an order and pattern that are in the mind but not in reality. (4)

TOPIC SENTENCE CLAIM (supports topic sentence claim)
Much of Bacon's scorn for the amateurish methods prevalent in his day was aimed at their faulty logical underpinnings. (5)

Arrange the topic sentence claims of paragraphs 6 through 11, using the same pattern to show the relationship of these claims to the thesis.

Lately, however, the idea that science is an exclusively logical, perfectly open-minded process has been seriously undermined. (6)

In economics, for example, the concept of "rational man," who always chooses in such a way that the expected benefits of his choice will exceed the expected costs, is not a logical deduction, or a fact derived from observation. (7)

> Even in the hard sciences, such as physics and chemistry, the minds of the great investigators have not been wholly free from the phantoms Bacon deplored. (8)

> Einstein did not bring an "open mind" to the riddles of space and time. (9)

> In scientific investigation, Gerald Holton finds, men and women of genius are especially apt to bring themes and other forms of subtle bias to their work. (10)

> Thus a form of prejudice, a certain point of view, creates a blindness that blocks a scientist's mental vision in certain directions, while extending it in other, perhaps more interesting, directions. (11)

3. *Relative clauses* are dependent clauses that add identifying information about a noun. Look at the following statements:

Petrakis, Wiesel, and Campbell are the men who wrote the three readings included in this chapter.

The essay that Campbell wrote is called "Farewell the Open Mind."

"Bias and Discovery," which is the title of this chapter, brings together two ideas that are usually not thought about as a unit.

The relative pronouns *who, that,* and *which* introduce statements that give more information about the nouns that come before. In the example above, the relative pronoun *who* introduces the clause that gives more information about *men;* the relative pronoun *that* does the same for *essay;* and the relative pronoun *which* does the same for "Bias and Discovery."

   Consider the following sentences from Campbell:

[According to Holton], themes force upon people notions that are usually regarded as paradoxical, ridiculous or outrageous. (10)

[Penzias and Wilson] were surprised to notice a large amount of microwave noise which scarcely varied in strength no matter where they pointed their antenna. (14)

An especially dramatic example of a bias of this sort was Newton's premise, which he tried to avoid stating openly, that God is the cause of all natural forces, including gravity. (12)

Identify the relative clauses and the nouns that each expands. Discuss what specific information the relative clause adds to the noun and how essential it is to the sentence. Note that the third sentence has two relative clauses. Is one of the clauses more essential than the other?

Referring to the patterns discussed above, write four sentences with relative clauses about Campbell's text using the following nouns: *theory, scientists, biases,* and *explanations.*

INTERPRETIVE JOURNAL

1. Campbell begins his essay with the following question: "Can an intelligence that is perfectly open make sense of the world?" (1). In a paragraph, answer this question from your own experience.

2. Campbell suggests that the climate or context in which ideas occur limits "what problems are to be solved" and what "puzzles" have solutions (19). What are the limits of the "worlds" proposed by Popper?

3. The title of the essay "Farewell the Open Mind" is striking because "farewell" is a formal and old usage of good-bye. Why might an author frame a contemporary discussion about the mind under a title that has associations with the word *goodbye?*

4. Campbell says that "No mind could be more open, more free from points of view, presuppositions, and biases, it might be thought, than the mind of a scientist" (3). What is Campbell saying in this statement? Which words show the reader Campbell's position?

ESSAY QUESTION

Early in his essay, Campbell affirms that "a form of prejudice, a certain point of view, creates a blindness that blocks a scientist's mental vision in certain directions, while extending it in other, perhaps more interesting, directions" (11). Discuss how certain biases can both obstruct and extend one's "mental vision."

Bias and Discovery
Sequence of Essay Assignments

READINGS

Harry Mark Petrakis, "The Judgment"

Elie Wiesel, "Fear," excerpt from *The Jews of Silence*

Jeremy Campbell, "Farewell the Open Mind," excerpt from *The Improbable Machine*

The following assignments form a sequence of interrelated topics. They become progressively more challenging as they ask you to interact with more texts. Assignment 1 asks you to write about a topic in Petrakis's story; Assignment 2 asks you to reconsider your first essay in light of Wiesel's text; and Assignment 3 asks you to consider all three texts as you establish your point of view on the assigned topic.

These assignments can be written as a sequence or they can be written individually. However you approach these essays, each one you write should be supported with citations from the text and examples. Whenever possible, include your own experience and knowledge on the subject.

ASSIGNMENT 1

PETRAKIS

In "The Judgment," Elias and Katina seem blind to each other's needs. Analyze the reasons for their inability to understand one another, and discuss how this blindness affects other aspects of their lives—such as their interactions with other people, and their reactions to new ideas, people, places, or things.

ASSIGNMENT 2

WIESEL AND PETRAKIS

Although Wiesel speaks Russian and Yiddish proficiently, when he interacts with various Jewish communities he realizes "that there was no common language between us, that they persist in thinking in terms of 'we' and 'you' " (10). Identify the biases that Wiesel and the people he meets bring to this situation. Use Wiesel's statement to analyze the biases that separate Elias and Katina in "The Judgment."

ASSIGNMENT 3

CAMPBELL, WIESEL, AND PETRAKIS

Campbell claims that "Unless the mind is partly blinkered, it cannot know the world at all" (1). Analyze Campbell's claim in relation to Wiesel's experience of fear and Elias's and Katina's experience of love and hatred. Does fear, which could be considered a blinker in Campbell's sense of the word, offer any insights to Wiesel or his people? Similarly, does the love and hatred in Elias and Katina's marriage offer them any insights?

Acknowledgments

Edward Abbey. "Water." From *Desert Solitaire* by Edward Abbey. Copyright © 1968 by Edward Abbey. Renewed 1996 by Clarke Abbey. Reprinted by permission of Don Congdon Associates, Inc.

Maya Angelou. "Mary." From *I Know Why the Caged Bird Sings* by Maya Angelou. Copyright © 1969 by Maya Angelou. Reprinted by permission of Random House, Inc. and Virago Press, London.

Jeremy Campbell. "Farewell the Open Mind." From *The Improbable Machine: What the Upheavals in Artificial Intelligence Research Reveal about How the Mind Really Works* by Jeremy Campbell. Copyright © 1989 by Jeremy Campbell. Reprinted by permission of Balkin Agency, agent for the author.

Sandra Cisneros. "No Speak English." From *The House on Mango Street.* Copyright © 1984 by Sandra Cisneros. Published by Vintage Books, a division of Random House, Inc., New York, and in hardcover by Alfred A. Knopf in 1984. Reprinted by permission of Susan Bergholz Literary Services, New York. All rights reserved.

Peter Freuchen. "Dead Man's Cache" from *Peter Freuchen's Book of the Eskimos.* Copyright © 1961 by the Peter Freuchen Estate. Renewed 1989 by Dagmar Gale. Reprinted by permission of Don Congdon Associates, Inc.

Eva Hoffman. "Paradise." From *Lost in Translation* by Eva Hoffman. Copyright © 1989 by Eva Hoffman. Used by permission of Dutton Signet, a division of Penguin Books USA Inc., and Random House UK Ltd.

Nancy Mairs. "Challenge: An Exploration." From *Carnal Acts* by Nancy Mairs. Copyright © 1990 by Nancy Mairs. Reprinted by permission of Beacon Press.

Rigoberta Menchú. "The Family" and "Birth Ceremonies." From *I, Rigoberta Menchú,* edited and introduced by Elisabeth Burgos-Debray; translated into English by Ann Wright. Copyright © 1984. Reprinted by permission of Verso.

Bharati Mukherjee. Excerpt from pp. 105–117 in *The Tiger's Daughter* by Bharati Mukherjee. Copyright © 1971 by Bharati Mukherjee. Reprinted by permission of the author and Penguin Books Canada Limited.

John G. Neihardt. "The Butchering at Wounded Knee" and "The End of the Dream" in *Black Elk Speaks* by Black Elk as told through John G. Neihardt, seventh Bison Book printing, pp. 255–270. Copyright 1932, 1959, 1972 by John G. Neihardt. Copyright © 1961 by John G. Neihardt Trust. Reprinted by permission of the University of Nebraska Press.

Liam O'Flaherty. "Going into Exile." From *Irish Literature: A Reader* by Maureen O'Rourke Murphy and James MacKillop. Copyright © 1987 by Liam O'Flaherty. Reprinted by permission of Syracuse University Press.

Harry Mark Petrakis. "The Judgment." Reprinted by permission of the author.

Nawal el Saadawi. Excerpt from pp. 1–19 in *Woman at Point Zero* by Nawal el Saadawi. Reprinted by permission of ZED Books.

Ronald Takaki. Excerpt from pp. 1–17 in *A Different Mirror* by Ronald Takaki. Copyright © 1991 by Ronald Takaki. By permission of Little, Brown and Company.

Elie Wiesel. "Fear." From *The Jews of Silence: A Personal Report on Soviet Jewry* by Elie Wiesel. Translated from the Hebrew by Neal Kozodoy. Copyright © 1973, 1987 by Elie Wiesel. Reprinted by permission of Georges Borchardt, Inc. for the author.

Index